This Reader forms part of the Open University course *Mental Health and Distress: Perspectives and Practice* (K257), a second-level undergraduate course and an optional course for the Diploma in Health and Social Welfare. The selection of items is therefore related to other material available to students. A companion book for the course is *Mental Health Matters*. Both books are designed to evoke the critical understanding of students. Opinions expressed in them are not necessarily those of the course team or of The Open University. If you are interested in studying the course or working towards a degree or diploma, please write to the Information Officer, School of Health and Social Welfare, The Open University, Walton Hall, Milton Keynes MK7 6AA, UK.

SPEAKING OUR MINDS

An Anthology of Personal Experiences of Mental Distress and its Consequences

Edited by

Jim Read
and
Jill Reynolds

The Open University

Published 2000 by
PALGRAVE
Houndmills, Basingstoke, Hampshire RG21 6XS and
175 Fifth Avenue, New York, N. Y. 10010
Companies and representatives throughout the world

PALGRAVE is the new global academic imprint of
St. Martin's Press LLC Scholarly and Reference Division and
Palgrave Publishers Ltd (formerly Macmillan Press Ltd).

ISBN 0–333–67849–4 hardcover
ISBN 0–333–67850–8 paperback

This book is printed on paper suitable for recycling and
made from fully managed and sustained forest sources.

A catalogue record for this book is available
from the British Library.

11   10   9   8   7   6   5
07   06   05   04   03   02   01

Printed and bound in Great Britain by
Creative Print and Design (Wales), Ebbw Vale

Contents

Acknowledgements

The editors and publishers wish to thank the following for permission to use copyright material: Ashgate Publishing Ltd for 'I Want to Become Part of My Family Again' extracted from Christine McCourt Perring, *The Experience of Hospital Closure: an Anthropological Study*, Avebury (1993); Richard B. for 'Afraid the Live and Afraid to Die'; Douglas Elliot Press for 'Stay Calm and Charm Them' extracted from Linda Hart, *Phone at Nine Just to Say You're Alive* (1995); Peter Good for abridged article, 'A Comparative Study of Application Forms for Housing Benefit and an American Express Card', *Asylum*, 8, (2) (1994); The Hamlet Trust for Igor Spreizer, 'Recovery at Home', *Out Loud*, Summer (1995); Bill Lewis for 'Therapy Room' from *Rage Without Anger*, Lazerwolf/Hangman Books (1988); Wendy Lindsay for 'By Definition' from *Looking Back: An Anthology of Writing From the Pastures Hospital*, ed. Rosie Cullen (1991) and for 'Treading on Eggshells' (originally 'Don't Go Back') from *Looking Forward: An Anthology of Writing From After the Pastures*, ed. Rosie Cullen (1991); Rufus McGinty for 'Good Stories and Stereotypes', his revised and updated editorial from *The Chronicle*, Broadmoor Community Magazine, Feb/Mar (1994); Macmillan Magazines Ltd for abridged article by Joan Tugwell, 'A Second Chance for Life', *Health Service Journal*, 18 Feb (1988); Mainsail Press for material from Diana Friel McGowin, *Living in the Labyrinth: a Personal Journey Through the Maze of Alzheimer's* (1993), Copyright © 1993 Elder Books, San Francisco, published by arrangement with Dell Publishing; Mainstream Publishing for 'Leaving Carstairs' extracted from Jimmy Laing and Dermot McQuarrie, *Fifty Years in the System* (1989); Mental Health Nursing for Vivien Lindow, 'What We Want from Community Psychiatric Nurses' (originally 'Now is Your Chance to Help Undo Some Wrongs'), *Mental Health Nursing*, 14 (1) (1994), and Jan Wallcraft, 'Becoming Fully Ourselves' (originally 'Empowerment: Professionals and Self-Advocacy Projects'), *Mental Health Nursing*, 14, (2) (1994); Mind for Richard Jameson, 'Schizophrenia from the Inside', *OpenMind*, 6 (1983), Leonard Taylor, 'ECT is Barbaric', *OpenMind*, 63 (1993), John Bell, 'Label Removed but Scar Remains', *OpenMind*, 49 (1991), Colin Hambrook, 'Healing Through Creativity', *OpenMind*, 62 (1993), Maureen Sangster, 'I Have Found Ways Out of Fear' (originally 'Obsessed'), *OpenMind*, 39 (1989), Brian Taylor, 'Reflections on Therapy', *OpenMind*, 59 (1993), and Terry Simpson, 'Beyond Rage' (originally 'Being Angry, Being Heard'), *OpenMind*, 75 (1995); National Institute for Social Work for abridged articles from David Keay, 'Who Do *You* Represent?' from *A*

Challenge to Change: Practical Experiences of Builder User-Led Services, eds Peter Beresford and Tessa Harding (1993), and Edna Conlan, 'Shaking Hands With the Devil' in *Building Bridges Between People Who Use and People Who Provide Services* (1993); Mary O'Hagan for 'Two Accounts of Mental Distress'; Open University Press for 'I've Lost My Innocence' extracted from Moira Walker, *Surviving Secrets: the Experience of Abuse as a Child, the Adult and the Helper* (1992); Michael O'Higgins for 'Ward' from *Every Other Weekend*, Bristol Mind (1986); Pavilion Publishing (Brighton) Ltd for material from Peter Campbell, 'What We Want From Crisis Services' (originally 'What Users Want From Mental Health Crisis Serivices'), *Mental Health Review*, produced in association with the Centre for Mental Health Services Development, Kings College, March (1996); Pluto Press for Peter Campbell 'Challenging Loss of Power' (originally 'Peter Campbell's Story') in *Mental Health Care in Crisis*, ed. Anny Brackx (1986); Quartet Books Ltd for 'Prozac Really isn't That Great' extracted from Elizabeth Wurtzel, *Prozac Nation: Young and Depressed in America* (1995); Marius Romme and Sandra Escher for Louise Pembroke, 'It Helped That Someone Believed Me' (originally 'Eleventh Contributor') from *Accepting Voices*, eds M. Romme and S. Escher (1993) Mind; Routledge for 'Neurotics at War: Art Therapy' extracted from David Wigoder, *Images of Destruction*, Routledge & Kegan Paul (1987); Sage Publications Ltd for abridged version of Rachel Perkins, 'Choosing ECT', *Feminism and Psychology*, 4, (4) (1994); East Midlands Shape for material from AN, 'Paying the Penalty', Miranda, 'I Don't Feel it's Right' (originally 'There's Nothing You Can Do'), and Terry, 'I Can Get About' from *Looking Forward: An Anthology of Writing from after the Pastures*, ed. Rosie Cullen (1991); Survivors Speak Out for 'Silent Scream' (originally 'Maggy Ross') in *Self Harm: Perspectives from Personal Experience*, ed. Louise Roxanne Pembroke (1994); A. P. Watt on behalf of the author for 'Thunk Among the Jolly Bunks' extracted from Lucy Irvine, *Runaway*, Viking (1986); John Wiley & Sons Ltd for 'I Suffered From Depression' (abridged from 'Thro' A Glass Darkly') in *Wounded Healers*, eds V. Rippere and R. Williams (1985); The Women's Press for Pam Mason, 'Agoraphobia: Letting Go' from *Mustn't Grumble . . . Writing by Disabled Women*, ed. Lois Keith (1995).

Every effort has been made to trace all the copyright-holders, but it proved very difficult to trace copyright holders for the following pieces. The publishers will be pleased to make the necessary arrangement at the first opportunity.

A Survival Story, by Patricia Brunner, is an abridged version of one in McNeil, P., McShea, M. and Parmer, S. (eds), *Through the Break*, Sheba, London, 1986. *The Right to be Informed*, by Christine McIntosh, was first published as 'Who Needs a Label Anyway?', in *On the Level*, Newsletter of the Manic Depressive Fellowship Scotland (19 Elmbank Street, Glasgow G2 4PB), 1993, no. 1. Christine McIntosh is a pseudonym. *Why we Run for Cover*, by Anon, is reprinted in full from *WISH Newsletter*, London, Summer 1994. *I've Got Memories Here*, by Clive, has been extracted from *Boots On! Out!*, Hereford Mind and Logaston Press, Almeley, Herefordshire, 1995. *What we Want From Mental Health Services*, by Jim Read, is based on an article, 'The Contribution of Service Users in the Design and Implementation of Services', in Dean, C. (ed.), *A Slow Train Coming: Bringing the Mental Health Resolutions to Scotland*, Greater Glasgow Community and Health Services NHS Trust, 1994.

Notes on the Contributors

Richie B. is Irish and an active member of Brent Mental Health User Group. He enjoys walking, gardening and football.

John Bell is a self-employed plant operator and lives with his wife in Bridgwater. He is writing a book about life in the mental health system. he enjoys making model motorbikes in his spare time and is an animal lover.

Peter Beresford works with Open Services Project, is a member of Survivors Speak Out and teaches at Brunel University College. He has a long-standing involvement in issues of participation and empowerment as a service user, worker and researcher and has written widely on the subject.

Peter Campbell is a mental health system survivor. In the last ten years he has been involved in action by mental health service users locally and nationally. He was a founder of Survivors Speak Out and was active for many years with Camden Mental Health Consortium in North London. He was a founder of Survivors' Poetry and now works as a writer, freelance trainer and performing poet.

Rosalind Caplin is a mental health trainer/survivor who turned to alternative approaches when the medical model failed. She subsequently trained in herbal medicine, counselling and nutrition and now works as a naturopath and writer. She has a strong desire to see that creative alternatives be made available to anyone, with opportunities for choice and independence.

Edna Conlan is a member of Milton Keynes Advocacy Group and President of the United Kingdom Advocacy Network. She has worked as a lecturer, trainer and researcher for the Open University and the London School of Economics, and is a consultant for the International Mental Health Network.

David Crepaz-Keay is a freelance survivor trainer, researcher and desktop publisher who previously wrote economic models at the Treasury and computer models for the water industry. He was detained under the Mental Health Act 1983. After ten years' treatment, he joined the self-help group Survivors Speak Out for which he has been chair and secretary.

Veronica Dewan was born in England in 1957 of Irish and Indian parentage and adopted by an English father and Irish mother. Following a diagnosis of clinical depression and experience of mental health services, she worked with local, regional and national campaigning groups, including Mind. Veronica was also an active member of ATRAP, the Association for Transracially Adopted and Fostered People. She is a law graduate.

Diana Friel McGowin had to leave her career in legal research following her diagnosis in 1991 and has since gone on to found the early-onset support group for Alzheimer's disease sufferers in her hometown of Orlando, Florida. As her condition permits, she continues to write and provide active support for other victims.

Gloria Gifford is a survivor of the mental health system. She works for Brent Mental Health User Group and is a member of Survivors Speak Out. As a disabled lesbian, she has spent years campaigning on equal rights issues.

Peter Good is completing a PhD thesis on Bakhtinian approaches to psychiatry at Sheffield's Centre for Psychotherapeutic Studies. He has crossed the Sahara six times.

Colin Hambrook is currently editor of *Disability Arts in London* magazine. He is one of a small team who co-ordinated and produced the best-selling Survivors' Press anthology *Under the Asylum Tree*. He is also an artist and poet.

Chris Harrison was born blind and spent sixteen years in special schools. He is a psychiatric system survivor, a member of Survivors Speak Out and currently works as a development worker and consultant in the field of mental distress and disability with Waltham Forest Association of Disabled People.

Linda Hart was born in London in 1947 and is the mother of two adult sons. She was diagnosed as suffering from schizophrenia in 1985 and has spent long periods in a psychiatric hospital. During this time, however, she has worked for social services as a mental health project worker and wrote *Phone At Nine Just To Say You're Alive* which won the 1996 Mind Book of the Year award.

Martin Henderson is a librarian, and works at the Information Unit of National Mind in Stratford. he has wide interests in biology (entomology, evolutionary studies, conservation) beside his interest in literature and creative writing. He is an active philatelist.

Lucy Irvine is a full-time mother and sometimes writer. She spent a year on an uninhabited tropical island in the early 1980s, after which she wrote *Castaway*, which later was made into a film. She currently lives a quiet rural existence in the Scottish Highlands, much informed by her island experience. She is active in promoting education in the care of the earth for future generations.

Sue King has trained as a mental health advocate and is studying for a diploma in counselling. With her partner, Stella, she is involved with voluntary work around mental health issues and, with two of their five children still very young, they organise and run play initiatives. She is involved with various residents' groups and support groups, from reproduction rights to traffic management.

Jimmy Laing was born in Perth, Scotland, one of a family of nine. He was incarcerated in the mental health system from the age of nine to fifty-nine. His autobiography, *50 years In The System*, which he wrote with Dermot McQuarrie, was published in 1989. Since then he has married, been appointed visiting lecturer to Caledonian University, Glasgow and chair of the Scottish Users Network, and appeared on TV and the radio.

Bill Lewis is a poet, storyteller and mythographer. since being hospitalised in 1976 for clinical depression he has made a career as a writer. He has read, lectured and published on both sides of the Atlantic and currently runs an adult education course in Myth, Magic and Spirituality for Kent Education.

Vivien Lindow is a member of Bristol Survivors' Network and Survivors Speak Out. She works freelance to try and get people's objections to the mental health system heard, and lives with her cat and an aspidistra called Benjamin.

Wendy Lindsay's contribution was written as part of a therapeutic process. She has developed a professional career working with statutory and non-statutory agencies and in individual training and counselling, both in the UK and abroad, providing support for vulnerable others who have suffered the distressing consequences of disempowerment and abuse.

Rufus McGinty is the editor of *The Chronicle*, has travelled extensively and among many jobs, worked with homeless people and those with learning difficulties. A catastrophic and tragic breakdown led him to be sent to Broadmoor in 1988. He has since recovered and is waiting to be released. His interests range from photography to drama to spiritual growth.

Pam Mason was born in Liverpool and now lives in Norwich. She has had articles and stories printed in various publications over the years. She is currently working on a novel.

Jenni Meredith is a poet, columnist and computer artist, and lives on the Isle of Wight where she has worked in community arts since 1988; directing projects with young people in dance, sculpture, radio play writing and poetry. Her own poems often reflect her experience of disability and have been published in a number of anthologies and broadcast on radio. She has performed at literature festivals and recently completed a video of animated concrete poetry.

Mary Nettle has a HND Business Studies and Diploma in Advanced Marketing from Bristol Polytechnic and is currently self-employed as a mental health user consultant. She contributes a service user perspective to research and training working mainly in mental health but increasingly across disability. She was a member of the Department of Health's Mental Health Task Force User Group and has been appointed as a Mental Health Act Commissioner.

Michael O'Higgins was born in Dublin in 1935 and educated at Ruskin College and Magdalen College, Oxford. He has won an Elmgrant Trust Award for Poetry, a Southwest Arts Literary Award (1984) and a Friends of Mendip Poetry Award. He also won the Marth Robinson Poetry Competition in 1988.

Mary O'Hagan is a New Zealander and has been involved in the user movement in her own country and internationally for ten years. She lives in Auckland with her partner and child.

Louise Pembroke has been an active campaigner in the survivor movement for a number of years. she is current Chair of Survivors Speak Out. Her book, *Self-Harm: Perspectives from Personal Experience*, was short-listed for the Mind Book of the Year Award.

Rachel Perkins works for Pathfinder Mental Health Services NHS Trust as a Clinical Director and Consultant Clinical Psychologist. In addition, and in no particular order, she is a user of mental health services, a lesbian, a feminist, a writer, a trainer and a political activist. Her most recent book is *Women's Mental Health in Context: Working Papers on Women's Diversity, Mental Health and Good Practice*, which she edited with Zenobia Nadirshaw, Jeanette Copperman and Catherine Andrews.

Jim Read lives in London and is a self-employed consultant, trainer and writer on mental health issues. He is particularly interested in service user perspectives and is a member of Survivors Speak Out. He is author of *The Equal Opportunities Book*, a teacher of re-evaluation counselling and has been active in many left-wing and environmental groups.

Jill Reynolds lives in Bristol and is a lecturer in the School of Health and Social Welfare at the Open University. She has worked previously as a social worker, as a trainer with voluntary organisations working with refugees, and as a lecturer on social work qualifying courses. She has written on social work and refugees, on learning how to work with interpreters, and on gender issues in social work education.

Maggy Ross was for several years a copywriter for leading advertising agencies in London and Bristol. As a result of periods of intense depression she turned to self-harm, a topic on which she lectured to doctors and health workers. In 1986, she helped to found the Bristol Crisis Service for Women. Four years later, at the age of thirty, she took her own life.

Terry Simpson worked for several years as a mental health advocate and is currently co-ordinator of the UK Advocacy Network. He lives in a housing co-op in Leeds, is an active member of Survivors' Poetry, and has a beautiful baby granddaughter.

Igor Spreizer was born in Slovenia in 1967. He had his first manic attack in 1989 and has twice been hospitalised in Ljubljana. He was educated as a computer technician and is now secretary of Association ALTRA – a user-led mental health organisation. He is also leader of a number of projects, such as radio shows, publications and a social network. He is still on medication but he handled his last two episodes himself, with support form the ALTRA crisis team.

Brian Taylor worked for Rochdale Mind during an eight-year cycle of growth as a user/survivor-led organisation. Whilst out of action following a berreavement, he has found sustenance in the mysteries of nature. Various experiences as a mental health system avoider, in mutual support networks, and in men's groups, have led to an interest in 'masculinities' and emotional wellbeing.

Leah Thorn is a performance poet, who explores issues of liberation through the spoken word and runs workshops that enable young people and adults to explore and express their creativity. She is happiest when dancing, reading and bargain-hunting in markets – especially the one close to her home in Deptford, SE London.

Joan Tugwell lives in Sussex with her three cats. She spent over thirty-three years of her life in mental institutions but now has her own bungalow. She has lived independently for ten years, supported by her keyworker, and has several stories published of her experiences.

Jan Wallcraft is currently researching user perspectives on community crisis services at South Bank University, London. She is a former recipient of mental health services, and now works to change and improve them. Her interests are women's mental health issues, aromatherapy, Chinese medicine and healing.

Elizabeth Wurtzel received the 1986 Rolling Stone College Journalism Award for essay writing. She was the popular-music critic for the *New Yorker* and *New York Magazine*. She lives in New York City.

Authors for whom we do not have biographical notes have preferred to remain anonymous or could not be contacted.

Introduction

We are proud to bring you this collection of writing by people who have experienced emotional distress. It includes contributions from people who have been supported through difficult times by friends and family, people who have used medication and those who have been detained in psychiatric institutions against their will. In this diverse collection, we include one account from a man who was depressed for a month and another whose stay in mental hospital lasted forty-one years. We have searched far and wide for material for this book. It includes extracts from autobiographies, articles from professional journals and new writing that we have especially commissioned for this publication. Although most contributions are from Britain, there is also writing from New Zealand, Slovenia and the USA.

In the great debates about mental health – psychological versus medical approaches, institutions versus community care and so on – the views of people who are most affected have rarely been considered. This is beginning to change, in these days of compulsory consultation and 'user forums', but discussion is still predominantly on terms set by politicians and psychiatrists.

Here, away from the world of busy agendas, short-term decision-making and political expediency, over fifty people share their experiences, knowledge and opinions.

If the feelings, behaviour and thoughts of people who receive psychiatric treatment defy psychiatrists' best efforts to categorise them into definable illnesses, we had a similar problem with their writing. In attempting to put a structure to this book we found that our desire for neatly described episodes of distress, courses of treatment and periods of recovery were constantly thwarted by the writers' insistence on bringing their whole lives into their accounts.

Patricia Brunner's crisis of identity should be seen in the context of the difficulties her parents experienced as strict protestants from rural Jamaica, coping with the life in the permissive atmosphere of 1960s

Britain. Elizabeth Wurtzel's feelings about her use of the anti-depressant Prozac have to be understood in a context of being 'young and depressed in America' at a time when Prozac has become a national obsession. Mental distress needs to be thought about in the context of individuals' whole lives.

Nevertheless, we have grouped these articles, as best we can, into sections, ordered in such a way as to reflect the path through life taken by many of the contributors.

We start with 'Emotional Distress and Its Causes', which includes accounts of depression, self-harm and agoraphobia. Cultural conflict, parental neglect and sexual abuse are identified as some of the causes of distress. We move on to 'Psychiatric Treatment' with accounts of encounters with doctors, and experiences with medication and electroconvulsive therapy.

'Life as an In-Patient' takes us inside mental hospitals. There are some horrific accounts of mistreatment, plenty of humour and some generous praise for staff who are prepared to ally themselves with the patients. 'Moving into the Community' includes several contributions from long-stay patients who have been moved out under the care in the community policy, with varied experience of responding to the challenges and opportunities of 'a second chance for life'.

'Therapy and Self-Help' includes contributions from people who have turned their backs on psychiatric treatment and others who have never been diagnosed as mentally ill but have still felt the need for support to overcome difficulties in their lives. Finally, 'Working for Change' is about how people who have experienced emotional distress have organised in order to influence the way they are regarded by others, lobby for better services and treatments, and campaign for civil rights and against discrimination.

Reading explicit accounts of mistreatment and personal anguish can feel liberating and affirming, or shocking and numbing, depending on your own life experience. Putting this collection together kept us on a roller-coaster of emotion, as we became entangled in discussions and disputes about the views expressed in the articles. It soon became apparent that our responses reflected our own allegiances. What one person views as justified anger another may experience as an unfair attack. Even if we both agreed on the validity of an argument, one of us might feel vindicated and the other defensive. If you feel shocked by any of these accounts we hope you will agree that if this anthology leads to more understanding of people experiencing mental distress, and to better services, then it has been worth while.

It has been a pleasure to track down many of the contributions to this book and bring them to a new audience. It has been a privilege to be able to offer several people a first opportunity to go into print. We are all too aware of the wealth of good writing that we were unable to include and many areas of experience that we were not able to cover.

There has always been protest by people designated as 'mad', but in the last ten years, the movement of independent action groups of survivors and service users has flourished beyond any expectation (Campbell, 1996). Writing has played a significant role in raising consciousness; and in the development of a shared body of expertise and ideas within this movement. By bringing some of the best of this writing together with some substantial new contributions we hope to have added to its growing influence.

Reference

Campbell, P. (1996) 'The History of the User Movement', in Heller, T., Reynolds, J., Gomm, R., Muston, R. and Pattison, S. (eds), *Mental Health Matters*, Macmillan, Basingstoke.

Part one

EMOTIONAL DISTRESS AND ITS CAUSES

Introduction

Emotional distress covers a huge range of human experience in its depth and duration, the feelings and perceptions of the people experiencing it, and the symptoms they present to the world. The first four articles are stories of survival, taking us through the causes and experience of distress, then on to psychiatric treatment and beyond it to building a new life. By doing so, they offer some clues as to how distress can be overcome, which are taken up in later sections of the book.

Pam Mason was treated for agoraphobia – the fear of being away from home. But in 'Agoraphobia: Letting Go' she reveals what can lie behind such a diagnosis. For her, it was the feeling of being possessed by the devil which, with hindsight, she attributes to 'absolute burning fury about the way my life was'.

In 'Afraid to Live and Afraid to Die' Richie B. tells us how sexual and physical abuse in childhood led him to a life of 'drinking and drugging', and eventual breakdown. A psychiatrist decided he had paranoid schizophrenia, but this is one of several articles that question the value of psychiatric diagnosis and treatment. For Richie B. healing and recovery became possible when he had the opportunity to build trusting relationships with people with whom he could open up about himself.

'A Survival Story' and 'The Pressure of Being a Human Chameleon' are about racism and identity. Patricia Brunner and her parents moved from Jamaica to England. Veronica Dewan's biological parents were Irish and Indian, but she was adopted and brought up as English. These are the human stories behind the statistics that show high rates of psychiatric hospital admission among immigrants and their descendants.

The above contributors were able to look back on their emotional distress with some sense of having coming through it. Nicki's account, 'I've Lost My Innocence', was given to the counsellor and researcher Moira Walker. Nicki, who is sixteen, is in the midst of coping with the effects of beatings from her mother, being taken into care and witnessing the suffering of her younger sisters. She is wise enough to know the support she needs, but we are left wondering if it will be forthcoming and what the future holds for her.

Maggy Ross describes her self-injuring as a 'Silent Scream'. It may seem to have little in common with Pam Mason's agoraphobia and may evoke a different response from the reader. But she, too, recognises unexpressed anger to be a root cause. Perhaps this is why agoraphobia and self-harm are both experienced by many more women than men.

Leah Thorn's poem 'Finger Pickin' Good' takes up the theme of self-harm. It is a reminder that behaviour that may appear bizarre and frightening to others is often an extreme version of more socially acceptable habits which may, themselves, mask a great deal of inner pain.

In 'I Suffered from Depression' a psychiatric nurse describes his experience. In this instance it lasted only a few weeks but was still a devastating ordeal. The writer regards his depression as an illness brought on by a change in circumstances; yet he was reluctant to seek medical help, describes his GP as 'as much use as the milkman' and attributes his recovery to the support of his girlfriend and father. The scathing comments about his fellow nurses' attitudes towards people who are depressed prepare us for the fundamental criticisms of psychiatric treatment to be found in the following sections. This part finishes with 'Unplanned Journey', an account of the early signs of Alzheimer's disease. By the very nature of their condition, people with Alzheimer's have difficulty communicating about their distress and speaking up for themselves. Diane Friel McGowin gives us a rare insight into the experience of realising you are losing your memory.

Agoraphobia: Letting Go

PAM MASON

When I was five years old, I thought I was possessed by the Devil.

The Devil wasn't there all the time. He usually arrived in the school holidays, the only guest we ever had in our house, turning up when I was bored, when the family relationship had begun to crack under the strain of us all being shut up together, day after day. There were no trips to the cinema or walks to the park. We just all sat there separately, in front of the TV.

He usually came at night when I was in bed. My mind would wander, my self-control would slip, and he would slide into my head, splitting me in two, turning the world wildly surreal, as if it was another planet, a place bizarre beyond the scope of science fiction. When the Devil had me, I did not even recognise my own body: what were these white tubes of flesh that imprisoned me? When the Devil came, I wanted to shrug off body, self, experience, everything, and evaporate into space.

But the other part of me wanted to kill the devil and be an ordinary little girl again, and that part always won, though each victory seemed like a miracle. I would scream for my mother. Even though there was normally some hostility between us, my mother was the only one who could make it better. 'You shouldn't think so much,' she'd say to me, and I agreed. But how could I stop?

I knew I was the only person in the world who had this. I called it That Feeling, but I collected other (inaccurate) scarewords over the years: mad, schizophrenic; 'in the head', 'neurotic', 'head the ball' if you want to be Scouse about it. I never ruled out demonic possession. I hadn't been in a Catholic church since I was christened, but perhaps I got Catholicism by osmosis. I remember being about ten or eleven, sitting with my friend, playing with dolls on the kitchen floor in her house, thinking how outraged her mother would be if she knew that a consort of Satan was in

3

her house. And I feared dying because I knew what Hell was: That Feeling, for all eternity.

I couldn't tell anyone about it, not properly. I knew that if I ever did describe it accurately to anyone, they would get it too, and their lives would be ruined.

No one outside the house noticed anything much, except that I had what is now called school phobia, and that I was a very quiet child. But I did well academically, and at sixteen I was preparing to sit ten O levels.

And then That Feeling started happening in the classroom. Reality would swim horribly around me, and I longed to get up and run away home.

My mother called the doctor. He came to the house. 'What's the matter?' he said, tired, irritable. 'I don't know,' I said, smiling, with all the embarrassed incoherence of sixteen.

He wrote a prescription for Ativan. He carried on writing prescriptions for Ativan for the next eight years. Little blue tablets, crumbly on the tongue, instant salvation, the hammer to the Devil. Immense relief, and then, all too soon, the agony of waiting for it to be time to take the next one. They worked wonderfully at first, but after a while taking them had no effect on me, except to add addiction to my other worries.

I was preparing for my A levels, dreaming of studying English at Liverpool University. None of our family had ever been to university before. I was to be the first. If all went well.

But terrible things were happening at home – inexplicable frightening things. People very close to me, driven by their own sadnesses, were trying to harm themselves. Although I thought I was coping perfectly, That Feeling was swooping down on me with increasing regularity. I had no one to tell it all to – my best friend had just discovered boys and I no longer felt close enough to her. So, I threw myself into my schoolwork, convincing myself that I was fine, in spite of everything. I did my homework, wrote my essays, asked questions in class. And when That Feeling swooped down during lessons as if I was Tippi Hedren in *The Birds*, I would scribble notes frantically to keep it from completely engulfing me. That helped with my work anyway, so what was there to worry about?

But I began to feel frightened of being away from familiar people, familiar places. When I was seventeen, I had gone to London with the school. At eighteen I was afraid to go, afraid of That Feeling possessing me when I was hundreds of miles from home and help. I missed open days at Sheffield and Hull Universities because I was frightened of the journeys.

Then, one Saturday night, I was sitting in front of the fire reading *The Grapes of Wrath* when it happened to me. The Devil, or whatever it was, took full possession of me. I began to scream and I couldn't stop, the Feeling was so terrible. They called a doctor, a man I'd never seen before. He looked at me with terrible pity, insisted that I go and see a psychiatrist and gave me some sleeping pills.

I didn't see the psychiatrist because she was in Whiston and I was too scared to go so far from home and she wouldn't make house calls. But I did get repeat prescriptions for the sleeping tablets.

Before long I found the thought of going to Liverpool city centre, only seven miles away, a place I loved more than anywhere else in the world, too hard to imagine. And then Huyton Village, a quarter of a mile away, became too far. School was about three hundred yards down the road – somehow I got there during the last few weeks. I got through all my exams, breaking down on the last day, but battling on, doing the papers, getting some good marks, incredibly.

And then I just collapsed. It was a struggle to get as far as the garden gate.

By now I realised I had a form of agoraphobia. I fought. I made myself go out of the house, brief and terrifying as such trips were. Although Mum was fighting her own problems at the time, she offered to go out with me. This meant I could get further from the house and the freedom was as precious to me as it would be to any prisoner travelling under escort. But instead of curing our problems, we had pooled them. I became acutely dependent on her. We acted out the roles of extremely protective mother and sick, frightened toddler. She had to be there all the time now, to hold me and save me when That Feeling came, as it often did, blasting away at my self and all my hope. How could I ever live a normal life when I had this in my head? I read Claire Weekes's books and Open Door newsletters, desperate for a solution, but only terrified myself with other people's symptoms.

But agoraphobics sometimes take chances, shock themselves with their own achievements. I did this in 1982, when I tried to take up a place at Bangor University.

My mother and I stayed there for three days, three days when I couldn't eat and certainly couldn't go out alone, before we conceded defeat.

At home, I saw another doctor and insisted on being given better help.

And he referred me to a trainee psychologist who was prepared to do home visits.

Jacqui, her name was, a pretty young woman with a mass of hair and a slight Birmingham accent. She came to the house and together we teased out some strands of my life. I began to see that this agrophobia hadn't just come down on me like a thunderbolt, but was the result of years of pressure, twisting my mind out of shape so that nothing was where it should be any more. Together, we began to name the Devil.

Jacqui took up a post with the Liverpool Health Authorities and, after a lot of agony and fear, I got into a taxi (with my mother) and we went to Fazakerley Hospital to see her.

I saw her twice a week, for several years, at Fazakerley and Walton Hospitals. And afterwards, Mum and I would get a taxi into town, into Liverpool, and just being there was heaven. The long wide streets, the old buildings, the Mersey, all the sites of the struggles of my ancestors, Catholic and Protestant, of the workers, of those fierce, fighting women, the ghosts blowing round the corners of St George's Hall and London Road, whom I could sense, but whose names I would not learn for many years yet.

Jacqui and I were uncovering everything, every patch of misery and fear, every manifestation of the Devil in my life.

The years passed like this, and it could have gone on forever probably: I'd heard all those horror stories about agoraphobics who stay indoors for decades. People think it isn't curable. Would I ever leave home, I used to wonder, would I ever be able to go out without my mother? Jacqui was sure I could, anyway.

I had made up my mind that I had to go to university, to get so far away that there would be no going back, no chance of getting a lift home in the first week. I chose Exeter, Brighton, Norwich. Before that, I hadn't even known where those places were, except that they were vaguely 'down south'. I looked at the map in the front of my new 1985 diary and I could hardly believe that places so far away from home could exist.

I remember the interviews, the journeys, long tunnels of winter darkness, the long drab nightmare of late-night trains, changing platforms, pitch-dark stations floating in a nowhere dotted with stars and red and green lights.

I was terrified of the journey (three hundred miles, via London) to Norwich. So I didn't go. I phoned and made an excuse. And they offered me a place, unconditionally.

I couldn't believe it. I still can't. I used to sit and wait for them to write back and say, sorry, there's been a mistake, we meant to give it to someone else. But in October 1985 Jacqui met me on Lime Street Station and I boarded the London train alone. My mother was seven miles away, twenty miles, a hundred, two hundred.

Crossing London, I shared a taxi with a Russian woman, who told me that her mother had been far too stern and restrictive with her. 'So I gave my daughter a lot of freedom,' she said wryly, 'and now she says I don't love her.'

From Liverpool Street, I took the train through East Anglia, through the wide, bright fields which stretched to the horizon. The light was hot, everything was strange after the north – no cities, no towns, no big rivers.

And I got there. And I stayed. And I got my degree.

I'd like to be able to say it was all gloriously easy, but it wasn't. I was anorexic, obsessive, I got into all sorts of difficulties. After all, I had spent all my time from eighteen to twenty-four locked in the house or beside my mother, and I knew very little of life. I'd like to be able to say I'm fine now, but I'm not. I still have eating disorders, still get agoraphobic at times of stress, and I suffer from depression badly. But I think that this is to be expected. You can't spend twenty-odd years of your life thinking you're possessed, fearing death and hell every second, without being scarred by it.

But physically, I am free. I get around town without thinking about it much, I look after myself, I no longer have that (mutually) awful dependence on my mother.

I fought for my freedom, but I had a lot of help. And a lot of luck. It takes my breath away now, thinking how lucky I was: lucky to be educated enough to get to university, lucky to be offered a place like that, lucky to find a psychologist who was so adaptable and so good at her job.

All this happened in the early 1980s. Can agoraphobics still get home visits and intense attention on the NHS? I had a full student grant, and in those days students could still claim dole and housing benefit in vacations. That was vital: it was essential, for my sanity and my survival, that I did not go home between university terms. Agoraphobia is a disease incubated, hatched and sustained in unhealthy families. What do agoraphobics do about leaving home nowadays, when student grants are inadequate and students can't claim any money during vacations? Where do agoraphobics go if they can't get to college, when there are no council flats and housing association lists are years long and few landlords will let rooms to the unwaged and suitable special homes can be counted on the fingers of one hand?

It makes me furious that the escape routes I took have been closed off by government cuts.

Becoming free was all about learning about myself. What I once thought was the Devil was, mainly, anger: absolute burning fury about the way my life was, about the things that were happening to me. Like most women, I had learned to eat my own anger, not let it show. Suppressed and feared, it became concentrated, and sought expression in ways that terrified me. That Feeling was a bundle of 'wrong' emotions: anger, fear, need, love. I still get That Feeling. When I am most brave, I do not fight That Feeling, and though the feeling of dissolving is frightening, at the heart of it I always find a vital message.

I feel now that this is part of my life's work: letting go when That Feeling comes, and learning from it. Not fighting feels dreadful, almost impossible, like staying in the saddle of a bolting horse or not yanking your hands away from flames. Agoraphobics are prisoners of fear. I want all agoraphobics and all women to know that fulfilment lies in passing bravely *through* fear. At times I can be cowardly. But I now know what I want, and need, my life to be.

Afraid to Live and Afraid to Die

RICHIE B.

My father had been a farmer, a soldier, a boxer and a survivor. To me, when young, he was simply an alcoholic and a bastard. His past was totally irrelevant as I became tuned in to his ever-changing and bewildering present. He was never very loving, although sometimes he would display a cheerful disposition and temperament when drunk. At other times he would rage. My mother and I would both feel the full force of his left hook. No one heard as we defended and consoled each other from his almighty temper.

As a consequence, I have had the shadow of victimhood torture my personality. As a child I wasn't aware of this. The horror show happened, and there was no social reproof or accountability – therefore it was normal to my young eyes. However, unlike many others I have known, it was my good fortune at a later stage to discover that my childhood was anything but normal. The truth in my case has been a liberating force.

Within five years of my birth there were three further child-victims. A decision was made that the family was now heavily laden and thus complete. We had all slept in a large bedroom until the arrival of my third sister. Now, bedroom positions were to be rearranged and my mother and father separated. This geographical form of contraception was to prove costly to me, as the parental hierarchy deigned that I should sleep in the same bed as my father, lest he should die in the loneliness of his anguish and sorrows. I had an internal tantrum, but failed to verbalise it, in case it meant another beating. It wasn't the last time I surrendered, without expressed objection, to a highly distressing and absolutely unwanted situation.

He arrived drunk on the first night of the new arrangement and promptly collapsed into deep unconsciousness on the bed. I arose in the hope that my mother would provide some support and comfort. I knocked on the door of the other bedroom. No response. I knocked again.

No response. I knew she and the others were all awake. It was too silent. She was abandoning me. I was the trade-in. Loneliness and rejection shivered right through me. No one was there for me. I was all alone in life and I was five years old. I wanted to cry, but couldn't. He might awaken, then Mamma would be angry too. I quietly slid back to bed and stared vacantly into the dark until I lost consciousness.

The sexual abuse began fairly soon after the new relocation arrangements. Invariably, my father was drunk. He would arrive home, usually slobbering, ranting and much given to self-glorification. If I was lucky, he would fall into a deep slumber on entry into bed. Often, he would sing from his repertoire of three songs and would jostle me, attempting to engage me (as though I were a fellow drunk) in his inebriated revelry. Sometimes, these music sessions lasted until the small hours and usually were ensued by his being 'playful' with me. He would tickle my stomach and around the genital areas. This always confused me, as I enjoyed the tingly sensations. However, when he went nearer the genitals, I wanted him to stop, but couldn't muster any resistance. He was all-powerful. I was a little boy. I did not recognise that my physical, emotional and other boundaries were being invaded without my consent. Worst of all, I had no one to turn to with my dilemmas and pain. I had a sensation that something untoward was happening, but parents cannot be wrong in a child's eyes. Hence, I took on board the guilt of my father's actions.

Inside, I felt a lot of anger and rage, but was powerless to express it or stop him. My feelings of shame, self-blame, confusion and self-rejection ensured that my traumas remained firmly in my own head, never to be divulged to another. Sometimes, I would waken to find him masturbating and rubbing his wet penis against my bum (I had no underwear or pyjamas). Other times, I would awaken to feel something sticky and wet on the bed sheets. Over a period of time, I began to lie on the very edge of the bed trying to sleep on my front, so he could only touch my genitals by moving my body. I have no recollections of him attempting overt sexual abuse. My defensive and strained posture has led to long-term problems with my back.

Often, I had school the following day and was constantly bleary-eyed and in a state of trance in the classrooms, through lack of sleep and constant anxiety and tension. Even when sexual abuse didn't happen at night, the threat was always there. I was under constant stress. We slept in the same bed until I was fourteen and physically powerful enough to assert my right to sleep in an unoccupied ('haunted', my parents used to tell us children) bedroom. The abuse continued sporadically throughout this period.

Soon after the sexual abuse began, my mother began using me as a scapegoat and male replacement for her anger against my father. Many times, she beat me with a stick across the legs and arms for the slightest 'mistake'. I refused to cry, because I knew it frustrated her and also knew her anger was being misdirected onto me. She often commented on how 'awful' a child I was and how unfortunate she was to be cursed with such 'evil' offspring.

Around this time, I also began to have severe nightmares of being abused sexually by large groups of males. I became frightened of sleep. I often imagined that I was choking to death. The fear was horrific, although I couldn't label the feeling at the time. I just felt something very bad and mad was wrong with me.

I was smoking with maternal consent and supply at the age of seven. At about the age of eleven I began drinking alcohol. Because my financial status was next to nil, I embarked on a career of breaking and entering various premises, to acquire alcohol and cigarettes. This was fairly common for young people in the area. The estate was the local council's dumping site for all manners of social misfits. It was impossible to get a job. The area had a reputation and the police wouldn't come onto the estate after the fall of darkness.

I loved the booze. It gave me sensations of power and enabled me to express deep angers and resentments against authority. Consequently, I was engaged in much vandalism and attacks on people. My underage drinking was seldom challenged by my parents and when challenged was met with great defiance by me. I was becoming older and bigger. Someday, I would kill my father, I thought.

My pain was more acute when I was sober, so I felt the need to drink more often. Without alcohol, I was easy pickings for social predators. My esteem was nil and I was uncontrollably emanating signals that my boundaries could be easily smashed with no consequence to the perpetrator. Consequently, I was on the receiving end of many uninvited street beatings. My expectations of life were abuse. Between the ages of eleven and fourteen I was sexually violated by two male teenagers from the area. At the age of fourteen I was making regular visits to the GP who was prescribing Ativan to me 'for nerves'. I had had numerous overnight stays in police stations and had made several court appearances. I believe I was a fully fledged alcoholic at the age of seventeen.

School was one of my saving graces. Education became my main defence mechanism. Both of my parents encouraged my schooling, as I was considered bright and they had had no educational chances. I strove to achieve at school and wanted to be the number one pupil in the classroom. My sense of shame and inferiority underpinned this drive. My intelligence earned me some respect and helped me to feel somewhat equal to other boys from richer backgrounds. There was much sympathy and encouragement from teachers and fellow pupils. My education allowed me access to other social classes and a broader outlook on life.

This became important at a later stage, as my healing process involved having a certain educative background.

Having achieved the required educational results, I moved to a larger city to go to university and pursue an arts degree. On arrival, I became bewildered and intimidated by the largeness and anonymity of the city and I promptly got drunk. This continued until I acquired friends in college, when the drinking was tempered a little. I was introduced to drugs within a month, and they appealed to me. I knew at depth my drinking was alcoholic and hated this fact. (I swore I would never be like my father.) Using drugs was 'cooler' and more 'sophisticated' than drinking. However, I was never comfortable with illegal drugs, but the smug superiority over alcoholics and denial of my own alcoholism ensured a continual use of them.

My food and accommodation was paid for by a charity from my home town. Many people, including myself, had good intentions for me, but I was becoming oblivious to all things, including positive input from others into my life.

I failed my exams because of my drinking and drugging. I couldn't concede to this, so embarked on a crazy scenario of continuing unregistered and unfunded in college for a second year. I was oblivious to the fact that I was entitled to benefits and was homeless throughout that year. Sometimes I did stay with friends, although their altruism and patience ran out, as I was often drunk and stoned. As well as sleeping in doorways, I regularly broke into a house near college and slept in the front room. I was permitted, occasionally, to sleep in a cell at the local police station, if there was a 'vacancy' after midnight. I sold drugs to finance my drinking and other habits. Food was a secondary need. I failed my exams a second time. Soon afterwards, I broke down completely. My internal distress was mirrored by my external reality. I was in a seemingly endless nightmare and I was awake. I somehow managed to get to my home town.

My mother took me to my GP. He said my problems were now outside his jurisdiction and that I would need psychiatric help. We went to the local psychiatric unit and my 'case' was 'assessed'. The psychiatrist wanted to commit me for 'treatment', but my mother declined, for which I shall be eternally grateful. It didn't take long for the label of 'paranoid schizophrenic' to be pronounced over my dead spirit. I was tendered a large dose of Largactil (a major tranquilliser) to appease my reality. My bail from the hospital confines entailed a two-times-a-week attendance at the local psychiatric clinic. At first, I used to speak with the psychiatrist for an hour or so, divulging some thoughts and feelings. Soon my attendance at the clinic became a prescription collection service only. This discipline was to continue for a period of over six years, during which time I had many changes of psychiatrists and medication.

Some psychiatrists said I could drink, but not smoke dope; others said I could smoke dope, but not drink. I availed of a personal interpretation of the best of both advices. I drank and drugged on top of the medication. The pills were having the effect of merely dampening my severe distress and made me look very weird. I sought to block my whole reality out. Though plagued with constant thoughts of suicide, I had a very strong will to survive. This attribute was one of the better legacies of my parents.

My recollection of events from 1978 to 1984 is very clouded and almost like a dream. However, I acknowledge that every alert moment was extremely painful with constant fears of swallowing my tongue, my eardrums shattering, my mind snapping or my stomach collapsing. I used to break down in the middle of conversations and wanted to hide away from people. I was afraid to live and afraid to die. I was a shaking 16 stone-plus nervous wreck. I looked and felt like a zombie.

In March 1984 I met a member of Alcoholics Anonymous, who managed to reach behind my defences by opening up about himself. I wanted to stop drinking and drugging, and had reached the stage where I couldn't from my own resources. So his entry into my life was timely. Coincidentally, within a week, I met a new female psychiatrist at the clinic. She decided that I had been on major tranquillisers for far too long and gave me a final six-month prescription. Though stopping drinking, drugging and psychiatry were major blows to my 'security' at the time, I now see two people demonstrating a lot of faith in my ability to heal and recover.

In AA, I felt more at home than at any other time, as people's experiences in AA mirrored my own in many respects. I will forever be grateful to my surrogate family of misfits, who provided love, faith and encouragement to me, the unlovable and self-despising. I have not taken an unprescribed drug or a drink since I went to AA. In September 1984 I put down my last psychiatric drug. Stopping drinking was not easy. Staying stopped was even harder. The first three years were turbulent and traumatic, although I withstood them. The pain for the first time seemed meaningful and I felt some security that I was at last on the right track.

I began getting concerned at my slow rate of recovery when I witnessed other alcoholics of less sobriety time make quicker strides back into society. I carried a huge inferiority. I still had no concept of the horrendous abuses I had been through. I engaged in a relationship with a fellow alcoholic and lost my virginity at the age of twenty-eight. She was on vacation, it was very fleeting and she returned to Chicago after some three weeks. Within six months all hell broke loose inside me. I had no idea of the extent of the wounds opened up as a consequence of the relationship. I became sieged by feelings of dread, rage, overwhelming lust, suspicion, shame, guilt, being a victim and a perpetrator, sexual confusion and many other unpleasant sensations.

I became isolated and could no longer relate on some levels to my fellow alcoholics. It was disheartening to be with friends and be unable to disentangle and rationalise this seemingly endless maze of feeling. I managed to uncover some understanding and release through writing. Thankfully, I had a strong faith that AA would maintain my physical sobriety, if I continued attending, which I did. Eventually I moved to London in an attempt to address my difficulties.

Early in 1991, I had almost lost all hope when I came across a book called *Male Rape* in a charity shop. It was my second major brush with good fortune, following my discovery of AA. On reading this book, I began to see very clearly that I had been sexually abused. It seemed that every nonalcoholic idiosyncrasy I had was mentioned and it could all be tied in with being a victim of sexual assault. My heart leapt. A help line was advertised in the back pages. I rang at the earliest possible time, got a response and soon was receiving one-on-one specialised sexual abuse psychotherapy.

In therapy, I was scared and distrusting, but gradually opened up every nook and cranny of my personality. My sessions were free of charge, which was very important to me at the time as it helped me believe my psychotherapist was genuine. I devoted a lot of time to reading literature on sexual abuse and tried to access memories of abuse by regular writing. I am proud of the work I did on myself at that time.

The one-on-one sessions continued for a period of about six months. Then, I was encouraged to join a facilitated group of male survivors. After a further six months, the facilitator departed. I still attend this group once a week and gain valuable support, insight and perspective into my various life situations.

Over a period of time, I found that parental alcoholism and childhood violence were further areas I needed to examine, feel the childhood pain and share with others. I now receive counselling for both areas, although I find accessing memories of violence extremely difficult and painful. I have not yet fully come to terms with some incidents and areas of my life, although I now feel more in control than ever. My systems of support are of my own choice and I have input from very valuable people in my life.

My faith and trust in human beings is increasing daily and my sense of personal safety is getting stronger. I have always felt like a sitting duck and a target for various forms of attack. I exuded victimhood. Over the past few years I am gradually feeling stronger in myself, developing better self-assertion and belief, and have become more capable of self-protection than previously.

Because most of my healing and recovery has been freely given, involving self-help agencies and the voluntary sector, I am now heavily involved in voluntary activities. I write articles for various newsletters. I am particularly engaged in the area of mental health. I campaign locally for services for victims of sexual abuse and other forms of oppression. I am fortunate to be on many local forums and committees where my voice is heard and respected, although not always acted upon in ways I would like. However, I feel I have helped to shift the focus somewhat in the planning and delivery of local services for people with mental health difficulties. I enjoy this work, as my own personal experiences and skills combine to at least try to improve services. I also get to meet professionals, whom I used to fear and dread, on an equal basis. I am gradually losing my feelings of inconsequence and inferiority through participation in society on a basis I favour.

I have also spoken and run workshops at various mental health conferences. My skills are being gradually increased through training as a reward for my involvement with various agencies. Campaigning helps me to effectively channel my anger against all forms of oppression and provides me with a valid outlet to endorse my outrage at my own childhood experiences. With the passage of time, I am seeing the black clouds of my long winter of distress and despair gradually depart from my life. I am a strong and resilient survivor and I am becoming stronger.

A Survival Story

PATRICIA BRUNNER

My name is Patricia. My parents, Enid and Clovis Brown, grew up in rural Jamaica, both receiving a rigorous Protestant upbringing, both deeply imbued with its ethic of work, respectability and abstinence, and with its guilts and fears. They lived in a society which, in theory, lived up to certain sexual mores, but which in practice ignored them. This I think contributed to their problems in adjusting to life when they came to England, and in raising a child here. It was particularly hard for my mother. She had been reared in a much stricter manner than my father, as is usual I suppose for girls, and in consequence had become very prim and prudish, in a manner which was anachronistic even for England in the 1950s. 1955 was the year in which we arrived to join my father.

Back in Jamaica her family connections and, it has to be said, her light skin (very much an asset in those days) had made her a person of some importance in her small community. But in England she was just another 'coloured' woman, an immigrant. At first she worked as a housekeeper in the vicarage where we had rooms to stay, and I suppose it was not much like the stiffly formal church manse where she had been raised. She felt herself misunderstood, brushed aside, probably humiliated, by people whose freedom of manner was to her immoral, unacceptable. Yet these were white people – the very people whom she looked up to, the people by whom she and her generation measured their standards of excellence! The confusion was too much for her and she had a breakdown. I was three in that year, the same year of our arrival in England. So I have no clear memory of my mother before she became disturbed.

As a child I never really knew how to cope with her. Mostly I hated her because of the stigma of mental illness which overshadowed our family life. Her behaviour was sometimes strange and unpredictable. My father thought that when we finally got a house of our own she might feel better, but it was not so.

16

Things continued as before. She would imagine that people were insulting her. Once she spat at a man in the street for no reason I could see . . . I cringed and tugged at her hand. I was ashamed of her. She came shouting into my school a couple of times, and everyone knew I was the mad woman's daughter. I had very few real friends. Our house was a lonely, isolated place.

I can't remember exactly how many times I came home and found that my mother had been 'taken away'. I knew all about Prestwick, the famous asylum in the Manchester area, before I was out of junior school.

I have to admit that I hated my mother for all the selfish child reasons that had to do with the way her illness affected me, the way it made me unhappy. I did not spare a thought for her pain, her problems, the darkness in which her own mind must have been wandering in its dreadful loneliness. Now I can.

My parents now live back in Jamaica, having gone there when my father retired. When I see my mother in that setting, doing her chores, ministering deftly and sympathetically to a sick relative, being hospitable to neighbours and old friends, I think of the woman she might have been, and of the appalling waste of a human being this signifies. All those years in England – all those years of grief, heartache and racism. Perhaps there had always been a rational person inside her struggling for assertion, but conventional methods of treatment failed to achieve much. Yet the simple act of returning to a society in which she could be both accepting and acceptable has done more than years of shock treatments and drug therapy.

My father responded to my mother's condition by getting out of the house. He had plenty of reasons to do so. He was a teacher, and he was involved in community and church work. There were long periods in which he would only appear at mealtimes and then disappear on whatever pretext he could find. At night he was rarely in before ten o'clock. But when he was around, he totally eclipsed my mother in my affections. For his part, he invested a lot of hope in me, hopes for my future, me becoming a successful career woman he could point to and be proud of, since the other woman in his life had turned out, in his ungracious term, to be 'a millstone round his neck'.

It strikes me now as odd that he could not see how impossible it was going to be for me to 'succeed' in any significant way, given the severe restrictions that he and my mother both placed on my life. I believed that I had a talent for writing; certainly the isolation and intense boredom which I suffered gave a rise to a desire, a need, to fantasise, to invent imaginary worlds in which to live. I tried poetry and my favourite classes at school when I moved up into grammar school were English and language classes. I wallowed in a wealth of literature and my own efforts were recognised to some extent at school. But to my father this was a hobby, not to be discussed practically; what he wanted was for me to become a teacher like himself and to follow in his footsteps. So enormous was the pressure put on me about this that it did not occur to me to search for alternatives.

As I advanced into puberty and adolescence, and began to cross swords with my father on this and other matters, the controversy became more and more bitter. Unfortunately my mother was unable to provide any counterbalancing viewpoint. I knew that I had to find my own path but I was in confusion; I was afraid. I was certainly not like my schoolfriends, confident and matter-of-fact about the basic facts of life, work, money, sex. And it seemed to me that when I tried to get my father's help on these subjects, particularly about sex, he would turn on me as if my desperate need to grow up was an attack on him. Yet he could choose so demanding and exacting a profession as teacher for me! From the strain of living in such a perpetual dilemma I began at fifteen to turn now and then to drink. My parents left me alone on this. I think it was something they, in their respectability, could not bear to think about, and they could not cope with it. Ever since then I have been a regular drinker.

I once read a phrase in a story which seemed to me to be very enlightening on the subject of 'why' people drink. It was simply 'so my brain would be quiet and leave me alone'. For me, peace of mind was unattainable without some kind of artificial help. When I drank , none of this sorry mess seemed to matter. If I could not find happiness, drink seemed to be an acceptable ersatz.

After taking my A levels at eighteen I got a place at Birmingham University, and since my father had convinced me that I was going to teach, I decided to major in modern languages. Despite being eighteen, legally an adult, I was still very much a child, afraid of taking my life in my own hands. Any activities I had initiated myself had always been frowned on, disapproved of; my interests in the Black movement had been dismissed as nonsense. Nothing I could produce myself had ever been taken seriously; even my writing was thought of as something I would 'grow out of'.

Now that I was free from my parents' chaperonage I wanted to try out relationships with men. Inevitably, though, I could not handle men. Sex itself I found painful and difficult; also, to put it bluntly, 'dirty'. The modern, liberated girl I wanted to be was infected with my parents' prejudices more than I was prepared to admit. But you just had to sleep around at university, I thought. That made you 'grown up', acceptable to the other students as one of them. Without knowing what I was doing I became the campus lay, all right for a few nights, but not really capable of a proper relationship. Men said they found me attractive but in the end my distaste for the whole business, my lack of experience, would militate against any real satisfying partnership, so eventually I found myself alone. I had no friends to speak of among the women students. The simple ability to make friends seemed to be beyond me as well. I might find myself among a group of people but always on the periphery, not really knowing what was going on.

At the time of my finals all these troubles came to a head, prompted by the pressure of exams and the anxiety about whatever future might lie beyond those exams. I withdrew into myself. The other students with whom I was associated had little or nothing to do with me, and I began to feel totally isolated and rejected by the world. At this time my parents had moved to Birmingham, my father having found a job there as a peripatetic teacher operating from a language centre, dealing with the problems of children in inner-city schools to whom English was a second language.

I was once more living with my parents. Paradoxically, as my situation worsened, theirs seemed to have improved. They seemed to have a new lease of life which made me feel all the more inadequate. My father got involved with various grassroots community projects and met forceful, active, self confident, young Black women whom he admired. I could imagine him measuring me against them, and as a result became obsessive about my studies, wanting to excel at least in that direction.

I would study all day and sometimes far into the night, neglecting food sometimes and taking caffeine pills constantly to stay awake and alert. Nevertheless, my academic work suffered and I simply could not take in all the things that I read. As I sat in the study hall, or outside in one of the quadrangles, I became convinced that people were watching me disapprovingly or suspiciously. A hopeless despair came over me, a feeling of being loathed and loathsome. As this state of mind took hold, my behaviour did become noticeable to the point where people did start to look at me and perhaps talk in hushed tones about me. My delusions began to mingle themselves with reality, and thus I expect it became harder and harder for me to tell them apart. When I heard whispering voices in my ear they were sometimes real whispers, but sometimes they were not, just an indefinable 'susurrus', a buzzing clamour, and I would wake up with a start, realising that I had lost the last minute or so of consciousness and had been walking or sitting in a daze.

I was taken home from the university clinic, then 'committed'. Mainly I remember the nurses at that time, and their patience and understanding. My parents told me later that some of them cried over my condition, as the doctors found my case so baffling to deal with that they feared I would never get better. My treatment consisted of having everything possible done to me – drugs in various combinations, all kinds of physical checkups and examinations. I began to have the most vivid hallucinations, terrifying delusions of a cosmic nature, a patriarchal god summoning me to be judged, damning me. Then, at last, something 'worked'. I recall sitting upright at a table suddenly, where a nurse, another patient and I were seated, and asking where I was, what hospital I was in, and how long I had been there.

After this I was gradually weaned off drugs and had a course of ECT treatments. The actual convulsion itself was done under a general anaesthetic, so all I knew of it was a slight headache afterwards, and a sensation of almost eerie calm. My attitude towards ECT is somewhat ambiguous. The old lady doctor in charge, with her Middle European accent, was herself such a pleasant person, gentle, dedicated and convinced that she was doing needful, merciful work, that I felt reasonably willing to comply. I did feel better afterwards in some way. But, like drug therapy, I still regard it as being an experimental form of treatment. Also, I feel that it may have some kind of residual effect afterwards. I find I suffer from lapses of memory which I never had before: problems with direction and orientation, finding my way round places or large buildings.

Then, too, there was always this attitude that the doctors knew best and that I had to conform to their notions of recovery in order to get out of the hospital. I never had much of a chance to discuss my problems with them on an equal basis; I was mostly summoned before a group of them, rather like someone on trial, and expected to answer their questions, such as how I was getting on, whether I felt that the treatments were helping me, and why I wasn't going to 'therapy'. Therapy consisted of weaving or making stuffed toys and I saw it all as a waste of time; I preferred talking to other patients in the common room, reading a paper or a book, choosing my own activities. In the end I had to comply; it was a question of 'they knew best' and I was not in a position to argue. It was clear that I would have to go through the motions if I wanted to get anywhere. In that way I graduated to being an outpatient.

One point in my favour was that in the desperate weeks before my finals and my breakdown when I had been searching for something to do, I had come across an advertisement for international telephonists in London in what was then the GPO. I had filled in the forms and done preliminary interviews; now the job was waiting for me. I had spent nearly two months in hospital and had to contemplate this move to London within a very short time. My parents fixed it up for me to stay with some old family friends there, and so in September of 1978 I found myself living and working in the capital with all the excitement and upheaval this entailed.

I continued to take tranquillisers for a while and then stopped as they made me dozy and dreamy, which was a state of mind I wanted to leave behind. Yet underneath I knew that I was not really 'cured' in any real sense. The psychiatrists and the hospital environment had managed to patch together a thin veneer over ingrained problems that were still there. I was still seeking. I tried 'men' and got pregnant, so was doomed to lose my first real job only months after I had started it. I tried running back home with my child, with the result that my parents, still intent on ordering and controlling what was left of my life, encouraged me in as many ways as possible to abdicate my claim on my daughter.

They wanted me to be a child again. I remember my father using the phrase 'pickney mumma' meaning an underage mother not to be taken seriously, even though I was twenty-five. If I railed against this, protested, got upset, I was threatened that they would 'call the doctor' to me again.

Patricia's parents returned to Jamaica, taking her child, Heloise, with them. Patricia set about building up her life, found work and married a Swiss man. They had a baby and prepared for the return of Heloise.

I was helped by Willy's unfailing support. Whatever I did he backed me to the hilt, an attitude which gave me more and more confidence. As opposed to 'Father knows best', which I had suffered from, it very often tends to be in our house that 'Mother knows best', in the sense that my point of view is accepted as valid. For instance, when it became more and more obvious that Heloise was in no shape to contend with the problems of coping with an alien culture like Switzerland, I was the one who prompted our return to England.

Settling down in London once more brought its own strains. I was on my own for six months with the two children while Willy worked out his notice with his Swiss firm. When Willy arrived he went through a period of unemployment and I worked on and off in low-paid jobs: school cleaner, packer in a warehouse, hospital cleaner. The last job was in Hackney Children's Hospital, and my experiences with other women there, their friendship and their raunchiness, which appealed to me, were a factor in choosing this place to settle, to put down roots, a place preferable to the rather 'straight' middle-class, cold neighbourhood we first came to. I think the feeling of coming home that I have here, the feeling that I am no longer drifting pointlessly has helped a great deal.

Now I am living a life that is quiet, reserved and gentle. That is how I am and I have finished trying to be something I am not; for the sake of my father, for the sake of the neighbours or what other people think, or for some God looking down the back of my neck. I am learning gradually – this is an ongoing process – not to dwell on the traumas of the past, to try to deal with things as they happen, and not to worry too much. My drinking problem hasn't gone away and I don't imagine I will ever have a trouble-free life; but I am not dismayed by that. My alcoholic relapses are less frequent than they used to be partly, to be quite plain about it, because I can't afford it. I don't want the children ever to go hungry because I want a bottle of vodka. On one occasion that did happen. I fed them what food there was and told myself 'no food for you, look what you've done'. I act as my own watchdog. This is the answer I've found.

Not that I want to tell other people; rather, it is the answer I have found for myself. And I think that's a step in the right direction.

The Pressure of Being a Human Chameleon

VERONICA DEWAN

I walk into Accident and Emergency (A&E). The receptionist asks me to explain. I can't tell her. I run out. Three days later I try again – can't describe what I'm feeling, say I feel faint, start to cry. Sit down and wait. And wait. It's crowded when I arrive. Made it this far. I wait. People bleeding, children screaming. I wait. They file past me. One, two hours, maybe more. Last one in the waiting room. A nurse calls me into a cubicle. 'What's the matter with you?' she barks. I say I don't know, feel faint. She takes my blood pressure. I burst into tears, say I feel bad, suicidal. She shrugs her shoulders and disappears. The duty doctor comes. His eyes do not hide his feelings. I'm the last kind of patient he needs at the end of an eighty-hour shift. He struggles, worn out, tries to ask the right questions. I feel okay – want to go home. Sorry for the trouble. 'No, don't go – let me call the duty psychiatrist.' He arrives after a few minutes. I'm okay, really, a mistake, I'll be fine when I get home. 'What will you do? Is there anyone there? Do you have any food? When did you last sleep? You are clinically depressed – we'll have to admit you. For maybe two or three weeks – it depends how you respond.'

Back at A&E reception, they ask you lots of questions. I don't remember this happening before. 'Your name?' Why do I have to remember my name? I don't know which name – I've had so many. There are people crowding behind me. 'Ethnic background?' Why? I have to tell someone – I don't know how to explain. Well, I was born here. He keeps staring at me. 'I'm British.' He taps his pen on the desk. 'Where are your parents from?' he insists. Which parents, which ones? English and Irish, Irish and Indian. 'Where were your parents from originally?' 'I'm mixed Irish and Indian.' 'Indian – that's what I thought', he snaps and ticks the box for Asians. But I'm – it's just that – oh, what's the point?

I am emotionally distressed about my identity and whenever I am asked what to some people may appear to be a simple question such as 'where are you from?' I get confused. There isn't a simple answer. When I say I'm from London very rarely will my reply be accepted. 'Where are you from originally?' or 'When did you come to England?' or 'But where do your parents come from?' It has taken years to come up with some kind of comfortable answer, 'I have both an Irish and Indian heritage.' This feels more comfortable for me at least.

So why is it so complicated? What's the problem? What does it matter? I am transracially adopted. My adoptive parents brought me up in England, but my adoption and the circumstances under which I was placed with my parents did not take into account my racial and cultural identity. From examining my adoption records, related correspondence and verbal accounts given by my adoptive parents and my birth mother, there was an overriding factor to be considered – that I should be brought up as a Catholic.

My Irish birth mother met my biological Indian father while both were studying in London in the late 1950s. My father denied paternity and this unmarried Irish Catholic student nurse was terrified that if she returned to her home town she would be stoned. She turned to the church but was fed with shame and remorse, told that if she didn't give up this child she would have a lifetime reminder that she'd had sex with an Indian. By giving me up for adoption she would be able to get on with her life. The adoption society coerced my parents into adopting me. They had only wanted to foster a child; they were poor, and at least there would have been some remuneration. But the letters the society wrote to my (adoptive) parents made it very hard for them to refuse to accept me. They were advised to tell me I was orphaned, but they were respectful enough to pass on to me what little information they had been given about my roots.

My adoptive parents received no counselling for infertility and my adoptive mother, my mum, was seriously depressed and could not show affection. She was constantly in tears and threatening to leave me or kill us both. She was desperately unhappy and believed we would be better dead. I tried unsuccessfully to mother her. Devoutly religious (also from Ireland), she was frightened that she would be accused of not bringing me up as a good Catholic. The pressures on us all were hard to bear.

I didn't know what it meant when they said I was Indian. When Christian Aid envelopes were posted through the letter box I was told I would have been one of these starving children. At the same time my parents insisted I was English, so when I started school I was not prepared for the classroom or the playground racism. My parents did not believe me when I tried to explain I wasn't coping: 'You're English now'. Denial the only way they could cope. I suppose that's when I retreated into fantasy, the Red Indian squaw being terrorised by cowboys, the gypsy child who had strayed from her encampment. There were no

Indian role models and the only images I saw on TV were of poverty and destitution. Somewhere along the line, an image of an Indian prince astride a white stallion wearing a jewelled turban fed into my psyche and I hoped and prayed that my real father was searching every kingdom to find his long-lost daughter.

We lived in a small village in southern England. My mother had to deal with a lot of discrimination against the Irish. There were no non-whites apart from me. It was acceptable at school that I was good at athletics – that seemed to fit the norm; but to achieve academically was certainly not 'pukka'. I was not encouraged by my mother's remarks that Indians were less intelligent beings, but somehow I did well enough to pass the eleven-plus exam. The relationship with my mother by this stage was almost irretrievable, but I was finally given the opportunity to attend a Catholic grammar school and foolishly thought this would solve the problems between us. Instead, it made life unbearable.

We had no money, and my mother had to take cleaning jobs to pay for my school uniform. She had never been given the chance to finish her education because her father had died when she was thirteen and her mother had forced her to leave school and take a job in a tobacco factory. She had had a breakdown at thirteen, and several subsequently, but had managed to keep her job for fourteen years until the youngest of her four brothers and sisters had completed her own education. Naturally my mother felt bitter. She had sacrificed her education for her blood relations. Now history was repeating itself, but with a child whose birth mother she called a whore.

The bitterness she felt was so raw and our relationship had deteriorated so badly that something inside me snapped. I had first contemplated suicide at the age of seven, and such thoughts continued to haunt me throughout my childhood. I needed to get back to my roots. The only way I could think of was to become a hippy. I took a lot of illegal drugs over a twelve-month period, tried to kill myself a couple of times, and stayed away at nights. The police, psychiatrists and social services became actively involved in our family life. Inevitably I was asked to leave the school. Although I was given the opportunity of a respectable girls' boarding school, things had gone too far, and I ended up at an approved school. It was there that I met other adopted or fostered black children whose relationships with their white families had broken down. The psychiatrists had no difficulty in overprescribing tranquillisers and other concoctions to keep us under control.

When I was released back into the jaws of life, I tried to deny my heritage. I told people I was English, until I could no longer accept being patronised with remarks like 'It's okay – you're one of us,' and 'You're quite light-skinned – anyone would think you were Italian or French.'

Obviously the guilt of trying to deny who I really was ate away, and the pressure of being a human chameleon was too much. As a result I've had a number of breakdowns and serious bouts of depression. I started to trace my roots about ten years ago and succeeded in meeting both parents and siblings from their respective marriages. By this time I had an Asian partner. I believe I had chosen to be with him because what I really wanted was to experience being a member of an Asian family. When I met my birth mother she burst into tears, perceiving history repeating itself. She had left England over twenty years earlier with 'No Blacks, No Irish' ringing in her ears. She had felt a great deal of anger towards my biological father, but had turned her wrath towards India in its totality. In her mind she had imagined me growing up with an English family, being English, rather as my adoptive parents expected me to be.

Each of my parents exhibited racist behaviour and I could not change the way I felt or the colour of my skin. My biological father finally accepted me as a child of his seed, but he perceived that those in his social and professional milieu would not accept this little indiscretion from his past. Mostly they didn't; he was right. I was not matching up to anyone's expectations and they weren't matching up to mine. My life fell apart and although I'd had some emotionally debilitating bouts in the past, none were as severe as at that time. It was precipitated by my first-year exams after returning to full-time education to read law. I was convinced I had failed my exams, although in fact I had passed. My expectations of myself were bound up in not being bright enough, a reflection of the society in which I had been brought up, as though I was walking around with a big stamp on my forehead saying 'Bound for Failure'.

I have a law degree now. I also have a greater insight into the racism that prevails in the National Health Service. I have been admitted to hospital on many occasions over the past few years. On each occasion I have witnessed or been subject to racism from staff and on occasion from other patients. It is not actively discouraged, and remarks are allowed to slither and slide without comment. Racist behaviour is most frequently meted out by local staff who receive little training, and bring all their prejudices to the workplace from the community in which they live. Their value judgments are mostly verbalised at an early stage of discussion with a patient. While a few show sensitivity, many will impose their stereotypical views on the person who is supposedly being treated and what they may think of as chit-chat is instead often very distressing.

I won't even attempt to discuss the value judgments of psychiatrists. There is enough evidence. I don't care where a person comes from, but what matters to me when receiving treatment is that I am not cast in a false role. However much I would like to have been brought up as an Indian child, I was not. To be referred to an Indian psychiatrist is not necessarily helpful. Any mental health professional will only help me if he or she understands racism, cultural conflict and the reasons for denial of identity.

This takes me back to my experience in A&E. My mental health, race and culture are inextricably linked. This link has been ignored, denied, mocked, excluded, avoided, misunderstood, rejected by institutions and individuals – and also by me in the many disorientated moments of my life. I think it serves little purpose to be placed in one of a limited range of ethnic categories. Is the information necessary and appropriate to the circumstances? If so, I would suggest that only someone who is sensitive to the wider implications of the questions being asked should be permitted to ask them.

I've Lost My Innocence

NICKI

I was first in care from when I was about eighteen months old to when I was five and those years were the happiest days of my life. I was in care then with foster parents, and it was really good. I was happy and looked after properly.

My mother got me back from care, and I went to live with her and my new stepdad. Even at that age I knew I didn't want to go back to my mum. I wanted to live with my dad, and he did try for custody when I was five. But they thought I should be with my mum, and I don't suppose anyone asked me what I wanted. My mum got what she wanted, I didn't. And once she got me she didn't want me.

She was very cruel. Now I think she must have had a mental illness: her idea of reality wasn't anyone else's. But I didn't understand that when I was five. My stepdad was on the buses and had these heavy jackets and boots. If I or my brothers and sisters did anything wrong my mum would make us stand with our arms outstretched with a boot on each hand and with the jacket on. She'd make us stand for ages, and if our arms dropped she'd beat us and force our arms up again. In the winter she used to stand me outside naked.

She just never cared for us. My brother and I would be made to clean the house at night. She used to go out and come back in the early hours. If anything was out of place she's beat us. My brother and I used to protect one another as much as we could. We were very close. One day my mother battered by brother and he had two black eyes and a cut along his back. She put make-up on him, and sent him to school with a note to say he'd fallen off his bike. And they believed that. How could they? I did have one teacher who was really nice. She didn't know what was going on, but she was kind – I'd like to thank her.

As I got older I used to look after all the younger children, do the shopping, make sure they went to school – everything. I was always mum because I was the oldest, but that meant I was the scapegoat too. I got into trouble if anything went wrong. And we were always moving, so I could never settle. In all I've been to fourteen schools and had thirty moves.

When I was younger I used to see my father sometimes. I don't think he knows the half of what my mother did to me. And neither of them know I was sexually abused by a family friend. That went on between the ages of eight and ten. I didn't tell anyone. Who was there to tell? My mum wouldn't have believed me anyway, and I'd have been scared what she'd do to me. She certainly wouldn't have believed it wasn't my fault, because everything always was my fault. I don't know if social workers were visiting. They know about her now. They know her three eldest children were physically abused for years. Three of us have been in care. But nobody is protecting the two youngest. My stepdad gets drunk and beats my mum up in front of them, and one of my little sisters got hurt recently. And she's child-minding. Social services say they can't do anything yet.

I went back into care a couple of years ago and I got sent to an assessment centre. They said my head was totally fucked up and they were very supportive of me. But I was only there two months, and then I was moved to a long-stay unit and things deteriorated. One thing was that I'd have a key worker for about two months and then they'd leave. I had five in all, and the last two I really didn't get on with, because I was just so sick of what was going on. One man I found impossible. He was really unfair and used to throw his weight around. I really didn't like it. He was quite subtle about how he did it, but he used to get at me. No one did anything about it – staff didn't support you: even when they knew someone was in the wrong, they'd stick together.

Being in care is awful. You have no privacy in children's homes. You can't have your friends to stay or even to come in. There's no space of your own. You don't have any possessions: it all belongs to the local authority. It's not your room, or your bed or your duvet – it's all theirs. Nothing is yours. When you get moved you just chuck everything into a black bin-liner – and it all goes in, you've go so little. I got moved into a semi-independent unit when I was sixteen. I had nothing. It took them weeks to even get me blankets and things. It's just a room, and I hate it there. It makes me feel claustrophobic. I just have to get out all the time.

Where's it all left me? I find it difficult to settle anywhere now; I'm really restless and unsettled. I can't be still. I think it's because I've had so many moves, and because it all eats me up inside. I'm very bitter and resentful, and I know I need help with all that. They didn't help me with any of that in care, except for the two months at the assessment centre. Then I just got left with it all again. They just didn't want to know.

I desperately need some support for myself, because I've go no one now. I want to try to find a counsellor, but I've got no money. I really want to go to college and get my exams, but I can't go, because I haven't got any money and no one will fund me. So I have to try to get a job. But what I really want to do is to study and get myself trained. I've missed out on my education.

I've lost having a family. I hate my mum and I can't forgive her for what she's done. She won't face up to any of it, and she has a lot of power in the family. I did see her once last year, and she threatened me and screamed abuse at me. I do see one of my brothers, but my two little sisters are with my mother still and she's told them I'm dead, so I can't see them. I did visit one of them at school once, on her birthday, but it was too emotional for her and she burst into tears – and so did I, because I couldn't handle what my mother was doing to them. So I don't see them. There is another brother, and I don't even know how old he is. My father has got three children, and I see them occasionally, but only when my stepmother says I can. Christmas is worst, wondering where I can go.

Something else it's left me with is difficult to explain. It's a trick I learned when my mother was battering me. I learned to turn off my nervous system when she hit me so I couldn't feel it. It protected me then. I'm not sure I could have stood it otherwise, the pain. But it affects me really badly now. Because if anyone threatens me or attacks me, I can't protect myself – I just freeze.

I think what I'd like to say to people who read this is that some of the residential social workers, at least the good ones, really have tried. But others didn't try – they really misused their power. They are abusive, and lots of us would tell you the same. You go from being abused at home to being abused in care. And they have a lot of power, because in the end they're always believed. It's not been good enough, and the ones who try need to work with us against the ones at the top who really make the decisions. Because the system is not good. It does not work. Being in care has not worked. And I really need support, and somewhere that's nice to live, and help to sort my head out, and help practically to live; and I need to know my little sisters are safe. They should not be in that home. But I'd fight to have them kept out of care. I'd look after them, I'd have them live with me, if people would help me to. So you can see that I don't have any of the things I need. What good was being in care? None.

The worst two things about my life are that it's been just soul-destroying and that I've lost my innocence. I've never had a childhood. If I'm ever around kids, whatever they're doing – playing, climbing trees – I want to join in. I never had any of that. My home started to destroy my soul. Being in care finished it.

Silent Scream

MAGGY ROSS

This article is the transcript of a presentation given to the first national self-harm conference, in 1989.

I'm Maggy and I started to cut my body five years ago.

It all started innocently enough. I was sitting in the sun outside a psychiatric hospital and noticed some glass glinting in the sunlight. I picked up a piece and started to cut the back of my hand. Since then I've used broken wine glasses, knives, scalpels, even a watch buckle. I then 'progressed' to razor blades. I've cut my arms, face and right leg. The left leg remains untouched – it's important to me that one part of me remains scar-free. Don't ask me why!

When I cut I do it in nice straight lines in criss-cross patterns, generally about fifty cuts each go. I've cut up well over a hundred times. On occasions I have had to go to casualty and immediately get hauled onto the psychiatric bandwagon. I cut up and if it's deep, I'm sent to casualty. I'm stitched up and inevitably the shrink is called in. I am urged to to into hospital. Sometimes I'm sectioned, so the right to choose has been taken away from me. I am then given a nice little 'label' by the consultant. The current label, incidentally, is schizophrenic. Then the 'treatment' begins. Drugs, of course, and once ECT. I am then totally bombed out and regarded as 'well again'.

The last two weeks have not been untypical. On four occasions in the last fortnight I have been 'strongly' advised to go into hospital. Knowing the system as I do, I have refused point blank. So instead, it's drug treatment – a jab of Depixol in my bum – that'll last a month. They know that I regularly refuse to take mind-altering drugs, hence the jab. At home I have supplies of other 'anti-psychotic' drugs, 'mood stabilisers', Valium and sleepers. I know all their contra-indications. That's why I don't take them. If I did take them I would be standing there like a monosyllabic zombie.

So. That's how the professionals see me. I'm a self-destructive schizophrenic.

31

But how do I see myself? First and foremost, I am a survivor of sexual abuse and a survivor of the system. I won't play ball. I know why I self-injure. I do it at times of extreme emotion: anger, self-hatred, stress, grief and guilt. I do it to punish myself. When I feel I am losing control, I reach for a razor and prove to myself that I can, at least, have control over my body.

The cuts are a visual expression of my distress. When I am lost for words, my cuts speak for me. They say – look – *this* is how much I'm hurting inside. So. Is that schizophrenic? I think not.

When I first cut up I thought I was mad. I didn't know anyone in the world did it. I felt a freak and very isolated. Joining the Bristol Crisis Line was a real turning point. Here were other women – bright, lucid and accepting. The majority of them self-injured too. So I was no longer alone. Now I know for a fact that we are not alone. I wrote a magazine article last year on cutting and had over five hundred replies from women who thought they were totally isolated and crazy because they self-injured.

There are many ways of self-injuring – cutting up is just one. Anorexia and bulimia are others. So's alcohol and drug abuse. Not to mention hitting things, burning and scolding oneself, or swallowing non-ingestants like bleach.

I'll tell you what self-injury isn't – and professionals take note. It's not masochistic. It's not attention-seeking. It's rarely a symptom of a so-called psychiatric illness. It's not a suicide attempt. It is not silly and definitely not selfish. I know – because I've been accused of all these things.

So what is it? It's a silent scream. It's about trying to create a sense of order out of chaos. It's a visual manifestation of extreme distress. Those of us who self-injure carry our emotional scars on our bodies.

It can and often does stem from our pre-verbal childhood. When we suffered the trauma of sexual abuse or abandonment. We were left, young and hurt and often angry. But because we couldn't express ourselves, we stayed silent and hid our feelings. Self-hatred inevitably creeps in. Eventually, for many, the only way to deal with terrible childhood experiences and give vent to them is through self-harm.

Women self-harm more than men. As little girls, we are taught to be ladylike and bite our lips. Little boys are encouraged to shout and let off steam. This conditioning inevitably stays with us in adulthood.

But what do we gain from harming ourselves?

Personally, when I've seen the blood run I've felt relieved and purged. The stress recedes and I've felt as though I am back in control of my mind. Once more I have deflected those emotions and painful memories.

Physiologically, when we inflict pain, our body responds by producing endorphins, our natural opiates or pain relievers that give us a lift and even a temporary feeling of peace.

Now I've told you what the professional's solution to the problem is.

But what about what we want? I want a lot of nurturing and the chance to talk, cry, shout and understand. In this respect, my lover, my parents and my friends have been brilliant. They may not understand, but they accept. They don't judge me or criticise me. I also want psychodrama – the chance to get in touch with the child in me and understand it from an adult perspective. A nurse once suggested to me that I could inflict pain on myself without cutting. She'd plonk two ice-cubes in my hands and I had to clasp them until they'd melted. It hurt. But for a while it worked. This day is crucial for all of us. It's a milestone because it's making self-harm a public issue at last. It's easy to lie about scars. Now, though, if anyone asks me, I tell them what I do. I don't care if they're strangers, friends or work colleagues. I want to make them aware of the problem and it's enormity, and above all, I want to enlighten them. The normal initial response is shock, but once I've explained about it, they understand, and often feed back their own experiences of self-harm. Dialogue is crucial. I have never lost a friend or colleague through being honest.

Let's take that honesty away with us today and not hide behind our shame. We must destroy the myths and destroy the silence. We must do it for those women, who like us, will turn to self-harm in the future. We must make it easier for them than it has been for us.

Now, it might sound like I'm through with self-harm, having all the insight that I've learned from others and from articles. I'm not. I still cut up. I am still going through the battle. The battle is predominantly with myself, my past, and of course professional ignorance. You rarely come through a battle without scars. I, like many, am battle scarred. But I'm proud. Proud because I am going to win this battle. My scars are my proof.

Thank you for letting me share this with you.

Finger Pickin' Good

LEAH THORN

Look at my hand
It'll tell you

The story's there
                in the serrated cuticles
                the uneven swirls of skin
                down the side of the thumb
                in pink soreness
                a badge of my pain
                red shield of despair

I peck at a finger nail
its irregular pointiness irritating me
Smooth it off.   Make it perfect.
Perfect it.

Have to keep these fingers under control.

Pull insistently at the skin that just won't come
but thrusts up to taunt me

Nibbling.   Fiddling.   Prising.   Picking

My fingers are numb
until the skin tears
'Now look what you've done!'

My hand goes in my mouth
to stifle a scream
silent
like Munch

My teeth grind with the effort of chewing off
the ever present flaps of skin.
Red, yellow, pink thumb
comforting as I run my tongue over the roughness.
Polished skin, broken and re-broken over many years.

I can't not, you see.
I love the pain as I flick my fingers across the flakiness.

I Suffered from Depression

A PSYCHIATRIC NURSE

Families and friends know a great deal more about caring for the depressed individual than any health professional. That's the conclusion I came to when, for a short while only, I suffered from depression.

Anyone who has experienced this illness (and it *is* an illness) will know what I mean then I say others have no idea how devastating it really is. Everyone suffers from some form of 'depression' at one time or another, but to endure this lingering state for weeks or months on end is totally indescribable. Minutes literally drag by and one feels totally apathetic.

As a recently qualified psychiatric nurse, I had some knowledge of the present theories and trends in the psychopathology and management of this illness. I regularly came into contact with many individuals (patients, friends, and colleagues) suffering from some form of depression. However, in retrospect, I realise that I was totally oblivious to and ignorant of what these people, deep down, were actually experiencing.

My own experience of this illness occurred when I had returned to this country after a short spell of working abroad. I was convinced that it was a reactive depression precipitated by returning to a strange yet familiar environment. Yet even with my own insight, I didn't feel able to cope with the problem, I felt I couldn't be bothered to talk to anyone. I just wanted to be left alone. I just wanted to stay in my room uninterrupted. The first few days were hell, but I thought I would 'snap out of it'. It's so easy for people (and especially the so-called caring professions) to say this; I know I have done so frequently. But for the person concerned, actually to *do* as he is told is virtually impossible. I know I will never resort to repeating those words again.

To get out of bed at midday was an ordeal. I felt that I had nothing to look forward to, no interest in anything – in short, I felt totally apathetic. I couldn't even be bothered to talk to my girlfriend or father, the two people who were closest to me. I had not interests at all. I wouldn't listen to the radio or stereo, or watch TV, never mind go out. I never even felt the desire to drink beer! I think it was because of this that both my girlfriend and father realised that something was wrong with me. I would just lie on my bed, staring at the ceiling, or walk aimlessly in the garden. Often I would burst into tears for no apparent reason. Both my girlfriend and father would spend hours trying to communicate with me and encouraging me to socialise.

Eventually, for their sakes, I decided to visit my GP. Although I have the greatest respect for my doctor, in the context of my illness he was as much use to me as the milkman. I realise he is a busy man, but although he tried to appear attentive I suspected he felt that I was a neurotic nurse just wanting his time. He stated perfunctorily that I was just a bit 'run down' and would soon get over it. He prescribed me a tonic and told me to 'take things easy'. The tonic was useless. I did not want any form of medication because I have never felt the desire or need to take medication in any form. I suspect that what I really wanted was a sympathetic ear – and a push in some direction, any direction, just something to get me motivated. The sheer frustration of the illness was that I knew deep down I was severely depressed but could not do anything about it. My frustration and boredom turned to anger and despair. If people spoke to me I would rebuke them severely for no reason at all. As far as work was concerned, I should have taken a new post in nursing on my return to England, but I couldn't even be bothered to turn up.

My sleep patterns were totally changed. I would lie awake at night with feelings of despair and unworthiness. My appetite diminished, and accompanying the anorexia was weight loss. Attention to personal hygiene diminished, as did my patience with others. I was generally bad-tempered, ill-mannered, and cantankerous, with my girlfriend unfortunately taking most of the brunt. Despite all this, much to her credit, she would come to see me daily and try to motivate me to start back at work, to socialise again, and in general to take more pride in myself. I feel sure that it was because of her positive and understanding manner that I regained my former self. My father, by helping me to help myself, also played an important role in assisting me to regain my normal life style.

My depressed state continued for about one month. It took me about a week to come to terms with trying to resume my pre-depressive state. I started to socialise more and to frequent various places of interest. My girlfriend encouraged me to watch TV comedy programmes and to read short stories. We started to go to the cinema and night clubs. I gradually resumed writing letters to friends both at home and abroad. By doing these things, I forced myself to become more motivated. I applied for a new job not too far removed from home and much to my surprise I was successful in obtaining the new position. While relearning my lapsed skills, I was continually discussing my problem with both my father and my girlfriend. Other friends who were also aware of my depression were very helpful in motivating me.

Retrospectively I feel I have learned a lot in experiencing and coping with some degree of mental illness. If I had had this illness before becoming a psychiatric nurse, I would have had a totally different attitude towards my patients. I would have appreciated better that these people need a great deal of understanding and patience. When I was depressed I felt that I was neither of use nor ornament to anyone. Although I never felt suicidal, I often thought about it and I can now understand severely depressed individuals carrying out a suicide attempt. I appreciate that it is difficult for many to conceive that a mentally ill person is experiencing pain, yet, having experienced some of this pain myself, I know that it can be very real to the individual concerned. I find it harder than I would otherwise have done to believe the dismissive views sometimes aired in psychiatric settings, for example that patients are depressed because they are 'feeling sorry for themselves' or because they are 'just seeking attention'. But I also am fed up with hearing time and again that 'no one cared'; many people do care, but it is often difficult for them to know what to do for the best. And they are helpless to help someone who will not help himself.

No one really expects men to become depressed. With women it is somewhat more socially acceptable, but in general it remains true that mental illness has never really achieved the same acceptance as physical illness. People also expect a depressed nurse or doctor (especially if they are men) somehow to recover of their own accord; they seem to assume that people with some knowledge of the disease should somehow know how to extricate themselves from it unaided. This may work for some, but I found that it was other people that made the difference for me. With their help, I recovered quickly and did not require psychiatric treatment, which I feel is fortunate.

Even in this day and age it is somewhat frowned upon for nurses to suffer from mental illness. Everyone knows of instances where this disapproval has meant that a nurse is refused a job because of having a medical history of mental illness. This stigma creates an additional difficulty for nurses, who, because of the widespread expectation that they can somehow do without help, find it difficult to cope with their illness. Moreover, as I have suggested earlier, there is much ignorance of the condition within the profession. Many of my colleagues who are trained nurses have virtually no knowledge of mental illness, nor of how to deal with people suffering from it. They often seem to have no idea of how to approach a depressed individual or how to talk to him or her and they often react to such a person by ignoring the problem or by dismissing it with some vague comment. Yet while working in a psychiatric setting I found, much to my surprise, that it was not uncommon for some of my colleagues to be themselves attending psychiatric out-patient clinics. Most often their attendance was surrounded by a great deal of secrecy. The need for secrecy makes it more difficult for depressed professionals to use their own experience of suffering in their work with others. The nursing curriculum is also sadly lacking in attention to the general problems associated with mental illness. The problem of the depressed nurse is never mentioned. My own experience suggests that much unnecessary suffering might be avoided if both problems could be brought out in the open. Meanwhile, family and friends can do much to alleviate suffering that trained professionals would prefer not to know about.

Unplanned Journey

DIANA FRIEL MCGOWIN

Diana Friel McGowin was already having a battle with 'little memory losses and balance'. But she had dismissed these symptoms as being psychosomatic: 'just a woman realising that she was getting older, and not necessarily better'. 'After all', she explains, 'I was forty-five years of age. One would naturally expect some innocuous symptoms of the body slowing down.' In the following extract it becomes apparent that the problem is more serious, leading to an eventual diagnosis of Alzheimer's disease.

The telephone rang. It was my husband, asking me to prepare a lunch and deliver it to him at his workplace. He would only have a thirty-minute lunch break; not enough time to get to a restaurant.

Quickly I put together a rudimentary lunch, and went to my car. I hesitated for a moment, confused on exactly how to place both my purse and the lunch container on the seat beside me. After some juggling, I backed the car from the driveway.

As I drove to Jack's office, I noticed a strip of shopping centre, new to me. It was strange I had not noticed this mall previously. I travelled this route frequently.

I passed the street leading to the off-site, and drove several miles down the road before realising my error. No doubt the new shopping centre had thrown my judgement off, I mused, and turned around to retrace my steps. Near the driveway leading to my husband's office, I observed a fire station which was also new to me. That would be a good landmark to guide me to the company entrance in the future.

Jack saw my car approaching and came out of his building to greet me. Accepting the lunch with thanks, he leaned against the car.

'Jack, when did they build the new strip shopping centre on Kirkman

Road? Funny, but I don't remember it being built, and it is already open for business.'

Jack frowned thoughtfully then shook his head. I continued, 'Oh, well, I'm glad to see the new fire station near your entrance. It will give me a good landmark'.

Jack laughed and again shook his head.

'Diane, that station has always been here,' he chided. 'Even before my building was built!'

I suddenly became irate. I started the car and began to pull away from Jack, who leaped from his position leaning against the vehicle.

'Whoa! What's your rush?'

I braked, staring before me in confusion. Where was the exit?

'Jack,' I asked shakily, 'How do I get out of here?'

Jack now roared with laughter. 'Diane, shape up! You certainly have something on your mind! "New" shopping centres, "new" fire stations, and now you can't find your way out of a parking lot!'

I fought tears of frustration as I shouted at Jack, 'Don't laugh at me¡ Just tell me how to get out of this place!'

Jack bowed ceremoniously and pointed straight ahead of my car.

Without another word, I pulled away and drove from the parking lot.

Suddenly, I was aware of car horns blowing. Glancing around, nothing was familiar. I was stopped at an intersection, and the traffic light was green. Cars honked impatiently, so I pulled straight ahead, trying to get my bearings. I could not read the street sign, but there was another sign ahead; perhaps it would shed some light on my location.

One of my favourite songs was playing on the radio, I was still in unfamiliar territory, at another intersection, in the right-hand turn lane. I took the turn, and spotted an overpass ahead. There were usually signs indicating the name of the roadway at overpasses. Now I could get my bearings.

The news was now coming over the radio and I was alarmed to notice how fast I was driving. Where was the overpass? I looked around and discovered I was in open country, with a golf course to my left. Where was I? What was the matter with the radio? I slowed down to a safe speed, and read the name of the golf course on an entrance way. It was unfamiliar.

I drove on, with tears of frustration streaming down my face. Unfamiliar music blared from the radio. I could no longer see any buildings. I was hopelessly lost, and had no idea how to get home. Suddenly I saw a sign on a rock-walled entrance: *Turkey Lake Park*. That struck a chord. Hadn't I taken the grandchildren to this park on several occasions?

I turned into the entrance of the park and pulled off the road. My body was shaking with fear and uncontrollable sobs. What was happening? An irritatingly boisterous commercial was playing on the radio. I snapped it off in annoyance and tried to clear my head.

A few yards ahead, there was a park ranger building. Trembling, I wiped my eyes, and breathing deeply, tried to calm myself. Finally, feeling ready to speak, I started the car again and approached the ranger station. The guard smiled and inquired how he could assist me.

'I appear to be lost,' I began, making a great effort to keep my voice level, despite my emotional state. 'Where do you need to go?' the guard asked politely.

A cold chill enveloped me as I realised I could not remember the name of my street. Tears began to flow down my cheeks. I did not know where I wanted to go.

He prompted me, his voice soft as he noticed my tears.

'Are you heading to Orlando, or Windermere?'

'Orlando' I sighed gratefully. that was right. I lived in Orlando. I was certain of it. But where?

'Which part? East end, West end?' the guard continued.

I felt panic wash over me anew as I searched my memory and found it blank. Suddenly, I remembered bringing my grandchildren to this park. That must mean I lived relatively nearby, surely.

'What is the closest subdivision?' I quavered.

The guard scratched his head thoughtfully.

'The closest Orlando subdivision would be Pine Hills, maybe,' he ventured.

'That's right!' I exclaimed gratefully. The name of my subdivision had rung a bell.

The guard told me which way to turn as I left the park and to continue on that roadway until I approached the Colonial Avenue intersection. If I looked to my right, he instructed, I would see the entrance to the Pine Hills subdivision.

I drove carefully in the exact direction he advised and searched each intersection to see if it were Colonial Avenue. Finally, I came to it and looking to my right, recognised the entrance to the subdivision. I negotiated the streets leading to my home without further difficulty.

Once home, a wave of relief brought more tears. I rushed through my home, closing drapes and ensuring all doors were locked. I looked at my bedroom clock. I had been gone over four hours. I took refuge in the darkened master bedroom, and sat, curled up on my bed, my arms wrapped tightly around myself.

It was thus that Jack found me when he returned home that evening.

Part two

PSYCHIATRIC TREATMENT

Introduction

The contributors to this section offer a variety of experiences of and reactions to psychiatric interventions. Some are positive and others critical, but some common themes emerge.

One such theme is the importance of gaining some measure of control over what may threaten to be a disabling experience. Igor Spreizer, from Slovenia, describes in 'Recovery at Home' how he avoided going into hospital for a manic episode. A crisis team was created from members of his user group, friends and family. The team agreed some rules with him as to how he and his family would deal with the crisis; for instance how much medication he would take, what time he would be in bed. Igor Spreizer's psychiatrist supported the arrangement by reducing the amounts of medication each week.

Richard Jameson in 'Schizophrenia from the Inside' recounts the terror of his imagination running riot in periods of insanity. He gains control for himself through the drugs which suppress his symptoms – for him this is as good as a cure.

In contrast, Peter Campbell in 'Challenging Loss of Power' has found that his need to maximise his self-control during the process of breakdown is ignored and thwarted by psychiatric professionals. He points to the pervasiveness of 'illness' models in psychiatry as leading to feelings of being a powerless victim in those diagnosed as 'mentally ill'.

Peter Campbell comments on the failure of professionals to provide proper information concerning treatments, which restricts the choice and control available to recipients of psychiatry. The same concern is expressed by other writers in this section. Leonard Taylor ('ECT is Barbaric') and Rachel Perkins ('Choosing ECT') had dramatically different experiences of electroconvulsive therapy (ECT). Their responses may have been related to their different understandings of their depressions. Leonard Taylor sees his as the reaction to a dilemma about his sexual identity, while Rachel Perkins was alarmed at entering a second bout of severe depression and wanted a speedy recovery. One point on which they agree, however, is that they (and their friends and relatives) were not given sufficient explanation about the treatment and its risks to be able to make an informed choice.

Many mental health service users who are critical of 'illness' models find the stigma attached to their psychiatric label particularly objectionable. In this book, Maggy Ross, John Bell and Vivien Lindow, among others, write critically of the effects of a label that is hard to remove. It therefore may come as a surprise to read Christine McIntosh's description in 'The Right to be Informed' of the torment she went through in her teenage years and up until she was twenty-three when she was first told of her diagnosis (manic depression). She would have welcomed information about psychiatric understanding of her condition as well as relevant treatment. The could have given her some control over her frightening and bewildering experiences.

In a different vein, in 'Prozac Really isn't that Great' Elizabeth Wurtzel reflects on her experience in the USA. As a teenager and young adult Elizabeth Wurtzel had 'no idea how to function within the boundaries of the normal, non-depressive world'. She was later helped by taking Prozac, the anti-depressant drug. Yet she fears that in time her depression will 'outsmart' the drug and re-emerge in another form. She queries the extent of the biological roots of her problems, but suggests that regardless of how her depression started, after years of misery her internal chemistry was messed up so much that only a drug could get it going again. She wonders whether competent therapy at an earlier stage might not have avoided the need for a drug solution.

The section opens with Mary O'Hagan's account, or indeed 'Two Accounts of Mental Distress', as she juxtaposes medical and nursing notes against her own writings while an in-patient in the grip of mental distress. She provides a fascinating glimpse of the gulf between her felt experience and the psychiatrically informed observations. Early in Mary O'Hagan's admission, the psychiatrist comments 'You need a high degree of control in your relationships don't you?' as though her questions on his ideas and values are out of place. Yet is is not so much the lack of information or explanation which shocks: more the complete lack of understanding of her communications at any level.

Two Accounts of Mental Distress

MARY O'HAGAN

This paper is a 'cut and paste' of excerpts from my journal and hospital file written during one of my episodes of mental distress.

I wrote most of the journal entries during my last stay in hospital while I crouched in the safety of a locked toilet. With enormous effort I created coherent sequences of words out of the chaos inside me and recorded them in tiny faint handwriting. This was one of the most intense and profound experiences of my life – but down the other end of the long polished corridor, others recorded their own version of my distress in the course of a very ordinary day's work.

Several years later I read what they had written about me and I couldn't believe that my journal and their notes referred to the same person and events. The incongruity between these two accounts of my mental distress is disturbing and I believe exposes the fundamental reason why mental health services so often fail to help people.

My journal entries are in italics. The psychiatrist's and nursing notes are in plain text.

The accounts

Today I went to see a psychiatrist. He is a little man with a beard and glasses and he wrote his notes in small, tidy handwriting. He stared right through me. I kept thinking he could see into every corner of my mind. Every time I moved – the way I sat, where I put my hands – I thought would be used as evidence of my badly diseased mind. I was afraid he had the power to trick me into letting out my biggest secrets. I was too terrified to talk to him.

Mary is a 25 year old Caucasian university student who has a history of Manic Depressive Psychosis. Now appears to be entering a depressive phase. Withdrawn and quiet. Dresses unconventionally. Not an easy patient to relate to. She plays her cards very close to her chest.

44

I stand alone, unable to move inside a dark bubble. I have no face or hands or feet. My veins are broken and my blood has nowhere to travel. Outside the bubble it is day. A rainbow appears but I cannot see it. I remain in the bubble, broken and hidden from the life around me.

Mary has an inadequate and confused sense of identity. She also has a long-standing picture of being an isolate; tending to live in her own world and always finding it difficult to fit in. In this way she presents a schizoid personality picture.

Today I saw the psychiatrist again. I wanted to cry out and collapse against the wall to show him the pain I am in but I couldn't. I wanted him to show from the core of his being that he understood my pain but he didn't. Instead we had a rational discussion. I asked him:

(DIALOGUE STARTS)

What do you think is a well functioning human being?

Why do you ask that question? I think you're worried that I will judge you.

Yes, I am worried about that. I want to know if your ideas on human beings are compatible enough with mine for us to be able to talk about me. How do you ensure that your values don't impose on mine?

Let me assure you, it's not my job to judge you. I'm here to help you know yourself better.

But what if you judged me without knowing it?

That was below the belt. You need a high degree of control in your relationships don't you?

(DIALOGUE ENDS)

Then, somehow we got onto sex. The whole time he just kept gazing into me. I felt terribly uncomfortable and was trying desperately to hide it. The sex talk stripped me right back to the raw. Now all I want to do is shrink back into myself. He had all the power.

Requesting my views on life, sex, religion etc.

1. Why she needs to know my views? Feeling of powerlessness that she knows little about me and my beliefs. Theme of control in relationships and how vulnerable she feels when she cannot label people.

2.   Problems with sex relationships – feels loss of control.
3.   For further discussion – importance of her control issues.
4.   Blood levels satisfactory.

Today I wanted to die. Everything was hurting. My body was screaming. I saw the doctor. I said nothing. Now I feel terrible. Nothing seems good and nothing good seems possible.

I am stuck in this twilight mood
where I go down
like the setting sun
into a lonely black hole
where there is room for only one.

Flat, lacking motivation, sleep and appetite good. Discussed aetiology. Cont. LiCarb. 250 mg qid. Levels next time.

I am lying face down behind a chair in the waiting room of the hospital.

I am a long piercing scream
All screaming on the inside of me
and out of the pores of my skin.
My screaming and myself are one.
This is pure pain.

The doctor comes along and snaps at me to get up. He tells a nurse to put me to bed. I have never ever been in so much shame.

Guilt swoops down on me
and pecks my sense of being good to bits
as I lie here snared between my sheets
like a whimpering animal.

I am full of red hot blame at myself for everything
I cannot bear being so thoroughly bad.

I am carrying hell around inside of me.

On arriving on the ward – spent the entire day curled up on the waiting room floor behind a chair. Could not talk. Impression of over dramatisation but with underlying gross psychological turmoil. She is difficult to engage and to that effect I have admitted her for a period of two weeks in order to consolidate her working relationship with us.

I am locked in here
alone in this black box.

I used to hide its blackness
with colourful decorations.
On its walls I painted windows
with pleasing views on them.

Now I have been stripped right back
to the bare boards of my mind.

My world has been emptied out,
as if burglars broke into my mind
and stole all my power.

On their way out
they pulled down my blinds.

Now, I cannot see the world
and the world cannot see me.

Poor eye contact, slow speech and movements. Stated her head felt empty and fuzzy; vision disordered, things appearing very ugly. Mentioned need to find meaning in her depression – not just a wasteful experience.

A nurse came to me and said 'Go to supper'. I said 'No'. She growled at me for
not making an effort, but all my effort is going into making these thoughts and
writing them down. The nurse punished me, saying, 'Well, I'm not bringing you
any supper, you know.'

Sitting in ladies' lounge with her head in her hands. Very difficult to involve in conversation. Not responding to activity around her.

Is attending the dining room with firm encouragement and eating small meals. Remains very withdrawn but occasionally gives vent to an incongruous sustained laugh – although says she isn't happy. Rx Chlorpromazine BD & Nocte as appears to be preoccupied with thoughts – hopefully medication will break the chain.

Last night they came to me
with Chlorpromazine.
I refused it.
I am afraid medication will dull my mind
and the meanings in there will escape forever.

Refusing medication. States she hasn't been taking it because it doesn't do her any good. Not persuaded by explanations or reassurance.

During the night

between sleeps
I felt bad.
I was on the rack.

Every thought
set off a shrieking alarm in my head.
My body would jerk and go rigid
As if electric shocks went through me
every few seconds.

I nearly didn't make it through the night.
I nearly asked for Chlorpromazine.

Awake at frequent intervals during the night. Found whimpering and thrashing around on her bed at 2.15 a.m. saying 'No, leave me alone.' Said she was frightened. Kept holding and massaging her head.

Every morning the night nurses
pull off my blankets.
They are rough.
I can't fight back.
Even their softest touches bruise me.

A nurse said to me
'Face the world.'
But I am facing the pain inside me.
I cannot face both ways at once.

Mary is not to hide away in her bed. She is to be encouraged to get up for breakfast and engage in ward activities.

My back is hard like a shell.
My front is soft like jelly.

I hate to stand
because I cannot shield my front
from the jabbing gaze of the world.

I must lie
curled up or front down.

Lying in bed under blanket. Face covered by hands. Wouldn't leave bed to talk – 'not safe'. Brief whispered conversation from under her hands. Sleeps worse than usual – can't eat – too frightened – body aching all over.

Everything hurts.
I am burning.

All the life in me
blazing out from the core of me
is getting stuck.
I can feel it
trying to burn through my skin.

I am almost on fire.

Experiencing frightening hallucinations, burning sensations, also brightly coloured shapes when eyes shut. Request Sunnyside notes of EEG. Repeat EEG to exclude Temporal Lobe Epilepsy.

I have lost my self
What is my name?
I have no name.
All I am
is shape and weight
rapid shallow breathing
and a black space inside my head.

Misinterpreting at times. Obsessed with the feeling of not wanting to be in her body – wanted to be a speck of dust. Also concerned as to her purpose of being alive. Describing feelings of 'emptiness'. Sleep poor, appetite poor.

My mind is a pile
of broken up smudgy thoughts.

I am searching for one
that is clear enough to have meaning.

But as soon as I find a thought
it gets sucked into the blackness.

Before, my thoughts were sliding off into nonsense. This terrified me so I tried to make some sense of things by taking bits out of nonsense and putting them into a story.

An old woman and her grand-daughter lived by a great ocean. Every day the old woman went fishing. She yelled in awe to the ocean 'Let me take the life out of you with my net.' She always returned with fish and cooked them for herself and her grand-daughter. One day she gave some of the fish to her grand-daughter and said 'Cook these for yourself.' The girl wailed 'I can't.' The old woman replied 'You must find your own power.' But the girl didn't understand and went to bed hungry. That night the girl woke from her dreams to a booming voice from the sky: 'You have the power of the old woman and the great ocean flowing into the core of you. Now, take meaning from the rawness of life and cook it for yourself without fear.'

Remains psychotically depressed. Reported hearing voices but no other bizarre symptoms noted. Thoughts still coming in 'fragments'. Unable to complete them. Still spending most of time on bed. On 150 mg Doxepin nocte.

Sometimes a speck of light gets into my black hole. The speck is a thought that has come back into focus.

I am coming up a bit but I feel all weak and wobbly from being on my bed for days. Before I looked up. This took courage. It was like coming out of a cocoon; the light was strong; it was strange. The next thing I did was walk around and say hello to people. It feels good to be halfway back and looking up.

Is beginning to interact. Says she is feeling much better. Asked permission to to out which was refused. Accepted this well. Enjoyed a game of Scrabble, giggling at times but this was mostly appropriate eg at mildly humorous antics of other patients.

Mary is to be discharged. The family have intimated that they would be glad if I continued to manage Mary. I will be ready to step in if she has any further psychotic breaks and needs the control of this ward.

Recovery at Home

IGOR SPREIZER

I have been hospitalised twice, with an average duration of five months. After being released I usually needed a year or so to feel myself again.

The memories of these times are still very painful, but I would like you to know about my crisis which began in the summer of 1994.

My job in ALTRA can demand very intensive work with psychiatric users, and in July 1994 I was among the organisers of its international summer camp for users. The camp is set up each summer outside a mental institution to provide some contact with the world for its residents. That year it did not proceed as planned. Many of the workshops were cancelled by the authorities of the institution, and too much of our time was left unstructured.

As an organiser of the camp, I took these setbacks personally. My upset was worsened when a friend of mine whom I 'did time' together with in hospital developed some mental health problems. They got worse, and the circumstances were such that he was eventually taken to a hospital. This was a big blow to me as a worker for an organisation which tried to help people stay out of hospitals.

I was overexcited, unable to sleep and worried about personal issues concerning my home life. When the camp was over I returned home to the house I share with my wife and parents. My family are quite dissatisfied with psychiatry and decided to keep me at home while I was in 'high speed'.

A crisis team was created with the help of Tanja Lamovec and other members of ALTRA, my family and some good friends. It aimed to reduce the burden to my wife and parents, and held weekly meetings where some basic rules were established:

I had to take medication regularly (starting on 2mg of Haloperidol).
I could not drive a car.
I had to be in bed from midnight until 8 a.m. and take sleeping pills.

51

If I did not follow these rules, my wife would go to her parents' home.

At first I did not want to follow these rules, but I signed the contract. Although it was planned a week in advance who would be with me at certain times, the greatest responsibility was on my wife. I tried to stick to the rules so that she would not leave me. She gave me a lot of support, as did my mother. My mother has been with me in previous manic episodes, and so knows me best of all. She remained calm and was very much against my hospitalisation.

During my manic episode it was very important that I received support from many people, because I had so much energy and felt elated. In our first crisis team meeting I tried to explain the insights I had about what was going on in the world, and about my personal importance in the scheme of things. I felt very much alive and convinced that I was the master of the universe. My world had no boundaries and I was sure, as many times before, that I was something special.

I had talked with my psychiatrist on the phone at the beginning, just to play safe. He suggested I take very little medication, but the team was opposed to this, since it was thought to be a way of getting people into hospitals. An amount of medication was agreed between my mother and the psychiatrist and he reduced this by 20 per cent every week. At the time of writing I am still recovering from the side effects of the neuroleptics and need to get down to my usual maintenance dose. With the present amount of medication (2 mg of Haloperidol) I feel very good; I can drive a car and work for four hours a day. Soon I will work full-time again.

This episode was quite different from those before. The acute crisis only lasted about two weeks, from which I gradually recovered. Compulsive treatment with enormous doses of neuroleptics in the hospital with all its ordeals provokes a much deeper crisis than I went through this time. The important thing was that I had support from my friends, my wife and my mother when I was in crisis. It is not possible to get such support in a hospital. The psychiatric system is repressive and a person is punished for every wrong move.

Being in a closed space, together with others who have the same condition, with no place to work, bad sleeping environment and bad food, only make a condition worse. It then takes a lot of time to recover. When I compare my crisis team to the staff in the institution I realise the former were my friends who wished me the best. Staff in a hospital do their job and nothing more. They can not do more because there is a shortage of staff and many things to be done.

In conclusion I would like to say how important it is to have reliable friends. They helped me beyond the level any professional could. They showed me that such an episode was not a problem for them, and that it could be managed. I think it was a success on both sides, since they learned something about psychoses and I did not have to go to hospital.

I am proud to be the first person with a full-blown psychosis to be helped by the members of ALTRA and to recover at home. I hope that we provided an example and that no member of ALTRA will ever need to go to hospital again.

Schizophrenia from the Inside

RICHARD JAMESON

Frequently I am told that the drugs I take only suppress the illness without curing it. There is, they say, no cure for schizophrenia. And yet the state I am in at present is, I am convinced, as good as a cure. I have a nice home, a good job, no sleepless nights, no disastrous mood swings, no hallucinations, no confused or disordered thoughts.

I am profoundly thankful because now I can get on with my life and not be pushed into the wings again. There is a lot of suffering involved in schizophrenia, but the main thing about it in my opinion is that is so confoundedly *inconvenient*. It completely destroys the thread of your life and forces you to start all over again from square one – if you are lucky enough to get round to that stage.

But schizophrenia is not the big, bad ogre that it is sometimes made out to be. It is suppressible if not curable. This light at the end of the tunnel must be held out to those who believe there is no hope. There are times, I know, during the illness when you are so removed from a cure that you are (in your imagination) living on another planet. You can be high or low, but these mood-stages are independent of schizophrenia. They can be cured separately by pills like Priadel.

Why are so many people so loath to take drugs and believe that coming off them is a major achievement? These are the chemicals that your body needs. You yourself may be totally unaware of what your body needs, so that to assert that your body functions best when you are not taking any pills at all seems strange. For example, most people manufacture their own lithium to stabilise the system. I don't, so I have to take it orally. What's wrong with that? These pills are not a punishment but are designed to help. Certainly there must be some experimentation to find exactly the right formula, and this can be painful. But it looks as if

54

the doctors have got it right in my case and I am very thankful indeed.

I don't want to give the impression that schizophrenia is any less of an ordeal than it is. The torture is as much physical as mental – and it hurts. Of course there is a lot of imaginative wandering, and when this is high it can be ecstatic: one is on Cloud Nine for prolonged periods, happier than you may ever be when you are normal. But the imagination can terrify too, and I can recall the terror now after twenty years. Even this, I believe, goes into the bank of experience and strengthens you for the future.

It is impossible to generalise about hospitals. Some are defeatist, ugly and overcrowded; others are constructive, kind and moderately sized. In one hospital I remember a military regime and beds thrown to the floor if they were not made perfectly. I remember the agony of being committed to hospital – it seemed to be be the end of everything. But can relatives really cope? My mother certainly couldn't have. It was only natural to send me into hospital to receive specialised treatment.

Psychiatrists are fine if you get the chance to see them and so bring your release nearer. In one of my hospitals I was lucky to see a doctor for five minutes once every three weeks. Even this interview was perfunctory and was carried out as a minor chore. But every week that passed I was more and more aware that I was getting better and screaming to get out. A more enlightened hospital sent me off to look for work very soon and when I had found it I commuted from the hospital until I was able to look for digs, since when I have never looked back.

It is said that only the strongest and most resilient get back to normal after bouts of schizophrenia. But I am not particularly strong. Perhaps I was a little more determined than some of my friends in hospital to get out and get going again . . .

In the back of my mind I still have these weird, vivid memories . . . being God in the Last Judgement . . . being at the court of the Emperor Tiberius . . . starring in a film being made all over London with hidden cameras and microphones . . . holding a senior diplomatic post during World War Three. My dreams were startlingly detailed and went on with my eyes wide open, walking all over London. Everything I saw bore out my dreams.

If anything, normality can be a trifle dull by comparison, but I thank God daily for my sanity and this is the most important consideration of all. I have an incentive now to stay as fit as I am, to help others if possible by sharing experiences and to try and give some idea of what schizophrenia is like from the inside.

Challenging Loss of Power

PETER CAMPBELL

On Tuesday I woke up an hour before my alarm clock ad wrote half a poem before going to work. I did a full day and worked an hour and three-quarters unpaid overtime. The Christmas rush was coming and pressure was building up. On my way home a down-and-out approached me in Euston Station. I bought him food and spent two hours finding him somewhere for the night. By the time I reached home it was already late, but I still managed to write three important letters before going to bed.

On Saturday I woke at dawn and left the house within an hour. I felt tremendous. Things had finally slotted into place and I was going to convert the 'natives' of the Upper Niger, equipped only with inspiration and a portable gramophone. Two hours later I tried to cross the Broadway opposite Hammersmith Odeon with my eyes closed. I laid my possessions outside the door to the church by the flyover and built a diagrammatic Calvary on the path. By mid-morning I was in custody, picked up by the police while standing in a bus garage, calling out about poisonous fumes in the earth. They locked me in a cell. I thought I was on the way down to Hades. Later they put me in a van and took me to a psychiatric hospital. I remember lying on the floor of a padded cell in my underclothes.

The above scenario is a distillation of events from eighteen years as a user of psychiatric services. Whatever else it may reveal, I believe it illustrates a major feature of life for those diagnosed as mentally ill: loss of control, whether truly lost or merely removed by others, and the attempt to re-establish that control have been central elements in my life since the age of eighteen. My argument is that the psychiatric system, as currently established, does too little to help people retain control of their

56

lives through periods of emotional distress, and does far too much to frustrate their subsequent efforts to regain self-control. Whatever power I may now have over my life, I have, to a large extent, won in spite of rather that because of psychiatry.

Before describing the specific processes of psychiatry as I have experienced them, I wish to make two general points which concern the context within which the system operates. The first relates to the medical model, or more accurately to the assertion that the phenomena psychiatry deals in should be seen in terms of 'illness'. Whether we accept this approach or not, there can be no question that it provides the current framework for society's view of the subject and that the psychiatric profession must take responsibility. Psychiatry would see itself as the servant of society. Yet it is naïve to suppose that a profession with such an individual and collective power does not form as well as reflect public attitudes. If we think of emotional distress as mental illness it is psychiatry that has seduced us so. And the pre-eminence of this concept does affect individual autonomy. To live eighteen years with a diagnosed illness is not incentive for a positive self-image. Illness is a one-way street, particularly when the experts toss the concept of cure out of the window and congratulate themselves on candour. The idea of illness, of illness that can never go away, is not a dynamic, liberating force. Illness creates victims. While we harbour thoughts of emotional distress as some kind of deadly plague, it is not unrealistic to expect that many so-called victims will lead limited, powerless and unfulfilling lives.

In the same way the feeling that the diagnosed mentally ill don't know what they are talking about limits the scope of our lives. The concept of insight – perhaps lack of insight would be more appropriate from the psychiatric perspective – is one of the most powerful and insidious forces eroding our position as competent, creative individuals. If I am to be confined to a category of persons whose experience is devalued, status diminished and rational evidence dismissed, simply because at a certain time or times I lost contact with the consensus view of reality agreed on by my peers, then it is scarcely possible to expect that my control over my life will ever be more than severely circumscribed. If my experience is not valued I cannot be whole. It is in particular discouraging to speak to some psychiatric professionals and have my experience validated only as a particular and very sad blemish in an otherwise benign conception. This is not validation whatsoever. I am not the one regrettable bacillus in the the sterile supplies room. My experience is shared and is relevant. It is not an interesting cul-de-sac. Tut-tutting and sympathetic frowns from those who are paid to intervene in my affairs merely confirms my powerlessness. They accept me as an individual pathology; they deny me as a cogent element of a social reality.

It is currently quite unclear whether those who work in the psychiatric system place a high priority on maximising an individual's self-control during the process of breakdown. In this respect I find it significant that no psychiatric professional has ever advised me on how to cope with a breakdown beyond the blanket exhortation to keep on taking the drugs. My own experiences suggest that once I start to lose control again I am expected to admit powerlessness, hand myself over to the experts and count to fifteen thousand. Such suspicions tend to be confirmed by the notably frosty reception my own ideas about my treatment receive from those who are attempting to process me back to in-patient status. It is clear to me that it is inconvenient to have to consider the integrity of the new admission too carefully during absorption into the psychiatric system. During admission, as at other times in the caring process, the system's needs dominate the individual's needs. This is bad enough as it stands. It is the more serious in view of the proposed shift to care in the community. A double dependency has been created. On one hand the users of existing services have been bred to accept dependency as a characteristic of relationships. On the other the caring team have based their operations on this inequality. The danger is that community care will come to fulfil these expectations, those standard practices. Instead of dependency beyond the community we will simply be creating dependency within the community – small and beautiful institutions on the next street rather than large and ugly institutions ten miles up the road.

Whatever the intentions behind the system, the reality of current provision is clear enough. For most who experience severe mental distress there is only one destination – the psychiatric admission ward. Many of us – particularly those whose crisis occurs after hours of sunset – will find the journey there extremely unpleasant. I have found my GPs reluctant to visit me after dark, casualty departments where knowledge of psychiatry or psychiatric medications is peripheral, psychiatrists' secretaries who do their best to persuade me not to bother the doctor in times of acute need. In short, a network of provisions designed to make it difficult for me to receive the help I many need and almost impossible to seek out the help I want.

If the admission ward met my needs I would endure the process of admission and the absence of choice as necessary evils. But it is becoming clear that for myself and for many others the admission ward is in no way a satisfactory environment in which to recover mental health. The existing system is not sufficiently sophisticated, and those who operate it are not sensitive enough, for whatever reasons, to meet the real needs of the many individual people who are forced through it year after year. What is needed above all are alternatives to prevent so many people falling into the psychiatric system in the first place – alternatives which do not rely on chemotherapy as a first-choice response to crisis, alternatives which address emotional distress as a problem of living and react to it more honestly than current psychiatric practices of 'patch up and put back on the road' allow. The impending closure of hospitals seems to have resulted in an obsession with the location of services. Character and quality of services is what really matters. Choice is essential. If provisions are to confront the real needs of people, it must first of all be accepted that people's needs are varied. It might even be worthwhile asking them what they want! What seems clear is that the same thing in different packages will be a golden opportunity tossed away.

In particular I object to the way in which power is stripped from me, the way that I am approached not as an individual but as a manic-depressive. It is not right that I should be casually drugged into unconsciousness on arrival in an admission ward. It is certainly wrong that I should receive this treatment regardless of whether I arrive handcuffed to a policeman or walk in of my own accord and calmly ask for help. On two occasions I have been given so much medication that I fell asleep before admission formalities had even been completed. I have not yet been allowed to complete my own process of controlled breakdown without such ham-fisted interventions. While such practices remain common it is not possible to claim that psychiatry respects individual integrity or is much concerned with self-education or change.

The psychiatric system is founded on inequality. By and large, the user is at the bottom of the pile. Our unequal position is symbolised by the compulsory element in psychiatric care. I do not intend to argue either for or against the use of legal compulsion in treatment. But the fact of its existence has repercussions for all service users, and these must be recognised. That an individual can be compelled to receive psychiatric treatment affects each in-patient regardless of whether his stay is formal or informal. It is hardly possible to be unaware that you are being cared for within a legal framework which allows for treatment against your will. Moreover, it is difficult for most in-patients long to remain ignorant of the belief – whether based on fact or on legend – that the threat of legal compulsion may be used to coerce individuals to accept particular treatments. Whatever the justification for compulsion in care, an inevitable result must be the diminution, whether physical or psychological, of the in-patient's control over his or her life. The implications of compulsion, the contradiction which may exist between the concept of compulsion and the concept of care, would seem to have some part in explaining why many psychiatric patients look back on their time in hospital as punishment.

Our self-image is further damaged by the limited extent to which we can participate in our own treatment and in that of our companions on the ward. While the resources of the medication trolley are over-used, the human resources of those living and working in the psychiatric unit are consistently under-used. I have been on wards where experienced in-patients have almost had to 'book' time to speak to nursing staff. I believe that many nurses whose prime impulse is to care for those in their charge are working in an environment which prevents them from exercising their most important human skills. Certainly the potential of the in-patient to be a creative resource for the community of the ward is seldom realised. Patients do support one another. But staff attitudes to this are often ambiguous. I have seen the inside of numerous admission wards. With one exception, none of them has provided structures which actively encourage patients to be involved in one another's care. Most ward meetings studiously avoid 'emotional' areas, and do more to confirm the powerlessness of the patients within a bureaucratic system than to encourage participation. I have a distinct suspicion that mental health workers in general don't like us to get too uppity.

I believe such an atmosphere belittles the standing of the so-called mentally ill. We are encouraged to be victims, to look vertically to experts for the solutions to problems they have defined, rather than to reach out for those around us who have a shared experience. The concept of care in the community will remain pretty hollow unless it confronts this situation. The ethos within which we tackle our problems and are helped to do so is in reality damaging our chances of becoming partners in the community. If we are made to feel victims and powerless by methods of dispensing care, if we are made to appear inferior by the systems supporting us, it is more than optimistic to expect that relocating the service-points will miraculously end our isolation. It is what the psychiatric processes are doing to our status and our self-image that is important, not where it is happening.

Our restricted role in our own treatment is of fundamental importance. The 'good' patient is usually the one who does what he is told. In one hospital a charge nurse told me that I would not be welcome on his ward in future because I complained about the quality of care. The implication that I should shut up and be grateful is disturbing. Participation not passivity should be the bottom line. I don't see conclusive evidence that the psychiatric profession always knows what it is doing. Simple to keep repeating their sagacity in a loud voice does not mean that the experts are entering into dialogue.

At the crux of the dilemma is freedom of information. I don't believe a patient can be otherwise than powerless until he or she has reasonable access to information regarding his or her treatment. When I was put on lithium carbonate I was told that it did not have side-effects like other psychotropic drugs. It was four years before I was given a kidney and liver function tests. Many of the side-effects of lithium are precisely the same as those of psychotropic drugs – dryness of mouth, tremor, for example – and there are significant possibilities of further effects from long-term use. All of this I discovered from my own researches. As a result I was eventually able to weigh the pros and cons and make my own decision to remain on Lithium. But no thanks are due to the psychiatrists. The initial withholding of information, whatever its motive, denied me one chance of exercising adult responsibility.

I am not aware of any conclusive statistics that revealing the true effects of drugs to patients ensures they stop taking them. Many of us stop taking psychotropic drugs because they do not do for us the things we have been promised they will do. Playing up the positive effects and playing down the negative ones is a recipe for trouble. The whole approach to medication in psychiatry seems to be tinged with a belief that the 'mentally ill' are by definition incompetent and unable to be adult even when returned to the community. Information is not volunteered, and even when asked for directly, is given grudgingly and in inadequate form. As a result of not being told the possible side-effects of the depot (slow-release) injection of Depixol when I returned to the community, I suffered sporadic side-effects over a long period, culminating in my collapsing with paralysis of the lower limbs in a North London street. This frightening experience could have been easily avoided. But to do so it would have been necessary for the system to recognise me as competent, adult, and a partner in charge, not as a non-responsible recipient of care, biochemicals and established wisdoms.

Every system has its faults. I would more easily tolerate the iniquities of the process if the psychiatric system returned me bright-eyed and bushy-tailed among my contemporaries. But this it does not do. The percentage of readmissions is high. Moreover, the diminished status we suffer while recovering from breakdown is not made right once we re-enter society. Discrimination affects us on major and minor levels, in personal and public areas. Discrimination in employment is standard. There are many with psychiatric records who are forced to rinse their talents down the sink and take jobs far beneath their capabilities. I find it humiliating to have to lie in order to be in with a chance of work. To be advised to lie, to choose to do so and hereby admit a shame about my past which is not justified and which I in no way really feel, has demeaned me more than any other single event of my life outside hospital. I want a chance to be what I am and for that to be recognised as natural. Society is not only ignorant, it stuffs its ignorance down our throats as well.

My argument against the psychiatric system is not that it is uncaring. I have met individuals at all levels – nurses, social workers, psychiatrists – who were clearly caring people and cared for me. But psychiatry must surely be more than custody and care. By approaching my situation in terms of illness, the system has consistently underestimated my capacity to change and has ignored the potential it may contain to assist that change. My desire to win my own control of the breakdown process and thereby to gain independence and integrity has not only been ignored – it has been thwarted. The major impression I have received is that I am a victim of something nasty, not quite understandable, that will never really go away and which should not be talked about too openly in the company of strangers. In short I have been ill, am probably still considered to be ill and am in some sense or other certainly handicapped.

I can find little evidence that psychiatry challenges the negative context within which the 'mentally ill' live. By losing control and having a nervous breakdown I seem to have entered a particular dimension of existence which is defined by the fact of its inhabitants' inability to have control – of themselves, their environment, their futures. The specific complaints I have made about the system's disempowering process are more worrying because they occur within an ethos that does not seem to challenge loss of power. Talk should be of creativity and change, not control and illness. Only then will the self-control I seek be a common object and not a by-product of protest.

ECT is Barbaric

LEONARD TAYLOR

Towards the end of 1969, 1 experienced the greatest crisis of my life regarding my sexual orientation. The crisis arose because I was married at the time yet fell in love with a person of the same gender. One part of me loved my wife and family; the other part of me loved my male friend from England, whom I had met quite by accident on a course connected with my job.

Clearly, to give up either person was one of the most traumatic decisions I had to face – yet a decision had to be made. I decided that my love and loyalties must be towards my wife and family, and that I would have to discontinue seeing my male lover. The pain of this separation was unbearable, the feelings of guilt and shame insurmountable.

Confused about my sexual orientation and suicidal, I voluntarily entered a mental hospital in England, where I was crying out for help in the form of counselling, acceptance and understanding. I needed reassurance that I was not 'dirty' or 'abnormal', that I was a decent, worthwhile human being no less than my heterosexual counterparts, but that I had the propensity or disposition to form a loving relationship with either gender.

Instead of being given the counselling I needed, together with a wealth of love, compassion and understanding I was promptly given about twelve treatments of ECT. I was also put on antidepressants and large doses of the major tranquilliser Largactil (chlorpromazine).

I cannot remember having been given any information as to the ECT procedures; neither was it explained to me that I may experience serious side-effects as a result of brain damage.

The treatment actually involves two electrodes being placed on the temples at either side of the head, and an electric current of about 150 volts sent through the brain. This shock induces 'grand mal', or a major epileptic seizure. I have been led to believe by certain experts in the field of psychiatry that the treatment causes a degree of brain damage.

That anaesthetic and muscle relaxants are given to prevent physical injury does not alter the fact that this electrical current has been passed through the brain which, in my case, caused serious side-effects for a very long time.

I can only describe this treatment as being barbaric or inhuman when it is apparently given to mentally confuse a person, or to give them a temporary lift by blocking out the problems which are bothering them. Even some psychiatrists who advocate the use of this treatment concede that its beneficial effects last for only four weeks after the treatment is given. Hence, although some short-term benefits may thus be apparent the degree of brain damage has been done.

After each treatment of ECT, I had severe headaches neck ache, loss of memory, disorientation, total confusion and a confused sense of time and place. Out of touch with reality, I would ask myself 'What am I doing here?' I was unable to concentrate or focus my thoughts and unable to read or write. Everything would blur and make no sense, and I would have to read over the article or letter time and time again.

While some people claim to experience euphoria or a high, 1 experienced the opposite.

Close relatives who visited me were shocked and upset by my vegetative, numbed or stupefied condition, and clearly would never consent to this form of treatment in their lives. I felt that I was losing my sanity and that if I did not get out of hospital the quality of my life would deteriorate still further.

When I returned to my job as a Ministry of Defence Police Officer what self-esteem I had previously had was now non-existent. I could not remember where specific buildings and roads were in the depot and my fellow officers had to try and cover for me when visitors arrived and wished to be directed to various places. Previously, though of a sensitive nature, I had been very efficient and intelligent, and had even successfully sat a written promotional examination, obtaining a position of first out of the eighty-five candidates who sat the exam.

At my own request I had to resign from my job, which I could no longer do efficiently. From then onwards I experienced about fourteen years of depression during which time I was treated with anti-depressants tranquillisers and a drug named Mandrax, to which I became addicted. I went from job to job with no confidence to do any of them efficiently.

While I can of course remember many events in my past life, there are some events which are gone forever. Relatives have often asked me in conversations, 'Don't you remember when so and so happened?' But it is just not there.

Even to this day I may be in the middle of a conversation when I forget what I am talking about and have to put much effort into remembering, or be reminded by my best friend. Often, I enter a room and forget what I am doing there.

I am convinced that ECT played a large part in the problems which I have experienced ever since my breakdown in 1969.

For the past eight years, I have received no ECT or any kind of medication for my mental health. Over this period of time, I have succeeded in finding self-acceptance and cultivating feelings of self-worth.

Having been medically retired due to periods of severe depression, I eventually joined our local Volunteer Bureau and I was able to do voluntary work which did not place me under any pressure. This type of work I found more in keeping with my personality, since I am a very caring person who enjoys helping people. I also worked on switchboard helplines, where I was able to identify with people who had experienced similar problems to those of my own. I began to read good books, and to write many balanced and informative letters to the press on homosexuality in order to tear down destructive barriers of prejudice which thrive on fear, ignorance and misinformation.

I sought out good, supportive and understanding friendships which further enhanced my self-esteem. I learned to assert myself and to stand up for my rights as an equal human being in society. I learned to like myself – to love myself – as the person I really was, as opposed to putting on an act to be accepted by society.

Although I'm still prone to depression when my confidence is threatened by cruel and insensitive people, I have a very dear friend who is also my confidant, and who gives me unwavering support and a wealth of love and understanding. To have such a great friend to turn to in times of despair is the greatest medication for depression.

In writing this article, it is not my wish to hurt or offend people who have had ECT and who have obtained short-term benefits. However, I am stating that whilst ECT seems to have worked in some cases, it certainly did not work for myself and others like me. Therefore, for any person to state that it is safe, reliable and effective for all people, is a travesty of the truth.

Choosing ECT

RACHEL PERKINS

I don't think I have ever heard the word 'choice' associated with electroconvulsive therapy (ECT) on the lips of a lesbian feminist or psychologist. Almost universally construed in *One Flew Over the Cuckoo's Nest* terms, ECT is seen (along with psychosurgery) as the ultimate in barbaric 'treatments' used to punish or control those who will not conform, especially women. How could someone like me, a radical lesbian feminist and a psychologist, choose to submit themselves to such torture?

Numerous women have asked me this question. I am writing now to address this question, as well as to outline some of the things that I wish I had known at the time, and some of the help that I would like to have received from my friends/allies, but which they were unable to provide because of their ignorance and my own.

The decision

I was two months into my second bout of severe depression. The first had prevented me from working (or doing anything very much) for about six months, and now I was back in the same situation. Although I was profoundly miserable, this misery that characterises popular uses of the term 'depression' is not what bothers me most. More important to me is being unable to think properly. Although I was receiving medication, I was still unable to work, read, drive my car, make even the simplest decisions or look after myself. I had all the classic symptoms: early morning wakening, loss of appetite, diurnal variation and amenorrhea. And I was terrified. Could I, like last time, face months of this?

One option available was ECT – and if it worked, it would at least be quick. I had seen its effects numerous times over the years: it hadn't 'worked' for everyone (neither has anything that I've seen) but it had for some. My primary interest in the possibility of ECT was its speed. I wasn't really able to make decisions at this time. What I wanted was someone I trusted (someone who knew me, my values, my situation and the options available) to tell me what to do and make sure that I didn't do anything too stupid.

When I asked friends, I received several long letters outlining the evils of ECT – not very helpful, as I really wasn't able to read what they said. Several telephoned and went on at length about how I would lose my memory and never be able to do anything again (at least that's what I think they were saying) – calls that generally left me in a flood of tears of indecision and hopelessness. Then there were the stunned silences at the other end of the phone, followed by some comment along the lines of 'Oh . . . Well . . . You must do what you think best' – again not very helpful: I didn't know what to think; I wasn't really *able* to think.

Fortunately, my family and a couple of friends (both mental health professionals) knew me well enough to provide what I needed. I am very grateful to them. First, they knew me and just how intolerable I found the inability to work, read, drive and the like. Second, they summarised 'pros' and 'cons' in a way I could grapple with. Third, they told me what they would do if they were me. Fourth, they made it clear they would help me whatever I decided.

I had ECT in the standard six treatments – two a week for three weeks; within a week of the sixth I was back at work.

What is it like?

Nothing really. I had an injection (anaesthetic and muscle relaxant), went to sleep and then woke up again a few minutes later. That's all I knew of the process. Some people get headaches: I didn't, although I did have some memory problems during the three-week course (could not remember who had visited and so on). I think my friends, found this more distressing than I did – if I wanted to remember something I simply wrote it down. These effects were not long-lasting: my job places heavy demands on my memory and I was able to resume it shortly after my final treatment. Now, some three months on, no one has complained about my having forgotten anything.

I tried having ECT on an out-patient basis, but having to cope with the demands of ordinary life as well as the effects of ECT made me rather agitated and confused. So for most of the course I was an in-patient: I left hospital the day after my last treatment. I did not notice any positive, effects until I had received my fourth ECT and then all of a sudden I could recognise me again. It may be difficult for anyone who has not experienced depression (or something similar) to understand what this means, but there is definitely a point at which I wake up knowing I am 'me' again.

Afterwards

One of the most irritating after-effects of having had ECT is the behaviour of those people who are so convinced that it causes irreparable damage that they 'test' my memory with their questions, or quiz me and/or my friends concerning my state: 'Are you/Is Rachel *really* all right?', they ask in hushed and ominous tones, and apparently seem unpersuaded by the answer 'yes'.

Now I am able to think back on the experience, I do not for one moment regret having had ECT. I would choose it again if I became depressed. But there are things that I wish I had known or, more importantly, that my friends and allies had known, to assist me in the process.

The classic feminist line of regarding ECT as a single, awful entity is inadequate. Ironically, this was brought home to me when the consultant psychiatrist with whom I work asked me questions like 'What equipment did they use?', 'How many volts?', 'What anaesthetic?', 'What was the seizure length?'. My rather pathetic answer – 'I don't know' – was greeted with the response: 'Why ever not? I bet you know the name of the medication you're taking, the dosage, the side-effects; you really ought to know the same for ECT.' I was ashamed: I have worked in mental-health services for years and I did not know these things. It transpires that they are important questions, particularly for women.

Things I should have known

I knew that ECT 'works' by passing electricity through the brain and inducing a brief fit/seizure, but that was about all. I did not know, for example, the optimal seizure length is 20 to 30 seconds: anything over this is more likely to result in cognitive problems. Or that the aim is to use the minimum amount of electricity to obtain such a seizure: 'the unwanted cognitive side effects of ECT are directly related to the amount of electricity used to induce therapeutic seizures' (Lock *et al.*, 1993). Or that different people have different 'seizure thresholds' (they require different amounts of electrical stimulation to produce a seizure).

Most notably (Lock *et al*, 1993), seizure threshold is about twice as high for men as for women and higher in older people than in younger people. The typical recommended starting 'dose' is 150 mC for women under forty, 200 mC for those aged forty to seventy, and 275 mC for those over seventy. It is important to minimise the amount of electricity used in order to reduce cognitive side-effects. It is also important that nothing is done to increase the seizure threshold. For example, I was given a 'pre-med' before receiving the ECT anaesthetic when I was hospitalised. I was not really 'with it' enough to ask what this was at the time, but I should have done. Benzodiazepines (often used as a pre-med) increase seizure threshold. I should also have known what type of anaesthetic was being used: some, especially Propofol, increase seizure threshold.

Other important aspects include the type of ECT machine and current employed. If a sinusoidal waveform is used then more electrical stimulation is needed to produce a seizure – a brief-pulse current is preferable. Five out of every six British ECT clinics are equipped with ECTRON models of ECT machine: 'It is important to note that none of the ECTRON models presently in clinical use meet the requirements of a good ECT machine outlined in the 1993 edition of the Royal College *ECT Handbook*' (Lock *et al.*, 1993; p. 8). The same document (Royal College of Psychiatrists, 1993b; p. 7) outlines how 'the problem with most ECT machines currently in use in Britain is that they have a narrow range of electrical output. The minimal output may be too high for individuals with low seizure thresholds, and these individuals will be at increased risk of cognitive side-effects.' As I have already said, these 'individuals with low seizure thresholds' are likely to be women, especially young women, whose seizure threshold is half that of men.

There are numerous other guidelines concerning the layout and practices of ECT clinics and the safety equipment they should contain (Royal College of Psychiatrists, 1993a). The Royal College of Psychiatrists' survey carried out in 1991 revealed that although anaesthetic practice was good, general patient care and facilities were deficient in 20 per cent of ECT clinics surveyed, and psychiatric practice was deficient in two-thirds – failing to meet even the minimum standards laid down in 10 per cent of clinics (Pippard, 1992).

Unfortunately, this sort of information is not generally given to patients or to their friends and relatives (Royal College of Psychiatrists, 1993b), and although more of the debate is available in the Mind report of the area (Mind, u.d.) there are still important areas missing. At the time I had ECT I could not have understood or dealt with information of the type outlined here, but I would have liked those who were with me to have known what to look for on my behalf.

I have no doubt that ECT has the potential for abuse and has been abused; it has the potential to cause harm and has been harmful. I would hate to think that my writing about ECT in this way might be used to coerce people into having ECT against their will. I also know from my own experiences, and those related to me by others that it can be beneficial. I reject the assertion that the potential for abuse renders anything, by definition, unacceptable. Most psychological therapies and most medications (both physical and psychotropic) can be harmful and can be abused. That harm and abuse can only by reduced if we are fully aware of the facts. Had my friends and allies been better informed about the details of the ECT I chose to have, I would have been in safer hands.

References

Lock, T., Freeman, C., Benbow, S., Scott, A., McClelland, R. and Pippard, J. (1993) *Electroconvulsive Therapy* (ECT), transcript of the official video of the Royal College of Psychiatrists' Special Committee on ECT, Royal College of Psychiatrists, London.

Pippard, J. (1992) 'Audit of Electroconvulsive Treatment in Two NHS Regions', *British Journal of Psychiatry*, vol. 160; pp. 621–37.

Mind (undated) *ECT Pros, Cons and Consequences*, Mind, London.

Royal College of Psychiatrists (1993a) *ECT Handbook*, Royal College of Psychiatrists, London.

Royal College of Psychiatrists (1993b) *Electroconvulsive Therapy*, Patient Factsheet, Royal College of Psychiatrists, London.

The Right to be Informed

CHRISTINE McINTOSH

I was first sent to a psychiatrist when I was fifteen years old, and my first admission to hospital was at the age of sixteen. I spent some eight years almost continuously attending psychiatrists and being admitted to hospital on a regular and frequent basis. I was twenty-three before anyone saw fit to inform me of my diagnosis. I have manic depression.

This brief, factual account of my 'career in psychiatry', as I like to call it, does not begin to convey the torment I went through during those years. I tried everything to get on top of my illness while at the same time trying to live a life that could be described as normal for someone of my age. While I was trying to build a life for myself – going to school, then college, setting up home, finding work, building relationships etc. – my poor mental health seemed to sabotage my efforts. Perhaps worst of all was the feeling of being in the wilderness, not knowing why my mind was in perpetual disarray.

My relief at finally being told what was wrong with me was marred by the intense anger I felt on discovering that it had been common knowledge among those treating me that my condition was manic depression. I immediately wanted some answers – I wanted to know why they had failed to inform me and why they had failed to offer me appropriate treatments. The complacent reply I received was 'we didn't think we should label you when you were so young and we thought you were doing okay by yourself.' The apology I expected was conspicuously absent.

Dissatisfied with this response, after much soul-searching, I consulted a lawyer and was shocked to discover that nowhere in law does it state

71

that a patient has a categorical right to be informed of their diagnosis. My only choices are to begin a costly attempt to sue on the grounds of negligence or accept the fact that as someone with a mental illness I have little recourse against the very people who were supposed to look after my mental welfare. I would happily trade the empty Patient's Charter for a few basic civil rights.

On a positive note, at least when I did learn of my diagnosis I was able to begin coming to terms with my illness and dealing with it on a constructive basis. I found out about my local self-help group and got involved with the Manic Depression Fellowship (MDF) and MDF Scotland. I discovered a common identity and a camaraderie with fellow MDs which has enhanced my life tremendously. Apart from my own personal experience, everything I know about this illness has come through contact with these organisations. No one should underestimate the power of self-help. I find that I can manage my illness more effectively these days and shudder to think that I could be blundering on in the dark, frightened and alone to this day but for a chance remark from a psychiatrist. I used to be running round in circles getting nowhere; at least now I know where I'm going – forward to better times ahead.

Prozac Really isn't That Great

ELIZABETH WURTZEL

Not too long ago, my friend Olivia brought her cat to the vetinarian because she was chewing clumps of fur off her back and vomiting all the time. The doctor looked at Isabella and immediately diagnosed the animal with something called excessive grooming disorder, which meant that the cat had grown depressed and self absorbed, perhaps because Olivia's boyfriend had moved out of the apartment, perhaps because Olivia was travelling so much. At any rate, the vet explained, this was an obsessive-compulsive disorder. Isabella couldn't stop cleaning herself just as certain people can't stop vacuuming their apartments, or washing their hands all the time like Lady Macbeth. The vet recommended treating the cat with Prozac, which had proved extremely effective in curing this condition in humans. A feline-size prescription was administered.

Now, you have to understand that Olivia had been on and off Prozac and its chemical variants for a couple of years herself, hoping to find a way to cope with her constant bouts of depression. Olivia had also recently insisted that her boyfriend either go on Prozac or take a hike because his sluggishness and foul moods were destroying their relationship. And I had been on Prozac for more than six years at that point. So when she called to tell me that now Isabella was on it too, we laughed. 'Maybe that's what my cat needs,' I joked. 'I mean, he's been under the weather lately.'

There was a nervous edge to our giggling.

'I think this Prozac thing has gone too far,' Olivia said.

'Yes.' I sighed. 'Yes, I think it has.'

I never thought that depression could seem funny, never thought there'd be a time when I could be amused thinking that of the $1.3 billion spent on prescriptions for Prozac last year (up about 30 per cent since 1992); some of them might even be for our household pets, who are apparently as susceptible to mental trauma as the rest of us. I never thought I would amazedly read about Wenatchee, Washington, a town known as 'The Apple Capital of the World', a place where six hundred out of its twenty-one thousand residents are all on Prozac, and where one psychologist has come to be known as 'The Pied Piper of Prozac'. I never thought that the *New York Times*, reporting on the eleven million people who have taken Prozac – six million in the United States alone – would declare on its front page that this constituted a 'legal drug culture'. I never thought there would be so many cartoons with Prozac themes in the *New Yorker*, illustrating, among other things, a serotonin-happy Karl Marx declaring, 'Sure! Capitalism can work out its kinks!' I never thought that in the same week I would stare down at both a *Newsweek* cover with a large, missile-like capsule beneath the caption 'Beyond Prozac' and a *New Republic* cover of some shiny, happy people enjoying their sunny lives above the headline 'That Prozac Moment!'

I never thought that this antidote to a disease as serious as depression – a malady that easily could have ended my life – would become a national joke.

Since I first began taking Prozac, the pill has become the second most commonly prescribed drug in this country (behind Zantac, the ulcer remedy), with one million orders filled by pharmacists each month. Back in 1990, the story of this wonder drug made the covers of many national periodicals. *Rolling Stone* deemed Prozac the 'hot yuppie upper', and all the major network news magazines and daytime talk shows began to do their Prozac-saved-my-life segments. In 1993, when *Listening to Prozac* Peter Kramer's book of case studies and meditations on Prozac as a pill that could transform personality, entered the *New York Times* bestseller list for a six-month stay, a new crop of cover stories and television pieces appeared all over again. While a backlash of reports, mostly promulgated by the Church of Scientology, linked Prozac with incidents of suicide and murder, the many people that it relieved from symptoms of depression had nothing but praise

The secret I sometimes think that only I know is that Prozac really isn't that great. Of course, I can say this and still believe that Prozac was the miracle that saved my life and jump-started me out of a full-time state of depression – which would probably seem to most people reason enough to think of the drug as manna from heaven. But after six years on Prozac, I know that it is not the end but the beginning. Mental health is so much more complicated than any pill that any mortal could invent. A drug, whether it's Prozac, Thorazine, an old-fashioned remedy like laudanum, or a street narcotic like heroin, can work only as well as the brain allows it to. And after a while, a strong, hardy, deep-seated depression will outsmart any chemical. While Prozac kept me pretty well levelled for the first several months I was on it, shortly thereafter I had a fight with my boyfriend in Dallas over Christmas. I took an overdose of Desyrel, an antidepressant I'd been given to supplement the Prozac, and ended up back in the emergency-room milieu that had once been so familiar to me. I hadn't poisoned myself terribly seriously (I'd taken about ten pills), and the hospital released me into the care of my boyfriend's parents. When I got back to Cambridge, Dr Sterling put me on lithium, both to augment the effects of Prozac and to even out some extreme mood swings. Regardless of my diagnosis of atypical depression, she was starting to think I was maybe cyclothymic or manic-depressive after all, going from gleeful revelry one day to suicidal gestures the next.

I stopped taking Desyrel once I started on lithium, but all my attempts to lower my Prozac dose have resulted in an onset of the same old symptoms. I have occasionally tried to go off of lithium altogether, because it is a draining, tiring drug to take, but those attempts to cut it out inevitably lead to scenes like one that found me spilled across my bathroom and wrecked out in tears and black chiffon after we'd had a huge party at our house. At times, even on both lithium and Prozac, I have had severe depressive episodes, ones that kept my friends in a petrified all-night vigil while I refused to get up off the kitchen floor, refused to stop crying, refused to relinquish the grapefruit knife I gripped in my hand and pointed at my wrist. After these difficult scenes, when I finally come to enough to seek medical help, the psychopharmacologist invariably will decide to put me on some additional drug like desipramine, or he will suggest I try taking Desyrel once again, or he will even ask if occasional use of Mellaril might not be what I really need.

Just as many germs have outsmarted antibiotics such that diseases like tuberculosis, once thought to be under control, have reemerged in newer, more virulent mutant strains, so depression manages to reconfigure itself so that it is more than just a matter of too little serotonin.

I believe, perhaps superstitiously, although my experience completely confirms it, that brain cells will always outsmart medical molecules. If you are chronically down, it is a lifelong fight to keep from sinking.

In the case of my own depression, I have gone from a thorough certainty that its origins are in bad biology to a more flexible belief that after an accumulation of life events made my head such an ugly thing to be stuck in, my brain's chemicals started to agree. There's no way to know any of this for sure right now. There isn't some blood test, akin to those for mononucleosis or HIV, that you can take to find a mental imbalance. And the anecdotal evidence leads only to a lot of chicken-and-egg type of questions. After all, depression does run in my family, but that might just be because we're all subject to being raised by other depressives. Where my depression is concerned, the fact that Prozac in combination with other drugs has been, for the most part, a successful antidote, leads me to believe that regardless of how I got started on my path of misery, by the time I got treatment the problem was certainly chemical. What many people don't realise is that the cause-and-effect relationship in mental disorders is a two-way shuttle: It's not just that an a prior imbalance can make you depressed. It's that years and years of exogenous depression (a malaise caused by external events) can actually fuck up your internal chemistry so much that you need a drug to get it working properly again. Had I been treated by a competent therapist at the onset of my depression, perhaps its mere kindling would not have turned into a nightmarish psychic bonfire, and I might not have arrived at the point, a decade later, where I needed medication just to be able to get out of bed in the morning.

As it stands, for a few years after I first began taking medication, after leaving Cambridge and coming back to New York, I stayed away from psychotherapy. I saw a psychopharmacologist who was basically a drug pusher with a medical degree, I filled my prescriptions, and believed that that was enough. After Dr Sterling, I could not imagine ever being able to find a therapist who was good enough. And besides, it seemed that with occasional lapses, drugs really were the answer. But then, as I found myself ruining relationships, alienating employers and other people I worked with, and falling all too frequently into depressive blackouts that would go on for days and would feel as desolate and unyielding as the black wave scares I'd spent much of my pre-Prozac life running from. I realised I needed therapy. Years and years of bad habits, of being attracted to the wrong kinds of men, of responding to every bad mood with impulsive behaviour (cheating on my boyfriend or being lax about my work assignments), had turned me into a person who had no idea how to function within the boundaries of the normal, non-depressive world. I needed a good therapist to help me learn to be a grown-up, to show me how to live in a world where the phone company doesn't care that you're too depressed to pay the phone bill, that it turns off your line with complete indifference to such nuances. I needed a psychologist to teach me how to live in a world where, no matter how many people seem to be on Prozac, the vast majority are not, and they've got problems and concerns and interests that are often going to be at odds with my own.

It has taken me so long to learn to live a life where depression is not a constant resort, is not the state I huddle into as surely as a drunk returns to his gin, a junkie goes back to her needle – but I'm starting to get to that place. At the age of twenty-six, I feel like I am finally going through adolescence.

Part three

LIFE AS AN IN-PATIENT

Introduction

We start this section with 'Thunk Among the Jolly Bunks', Lucy Irvine's account of an unorthodox way of becoming an in-patient. It is included for its humour and because it illustrates the ambiguous nature of 'craziness' – such a thin and wavy line between freedom from conformity and emotional distress! She also lets us in on a sometimes hidden reason for wanting to be an in-patient – free accommodation.

Although people may be admitted in dramatic circumstances, life on a psychiatric ward is often more notable for its tedious routine. Michael O'Higgins's gentle poem 'Ward' captures the sense of life passing you by that will be familiar to many people with in-patient experience.

The occupational therapy department may provide greater opportunity for activity and communication. For Wendy Lindsay the woodwork shop was where 'our lives started to be slowly put together again'. 'By Definition' is her generous tribute to the man who ran it. Any mental health worker can learn from reading this article.

Bill Lewis's poem 'Therapy Room' shows how humour and despair are so closely linked in patients' lives.

Wendy Lindsay was only allowed to do woodwork if she also agreed to go to a sewing class. More evidence of sexism in psychiatric settings is provided by a woman from Ashworth Special Hospital. In 'Why we Run for Cover' she explains how women are virtually excluded from occupational therapy by harassment from the men. The problem of sexual harassment in mental health services was highlighted by Mind's Women in Mind campaign. There has been a positive response, and woman-only space and activities are increasingly being made available. But how long will this reform take to reach the Special Hospitals?

There are three Special Hospitals for England and Wales – institutions for people detained under the Mental Health Act who, in the opinion of the Secretary of State, require treatment under conditions of special security – the others besides Ashworth being Rampton and Broadmoor. 'Good Stories and Stereotypes' by Rufus McGinty is adapted from an editorial in *The Chronicle*, the community magazine written and edited by Broadmoor patients. It is about the effect of patients absconding on public perceptions, and on the lives of all the patients, as security measures are tightened.

Carstairs State Hospital has an equivalent role to the Special Hospitals, for people from Scotland and Northern Ireland. Jimmy Laing's account, 'Leaving Carstairs', gives us further insight into the particular environment of these places. As someone who had always stood up for his rights and those of fellow patients, he felt obliged to compromise his principles in order to secure his release. This, and the preceding account, raise serious concerns about the role of the Prison Officers' Association. Both refer to times when conditions were even worse, but the more recent report, from Broadmoor in 1994, does not suggest a rosy future.

When Jimmy Laing heard he was being transferred from Carstairs he 'wanted to let rip a blood-curdling scream of ecstasy', but decided to keep his feelings in check because 'if I went over the top they might just change their minds and keep me in'.

Linda Hart is equally careful to 'Stay Calm and Charm Them' in her account (taken from her journal) of appealing against detention in hospital under the Mental Health Act, 1983. Earlier in this book, Patricia Brunner speaks of conforming to the doctors' notions of recovery in order to get out of hospital. Why is it that a psychiatric in-patient who feels and expresses the full range of human emotions is in danger of having them interpreted as a symptom of their mental illness?

Linda Hart introduces us to the baffling array of professionals and lay people she had to deal with in order to make her case. As a mental health social worker, she was at least familiar with the procedures. Her experience illustrates why ready access to trained, independent advocates, with time to listen carefully and explain, is so essential to psychiatric patients trying to secure their rights.

In 'Label Removed, but Scar Remains', John Bell tells us of his eighteen year struggle to prove he had been wrongly labelled and treated as schizophrenic. His account of humiliation and beatings by nurses in Tone Vale Hospital suggests why, despite the short-comings of community care, few patients are clamouring for such places to be kept open. His 'lucky break', shows the difference that can be made by doctors and nurses who are willing to risk the wrath of their colleagues and stand up for the rights of patients. His description of the changes at Tone Vale offer some hope for the future

Thunk Among the Jolly Bunks

LUCY IRVINE

By now I was expert in the art of using the hospital. An old file dating back to the days of truancy, and connecting my name with such terms as 'maladjusted', served as a sort of multiple re-entry visa. But still I could not just announce that I wanted to come in. I had to produce evidence that I *needed* to, something forceful enough to bypass the usual waiting list yet not so violent as to get me locked up indefinitely.

One weekday afternoon, having walked for hours along the Thames with no particular aim, I found myself within easy reach of a large shopping centre. I did not know where I was going to sleep that night – not 309 again with Kay's anxious, non-comprehending eyes and this worried me. I knew before I left the towpath and mounted the steps to the town that I was going to do something which would take the worry out of my hands.

The streets were busy, milling with shoppers and office workers hurrying on their lunchtime rounds. I held open the door of a department store for a well-dressed woman and two others took advantage of my portership to push through. I followed, entering a bright luxurious atmosphere designed to divert the weary shopper. Today, with a little assistance from me, they would be well entertained.

I lingered for a while on the household goods and china floor. There were tables laid up to display dinner services, apricot-coloured napkins folded into tongued cones, stylish placemats with elegant hunting scenes. In my mind I rearranged the settings, banishing the formality and making them warm and colourful as I would want for a family of my own. I passed on into the clothes section, taking my time, finding sudden value in the last quarter of an hour of freedom. Before the mirror of a hatstand

79

I tried on a wide-brimmed Garbo showpiece, tipping it down at the front so that only one middle-distance-gazing eye could be seen. Then I swapped it for a big Russian fur, drooping my mouth to look suitably proud and mysterious, and after that a Faye Dunaway beret, worn at a ludicrous slant. I liked hats for the clues they gave as to who I could be.

On the escalator to the restaurant floor, past lampshades and light fittings and long rolls of carpet, I stood behind two women discussing shopping problems. They were on their way to get their hair done but would stop for coffee first and 'a little something wicked to go with it'. I thought coffee a good idea too. My little something wicked would come afterwards.

The coffee shop was situated to one side of the main restaurant, surrounded by a low.white rail. It looked out over the rest of the floor which housed the store's lavish display of lounge and bedroom furniture. It was a busy time and most of the tables were full. The women from the escalator joined the counter queue ahead of me and filled their trays with quiche and tinned fruit gâteau. . . . I bought my coffee and headed quickly for the one vacant table near the front. I needed to be near the front. There were dirty plates cluttering the table and I smiled at the overalled waitress who came to clear them away. She did not respond and gave the surface a perfunctory swipe; red fingers wielding a damp cloth. Memory of Kay. My head felt full of irrelevant little snippets of the past, each one pointlessly clear, as irritating as advertising jingles repeating themselves uninvited.

I watched the traffic at the counter. Talk ebbed and flowed all round. It seemed to me as if the words were unimportant; it was the nods, the affirmations which mattered. Each separate table was like a cog in a wheel of ritual reassurance. When one removed the mind a short distance; the voices were reduced to a few simple patterns of sound: animals signalling. I was back to being a fly on the wall again. When the coffee was finished my gaze wandered to the wider spaces of the room and rested on the rich drapery of an ornamental fourposter. There were modern bunk beds in bright colours, long walkways of thick carpet; a yellow velvet divan.

With me I had a bag containing comb, purse, toothbrush and a library book with the address of the hospital clearly marked inside. I stood up and politely interrupted two women at the next table.

'Excuse me, would you mind looking after my bag a moment?'

After a slight pause there were nods. I laid the bag on a chair, bending as I did so to slip off my shoes. Then I stood up straight and took a deep breath.

One, two, three . . . Hup! Over the rail. Long diving somersaults down the nearest length of pile. Up on to feet with the last roll and three skips to the springboard of the yellow divan. Big leap and I'm on the Rest Assured mattresses, row of three. Spring! Spring! Spring! To land thunk among the jolly bunks and chintzy singles. Whumph! Air farting out as I hit a deep pink kingsize, satin bedspread all in a whirl. Short run up to a designer number, whoops-a-daisy it's on wheels – skid slide crump into a fat settee.

P-rrring! The bell. They're quick. Got to make it to the fourposter before they catch me. Come on run, short cut, dash towards the coffee crowd, brave it, brave it, oh look at their faces rolling back in a messy wave. Crash! A dropped tray. Yippee! Steady now for a big jump on to the final, the most inviting, row. Deep, satisfying springs, breaths . . . Damn! They're coming at me from the other end. So what! They're going to get me anyway but not before I've had a bounce on that fourposter . . .

We reached it at the same time. They came at me over the bed, one at the side and one at the end. Blue, this time, instead of whitecoats. At the last moment I dived under the valance to slide out unexpectedly the other side, dust up my nose and hands clinging trustingly to a pair of serge ankles. I kept my head down, mouth shut and went limp. Upside-down, dangling from their arms, I saw the pink satin bedspread crumpled like a bruised camellia.

Ward

MICHAEL O'HIGGINS

The view from the Ward
Is through a scenic window
Onto a trim, well-kept lawn
Where dancing starlings
Forage for grubs

In the window seat
The patients muse away
Drowsy afternoons
Either staring out wistfully
Or talking to themselves
In riddles.

The sun
Polishes the window,
Reaching long fingers in
To stroke the burning heads.

An occasional nurse flashes by
Like a busy fish,
Bearing antidotes.

In the office
A patient recounts
His favourite delusion
To the duty doctor:

'The government
Have put telepathic drugs
In the water supply
And the mice are telepathic
I have one in my head.'

Outside
A huge tree
Rustles in the breeze
And along the road,
The healthy drive by
In speedy cars
Aiming at distant houses.

But the people here
Have no journeys to make,
No destination to arrive at.

By Definition

WENDY LINDSAY

occupational therapy creative activities to aid recovery from certain illnesses (*The English Reference Dictionary*)

Part of my therapy was to go to somewhere called occupational therapy – this is a place where people are supposed to engage in activities which will rehabilitate them. Since I have always been a very active and busy person, this didn't seem too difficult a task and infinitely easier than staying on the ward watching the awful things happening to patients there.

To get to occupational therapy I quickly learnt that I had to be trustworthy, conforming, bright, reliable and I had to look as though I was really willing to 'be' rehabilitated!

I was asked what my interests were and to the therapist's surprise I replied, 'Woodwork'. My grandfather was a carpenter and as long as I can remember I have been fascinated by wood.

I couldn't have chosen a more difficult subject. The woodwork shop was a place where few or any women had been before. It was also a place of danger and, since I had been suicidal, most people were unhappy that I should go.

I made it clear that I had no intention of going to cookery or sewing classes, that the only alternative to woodwork was to sit on the ward. It was decided that the man running woodwork should come and visit me to make his own decision.

I liked Brian from the moment he walked onto the ward. He was a gentle man, neither threatening nor egotistical, not at all like any of the men I had ever known. He sat opposite drinking a cup of coffee, chatting as if he had known me all my life. He listened and didn't interrupt when I was speaking. He asked me what I enjoyed and why I had chosen woodwork.

I didn't know how to answer. No one had asked me questions before, or listened to my answer in the way that he was doing, showing such interest.

'I don't know what I'd actually achieve with the group,' I said. 'but I'd be happy to go in and sweep up sawdust or sand things down, I don't know if I can actually make anything.'

'Wendy, if I let you come into my group – will you give me your word that you will *not* harm yourself with any of the equipment in the workshop?'

'How do you know you can trust my word?' I replied, 'How do you know you can trust me?'

'I don't know, but I'm willing to, I'll give it a go. If you let me down Wendy, you won't *ever* be able to come back again. You will also be letting yourself down.'

Instinctively I knew I never would let this man down, never betray his trust in me, because this stranger was giving me a chance, without guarantees.

To get my one morning a week in woodwork I had to compromise, I agreed to go to sewing classes. That took the edge off my excitement, but on my first day I was so delighted to be going that I had a spring in my step – bursting to skip along the path!

I entered a light and airy room full of half-upholstered chairs and stools. Along the walls were two large cabinets brimming with braids and fabrics. This was the upholstery room. Through the open door I could hear saw and drill – there it was, life and activity. And coming towards me was Brian, soft brown dishevelled curls, a bright shiny face, rosy cheeks and a big smile. I scarcely caught what he said as I entered the workshop.

Then, 'Wendy, this is the Gang.'

'The Gang', those words were some of the most precious I had heard for many years. This was something we should be doing together, this was a place we could all be a team.

The room was long, surrounded with wooden benches, shelving, piles of wood, pots of paint and varnish, and a sink which clearly hadn't been cleaned for many a year. It was a pigsty.

At the sight my heart leapt – if I could do nothing else there was plenty to do in the way of cleaning up!

Very quickly I began to feel at home. I had looked immaculate in my dungarees when I entered but I was soon covered in dust and loved it. Dust and shavings were everywhere, and the smell – an aroma I was going to long for, to love being a part of.

These men, like me, were a little shy on this first day, unsure how to be with each other in the presence of a woman. Brian invited me to go see what each was doing and as I asked questions

I began to get the feel of the place. Brian stood back and let us talk.

Over tea-break a woman came in, clearly very upset, Brian asked to be excused for a little while and went away. We continued to chat. 'What ward are you on?' 'Are you married?' 'Have you got a family?' 'Do they come and visit you?'. All the questions patients ask of one another. 'What tablets are you on?' 'Do they help?' 'Do you sleep at night?' 'What are the nurses like on your ward?' These were the focal points of our days and nights, everything depended on our reactions to all of these issues.

I spent the next hour getting to know the equipment and surroundings – but all too quickly it was time to return to the ward. There it was obvious to everyone that I was brighter and happier than when I had left. I dared to ask if I could go back the following day. But of course I had to wait the long week.

I arrived as early as I could. The department was empty.

'Hi Wendy, who's an eager beaver?!' the men called as they arrived.

'Okay,' said Brian. 'what are you going to make? It's coming up to Christmas, what about a present?'

'A coffee table.' I decided. 'With tiles on top.'

Well, this was a fascination, no one had done this before. One of the men said he would like to do the same. We started to make the base, which was cut out for me because I never could use the saw without getting it stuck. The other man helped me off his own initiative and I was delighted, so was he. Brian said nothing, he looked at us both with a big smile and I thought, 'This is a very knowing man and a very wise man.'

I was determined to have my piece of wood, and the ready made Queen Ann legs, velvet smooth, with the grain as beautiful as I could make it. The hours of sanding kept me busy for weeks.

We had very few tiles in the workshop and certainly not the kind I wanted. So Brian arranged for us to go out shopping. He really put himself out a great deal to get us the things we needed. This shopping trip was my first outing from the hospital for months. I really enjoyed choosing the tiles I wanted and Brian never gave any hint to anyone that we were from the local 'madhouse'.

'Oh, the runaways have returned!' They jibed on our return. 'Why didn't you escape while you had the chance?!'

'How can I leave you?' I rejoined, 'You're my friends – we are The Gang, and besides, I want to finish my coffee table!'

Some continued to joke, but I could see that others were moved and swallowed hard, close to tears.

As time went by I could go to Brian's department every day – everyone had noticed how I had stopped being so isolated. Brian never told us what to do with our time, he allowed us to use it in our way. We had long discussions and often our work came to a halt. Brian saw our hurts but he never intruded, he let us retain our dignity in any way he could. But if we did cry, and many of us did, he would be there, offering his office, and he would go with us either to listen or talk on a one to one basis. This little office became a place of solace.

We were a great gang and Brian was one of us. He was reliable and trustworthy, he *never* let us down, never changed, he was consistent and constant. This was priceless for us in a hospital that was anything but constant in caring; here, with Brain and with each other, we had safety.

There was a time when a woman in upholstery came through and started to banter with us. Brian stood back and listened until it started to get out of hand.

'Right,' he steeped in, 'let's have a break.'

This made the woman really angry; she shouted at Brian, threatening to cover him in water if he didn't say sorry for interrupting. Brian stood still. 'I'll drench you if you don't!' she shouted, and she did.

We all gasped. Surely this would mean severe punishment.

Brian burst into laughter! The tension evaporated. The woman laughed too.

'Well, gang,' said Brian, 'you will have to work without me until I get changed.' And he gently returned the woman to her department.

We discussed the event for weeks after. Brian made it clear that this was not to happen again. But there were many times like this when patients found space to express frustrations in our woodwork group – without punishment.

Now and then Brian would fix it for us to stay for lunch, then he would go and buy fish and chips. And among the sawdust and paint smells we would sit on benches eating them out of paper with our fingers. These moments felt wonderful, a real treat, as normal as anything could ever be. We were relaxed, happy, having fun and feeling cared for. We laughed and there was endless talk of horses and races, who to bet on and the thrill of waiting for results after Brian had taken bets of a few pence each.

Many people could not understand the relationship which Brian had with his patients and for our part we couldn't explain it either, because it was something that was shared, 'from the heart'.

In the woodwork shop our lives started to be slowly put together again. Brian helped us, to understand the things which upset us, the things missing in our lives, or, to think about going home, to discuss, to communicate, to look for ways of coping and even to moan. He never rushed anyone. We could make mistakes and it wasn't the end of the world, and because of that we were able to attempt things we had *never* attempted before.

I often slipped back after a weekend leave and found I couldn't cope. But at these times Brian would stay in touch, he would come onto the ward and say, 'What's gone wrong, Wendy?' And we would talk and he would make me laugh. He would tell me what was happening with the gang, reassure me that my things were being safely kept. Out of the darkness was Brian reaching out and saying, 'I'm still here for you – when you are ready we will get it together again.'

What I had first thought would be a visit of a few weeks in fact lasted eight years. I had no idea then that Brian would play a major part in keeping me alive. What I gained from woodwork was not what I made but what I shared, what I saw, what I felt and what I grew to admire – a man who saw and acknowledged our pain, and did something about it!

Brian's therapy   recovery aided by humanity and gentleness.

Therapy Room

BILL LEWIS

Joe's making a stool
i'm weaving a basket
someone's making coffee
Dee says *I can sing*
and she does.
Jane won't make an
ashtray
Arthur's sulking because
the priest wouldn't re-
christen him *Jesus*.
Jane still won't make
an ashtray, instead
she becomes a dog
ggrrr Woof woof WOOF!
Dogs don't make ashtrays.
Dee's singing the
national anthem
Arthur blesses me.
Sydney hasn't spoken
all morning, or yesterday
or the day before,
gggrrrr Woof Woof!
Shit said Joe
I'm going to discharge
myself from this place
it's driving me mad.

realising what he had
said, he starts to laugh
i also start to laugh
the man on my left
(who didn't hear Joe)
starts to laugh as well.
we all laugh.
except Sid who wants
to die (and means it)
then we had coffee.

Why We Run for Cover

ANON

When I first came to Ashworth I remember thinking how strange it was to see people lying around in different parts of the ward. Was it lack of chairs I thought. But sadly the answer isn't that logical. People are lying around this ward because going to sleep is the only escape from the monotony of the days here. Need it be so? No, there are workshops to go to or there's leisure craft and education. So what's the problem? Why is everyone so motiveless?

The reason is – that all these occupational activities are male-dominated, there being an average eight men to every woman. As if that isn't daunting enough, any woman daring enough to venture to one of these groups will be bombarded by what can only be described as male harassment; this is enough to send any woman running for cover.

We are not talking about normal living here – these men are totally isolated from females. The only chance they have to see or talk to one is either at one of the occupations or at joint club venues. So you can imagine how they react when they come to a group, can't you?

There is a genuine need for us women to be respected and not have to live our lives as brain-dead, numb people. That is sadly how the regime of this hospital makes us feel and act.

If the male patients here are not capable of controlling themselves in company, then we should be allowed to have use of the facilities here without the men, not as it now stands. I am speaking here for the many women who I know of who are suffering because of it.

Good Stories and Stereotypes

RUFUS McGINTY

The year ended disastrously for Broadmoor. Two patients ran off on consecutive days while out of the hospital, and our profile was, once again, of the most notorious institution in the UK. Much was written and broadcast by the media, most of which was damaging to the hospital's patients and staff. Local people were reported as being in great fear as two convicted killers roamed free for twenty-four hours. *What was the hospital doing? Were they no longer safe in their homes?*

Gleefully, the Broadmoor Prison Officers' Association (POA) spokesman, Frank Mone, went on television to criticise the management of the hospital. He claimed that it was because of the liberalisation of the hospital that these people were escaping. 'The lunatics are running the asylum', one tabloid newspaper quoted him as saying, although he denies it. This stock phrase, with all its fantastic imagery, of a normal, healthy world turned on its head, of leering lunatics taking control, is what journalists realise will grab their readers' attention.

I couldn't resist but look at the matter, discussing it with both staff and patients, and the following points came out.

Will you ever stop the incarcerated from running away? Surely not. It is human nature. Of course, the majority of patients will be aware of the knock-on effects of mass-media coverage, and other negative sanctions such as capture, and being locked up even longer – yet people still go. Escaping from here has to be seen as a pathetic, useless, negative action. The vast majority of the staff and patients suffer as life here becomes more security-obsessed and the media feast on the sensationalism.

No one was physically hurt from any of these 'bids for freedom', or indeed, any of the previous ones in the last few years; yet the media react as if half the population was in grave danger. As usual, the media have gone 'over the top'. The historical notoriety of Broadmoor has given many of the papers the opportunity to do what they seem to do best: spread misinformation, titillate their readers, and play up to stereotypes and ignorance, all the while passing greasy back-handers to the 'moles', in both sides' immoral advance to make a buck.

Am I being too hard'? Let's look at the recent reaction of the media to a lifer escaping from prison. It attracted nothing of the same interest. It was the same with abscondions[1] from Ashworth and Rampton special hospitals, of which they had six and two respectively, last year.

The public conception of Broadmoor patients being the most dangerous of all inmates comes from it being the flagship of insanity. It was the first specifically built Criminal Lunatics Asylum and was opened in 1863. Since then, ten thousand men and women have passed through its gates. The horrific nature of many of their acts and the irrational, ignorant views of madness that preceded the bricks, bars and mortar, fuel the distortions. People are in prisons and other special hospitals for committing the same sorts of offences, yet they don't seem to make such a good story, of stereotypical axemen or baby-killers.

The damage the abscondions do to the hospital is enormous. Those patients who run off, obviously don't care about the harm that they do to their peers. But we have mixed views. Some patients think well of those who run off; others react with anger; some seem oblivious to it all.

Bridge-building visits to families and the outside community are stopped, as all patients get viewed in the same light as those running off. Could the positive anger of fellow patients ever prevent people going'? Over the recent Christmas holiday, in excess of five hundred prisoners, convicted of terrorist offences, were released for Christmas parole in Northern Ireland; yet not one abused that gesture. All returned to prison, being aware of the repercussions for fellow inmates if they did not. Could Broadmoor patients ever show such solidarity? I think not. The nature of mental illness – to use the crudest term – is that people are often isolated, unmotivated and alienated with an attendant lack of awareness. I suppose that if you don't think you've done anything wrong, you must feel you have every right to be free.

Last year, there were over 960 rehab (rehabilitation) trips from this hospital, from which two people absconded. Of the other incidents, someone went over the wall. a patient ran off from a general hospital visit and there was the disappearance of one from an outside working party. Rehab trips came under intense criticism and, although two running off is regrettable, it has to be acknowledged that it is a tiny percentage.

Frank Mone's attack on the management talked about their liberalism and lumped all the breaches of security under the responsibility of the new regime, which is patently unfair. Security has, as all patients know, been stepped up. The image I get of the Broadmoor POA is of a desperate, inappropriate union fighting for its survival. The damage that Frank Mone does to the hospital with his inflammatory statements is considerable. He, and others who act accordingly, are doing something that is characteristic of many POA members. They hold vested interests that have little to do with caring for people. In any case, many of them judge the patients here as bad people who should be punished by them. A good many people want the POA out for these reasons. There is no way, in the light of recent comments and past history, that the POA holds patients anywhere near the top of its priorities. It is not a union designed for carers but for prison officers. If this is a hospital and you treat people here, then trips are an essential part of treatment. They must go ahead. But what safeguards are there to protect the public? I see calculated risks being taken through the skills of the nurses and clinical teams, although they are never sure what is going on in people's minds. The public – from what I understand of the public – expects 100 per cent success.

May I state what is for some the unpalatable truth? People who are locked up are going to continue to run off. It does not seem to worry the prison service too much, but to ask the same question again, what can be done to stop it happening here? It is a thorny issue. Do you stop all trips and lock people up for longer? How can you change the selfishness, deceit and lack of responsibility of those who run off? Should there be more confrontation, in a positive way? (Not the old days of humiliation and degradation by staff – that just made things worse.) How about groups of peers voicing their opinions so that people will find it harder to hide from the consequences of their actions?

I am not advocating a witch-hunt, but making people aware of the effect of their actions on others, which is going to be painful, as reality tends to be. Being mad goes so far as an explanation, but if people turn around and say 'up yours' to the rest of the world then that deserves to be looked at. If you feel that you have not done anything really wrong, when you are locked up in here, with all its negative reinforcement, after doing something which, often, has been horrendous, then what are you going to be like when you are let loose'?

Finally, a word for those nurses suspended. They were doing their jobs and taking the calculated risks that all nurses take on escorting patients outside the hospital. That they have been suspended for over a month is really sad; a bad move by management. The word 'scapegoats' has been used. It gives no confidence to other nurses in Broadmoor, who may refuse to take people out now, and who can blame them? Someone is going to go at some stage in the future, 'out of the blue', and why should they put their heads on the block to have them publicly chopped? All said and done, the whole affair was an utter disaster, with the Home Office putting a block at ministerial level on the movement of all patients they have jurisdiction over, the gap between management and staff widening, and the image of this place terrible from all angles. Whatever will the coming year bring? No doubt it will take twelve months to get things moving again.

Update – February 1996

The other day I came across some wonderful photos of a sunny day spent visiting my young nephews. I had been accompanied by a social worker and my primary nurse, and had a chance to be 'normal' for a day. It was a marvellous experience. My nephews had a chance to play with their uncle and show him their toys, while their dad was able to share with his brother some precious moments of privacy and much needed communication. That was nearly three years ago, and as a result of the absconsions in December 1993 I have not been able to visit them again.

Note

1. This word is part of the language of Broadmoor, although it doesn't appear in my dictionary.

Leaving Carstairs

JIMMY LAING

I learned that I was being transferred to Murray Royal Hospital in Perth. It came about one day when Dr McDonald came round to my ward. She came into the kitchen and I gave her a cup of tea. I was on tenterhooks. Was she going to tell me? I daren't ask in case I was seen as being forward. Or was she going to keep me waiting yet another day? She turned to me and almost as an aside she said, 'You're going to Murray Royal on the twenty-seventh of August.'

I just wanted to let rip a blood-curdling scream of ecstasy. At long last I was going to be released. It is hard to imagine the delight that was racing through my body. Almost fifteen years had passed since I had been sent back to Carstairs from Inverness – for a 'short time' – and at long last I was getting out. Yes, I wanted to scream and shout but I couldn't let myself do that. This was a testing time for me, and if I went over the top they might just change their minds and keep me in. I said to Dr McDonald, 'Oh, that's great news, I'm so glad it's all worked out for me. Thank you very much, Doctor, for all your help.' She smiled and said it was her pleasure and she hoped that I'd do well.

I have suffered a lot in the years I was inside but nothing like the suffering that I went through in those last four months before my release. I prayed that I would get through each day without incident. For the first time, time was preying on my mind. Now that I knew my release date, each day seemed an eternity. Thank God it was only for four months. That was bad enough. Some nights my mind would play tricks on me, my imagination would run riot. I'd convince myself that everything was all right and then I would hear one of the nurses patrolling the corridor. Would he come into my room? Had I done something that day that they were going to complain about? Would he come up to my door and give it a kick, just for the hell of it, as they had done in the past? If I got up in the morning and complained would that go against me? All these things bounced around inside my head until I fell asleep. In the morning I'd awaken to the new day and begin to plan what I would do to ensure that that day would go smoothly and that there would be no slip-ups.

About two weeks before my release date an incident occurred that I have lived with since and which has tormented me ever since it happened. We had a particular patient in the admission ward who was in Carstairs as one of the many patients who was dumped there. He had a habit of keeping some of his bread from his meals and throwing it out of the window in his room for the birds. This was frowned upon. One day he was caught throwing the bread out by an enrolled nurse who called in another nurse, saying, 'Come and see this. What a bloody mess you've made outside.' Then I heard them slapping the patient and eventually beating him up. The next day, Thursday, was bathing day, and one of the nurses announced that we would get as many bathed as possible in the morning as there was a good film on television that afternoon. I hadn't said anything to anybody about the beating but Jock Reid came on duty and he saw that the patient was black and blue with bruises. Jock immediately called his superior officer, George Tait, who was the group charge nurse. George arrived and said that he was having nothing to do with it and called in the principal nursing officer Ian MacKenzie. He in turn called in Dr McDonald who called in the local GP from Carnwath who gave the patient a full examination. He pronounced that there was evidence the patient had been badly beaten. Dr McDonald called in the police. What a difference to the old days. In times past the whole incident would have been hushed up, but not in modern times, thank God. When the police arrived the patient told them that he had been beaten up for throwing bread out of the window to the birds. 'I feed them every day,' he said. He was a poor soul. However, an inquiry was immediately started and the union agreed that it would co-operate.

The police organised an identity parade of eight nurses from around the hospital and the patient was asked to pick out the nurse involved. He went up and down the line and picked out the one who had beaten him up. The other one wasn't there and as he hadn't actually taken part in the beating he was allowed to go free. The nurse involved was immediately suspended from duty. The police then began to question the other patients in the ward about the beating. Eventually they came to me. 'Good afternoon, Mr Laing,' said the policeman. 'We are making inquiries into the alleged beating that took place and we want to know if you have any knowledge of it. Did you hear any noises, screams or shouts ? ' My life flashed in front of me. I had just come from the bedside of a very young patient called Sammy. He had been sent to Carstairs as he was unmanageable at the other hospital he had been in. I had spent a lot of time with him as his story was so close to my own. I thought of him and the future that lay ahead. I thought of my own future and the fact that I was getting out in two weeks' time.

Later my reply was to tear holes inside me. 'I don't know anything about any beatings, sir,' I replied. 'I didn't hear anything at all. We have a patient here who tends to shout a lot, perhaps that's what I heard.' I actually wanted to believe that. My God, what a coward. All those years fighting for my own rights and those in the system and at the end I let myself and the others down. Why did I do it? Yes, I did it for myself but I also did it for Sammy. If I had told the truth all hell would have broken loose. The system, by this time, was changing, it had changed a lot, and was still progressing. I was leaving. Was I going to leave that young boy behind to the life I had suffered? No, I had to leave him to survive in a system which, I hoped, would provide him with a better life than I had ever had inside. But I was sick within myself. I excused myself and went to my room where I wept my heart out. In spite of my good intentions to help Sammy, I had betrayed my fellow patients. Self-preservation had eventually taken me to this awful stage. If I had spoken out I could have been kept at Carstairs for months afterwards for internal inquiries. Eventually the inquiry gave its result. No action was taken against the nurse in question as the case against him could not be proved. A whitewash. There was no court case as it was felt that Carstairs was doing so well that something like that would have set back the progress which was being made. It has to be said that the incidents of violence in those days, 1985, were few and far between, even in Medwin ward, and I heard later that the Scottish Prison Officers' Association had met with the Board to discuss the problem and it had been intimated that the spirit of co-operation wouldn't be maintained if the incident had been taken to court. One may ask how an incident such as that could be covered up. The Hospital is covered by the Official Secrets Act and once the authorities have decided that no action will be taken that is the end of the matter. While I believe that the Official Secrets Act can, and should, apply to patients' cases I do not believe that it should be used to protect someone who should not be allowed back to work at the State Hospital after he has assaulted a patient. Some things never change at Carstairs.

The nurse in question came back to the ward the day after the inquiry delivered its result and I half suspected that he would have his tail between his legs. Nothing could be further from the truth. I was in my room when he arrived and he came to the door and shouted, 'Right, you bastard, your fucking holiday's over. Get out of there.'

I said to myself, 'I'm having none of this.' I followed him down to the staff office and said to him, 'You're working here today because I lied for you. I heard you beating up that patient yet I told the police that I had heard nothing.' His face turned chalk-white. 'If you carry on with this kind of treatment then I'll be forced to go to the authorities and tell them all I know.'

'OK, Jimmy, I understand, it won't happen again,' he said.

However, one of the charge nurses, Frank Scott, came up to me and we had a long chat about it and later he also spoke to the nurse in question and that was the end of the problem.

By now I had only three days to go and Frank had suggested that I took some time off from working in the admission ward to get myself ready for going out. My initial reaction was to refuse. I was still officially based in Forth ward, and that is for long-term patients. I knew that when someone is leaving it affects the patients to varying degrees. Some are elated that a patient is getting out and some can crack up. Eventually I decided to go back to Forth with only forty-eight hours to go. I went back to my room, packed up my clothes and remained there for the next twenty-four hours apart from going out to the toilet. I didn't want to see anybody; not so much the patients, rather I didn't want to see or speak to the nurses. I didn't want to listen to the inanities of their conversation or overhear them saying, 'Oh, he'll be back.' I'd heard it all before and didn't want to listen to it ever again.

I read all day and I had my food brought up to me by another patient. On the final night, the twenty-sixth, surprisingly I was able to sleep. I laid my head down about midnight and slept straight through until seven the next morning. That morning, 27 August 1985, the nurse came up to open the doors and I got up, washed and shaved and dressed upstairs in my room, and waited for the car to arrive to take me out. Eventually the phone call came that the car was on its way and I went downstairs. I just wanted to get away. I didn't want any ceremony from anyone just a quick goodbye to those I knew best – the patients.

As we got towards the gates I began to panic slightly. Were the papers in order? One mistake and they would refuse to let me pass. But the gates slid open and we passed through. I was finally out of Carstairs. What a relief it was. I knew that I still had to do time at Murray Royal but that was a 'real' mental hospital. Not like Carstairs which is a hospital in name only. Before getting out I had been on 'training for freedom' days out with a nurse to Edinburgh – to see how I got on. Those had been fine but you always knew you had to come back to Carstairs. Now I was really heading for freedom. I suppose that it would be expected that I wanted to get out of the car, breathe in the fresh air and maybe even go for a walk in the fields, but that was not the case. I was delighted to be out but, while I don't want to be considered exceptional, I had kept up to date with what was going on in the world. I knew what the outside was all about. My room had overlooked the long Lanark Road, there was less than a field between it and the Hospital and, strange though it may seem, I had been able to mentally take down the fence that lay between it and the road. I always knew I would get out and that fence was not going to stand in my way.

All my problems at Carstairs were now behind me. I was leaving and I was determined never to return. I didn't even look back at the place as I left.

Stay Calm and Charm Them

LINDA HART

Some names and other identifying details have been changed to protect the privacy of the individuals involved.

3 December

When Graham, the consultant psychiatrist, came, uninvited, to my house that Thursday morning, 2 September 1993, I felt even my private space had been invaded. He talked to me for a while and said I had to go to Ward 20, the psychiatric department of the general hospital.

I'd been a patient on that particular ward before. I knew staff on 20 as colleagues as I worked for Social Services at the Mental Health Project which provided day care and individual support work with mentally ill people who were living in the community.

I didn't want to go into hospital, but Graham said he was going to call for an ambulance and if I didn't go voluntarily then he would get my GP and I would be sectioned under Section 3 of the Mental Health Act. He said if I didn't go into hospital I would be dead quite soon. I said I needed to see a physical doctor about the maggots in my stomach and he said it was a psychiatrist I needed. He said there was no negotiation; I had to go, and the sooner the better. I asked if I could go in the car with Rob, a work colleague, but he said I might try to get out of the car on the way. The ambulance came and I felt very scared. I was also conscious that it wouldn't go unnoticed by the local villagers. Rob said he would come in the ambulance with me and I was very glad of his support. Walking the short distance from my gate to the ambulance made me feel very humiliated and I dared not look around to see if I was being watched by anyone.

100

At a later stage Linda was formally detained under section 3 of the Mental Health Act and this order was extended for a further six months.

7 March

At 3 o'clock Laura, my key nurse, and Hugh, the junior doctor, saw me and they said they had been in touch with Graham and between them had decided that they were going to extend the Section 3 for a further six months. I feel ashamed and humiliated.

14 April

Laura saw me later than she said she would. I told her her manner was making me very unhappy and she said that she felt the need to challenge me. She said she was fed up with me always pushing at the barriers surrounding the restrictions that have been imposed on me. She said they would be reviewed weekly at the ward round and would not be up for negotiation in between times. She said I should be fighting the illness, not the restrictions.

27 April

I sat down with Annie, a fellow patient, and worked out a response to Graham's report for the managers' meeting. A managers' meeting is called when a patient has been compulsorily detained in hospital for longer than six months. It's automatic and comprises three managers, the consultant psychiatrist, a social worker and legal representation. Graham and the social worker have to submit reports, and these are also used for the tribunal, which is automatic after six months. For the tribunal on 16 May I have asked for Dr Sashidharan to do an independent report. He doesn't subscribe totally to a medical model, and so it should be interesting.

28 April

I'll describe the managers' meeting which occurred yesterday afternoon. The legal executive, Beryl, arrived at 1.50 p.m. ten minutes before the meeting was due to start, so I didn't have time to go through my response to Graham's report. She didn't have a copy of Graham's report either, so she only had time to scan it quickly. I decided she was useless anyway and so told her I would do my own defence and she could sum up at the end. I was cross with Beryl for being so late and told her so.

Jo, the social worker came and I felt comfortable with her.

At 2 p.m. we went up to the boardroom, and three associate or executive managers were there. Only one had a medical background and she was a general nurse. No one there had any psychiatric experience. Bernard was the chair and the other two had nothing to say. He was quite friendly and tried to put me at my ease, but he was dreadfully patronising. I kept my cool throughout and tried to woo Bernard with wit and charm.

Graham spoke first and said, among other things, that he expected a return of the psychosis whilst reducing the Stelazine and he didn't think I was psychosis-free yet. He said he had grave doubts about my safety. Graham was more positive than his written word, and did say my performance at work was excellent.

I then went through his report, paragraph by paragraph, and made my response to what he had said. He replied, and we had quite a sparring match, but I kept control and retained my dignity.

As regards diagnosis, he said I was complex but was more schizophrenic than other things, although he has seen me being hypomanic also. In other words, I've got everything.

Beryl, the legal executive, summed up but didn't say any more than I had.

We left the room and came back to the ward. Then Bernard came and told me they thought Graham needed the Section to stay for just a little bit longer. He said, 'You're a very intelligent lady', in almost an accusatory way and I told him my intelligence was irrelevant. He also said he'd never come across anyone who had argued their case so well. He was very patronising. He did also say they had told Graham to get me the drug information I had requested.

10 May

I'm now on thirty-minute observations and allowed off the ward alone for 30 minutes each day.

At 4 p.m. Dr Sashidharan came. He said he wanted to look at the care notes first, and at around 4.50 p.m. he called me in. We had a long conversation that lasted one and three quarter hours. He was amazed by the amount of drugs I'm on and said information was available. He said it didn't have to be 'lay' information, since it was written in English and I would be able to understand it. He asked me lots of questions about my experiences and was aware that being confined to the ward was detrimental to my health. He seemed very astute, and said he would strongly recommend my release from the Section. The interview was conducted with dignity and intelligence, and I'm very much looking forward to reading his report.

16 May

9.35 a.m. I'm feeling tired and subdued but confident I will win the tribunal today. I'm possibly prone to being unstable, so I must watch my anger levels. Stay calm and charm them.

7. 10 p.m. The tribunal doctor arrived and wanted to see me at 11.45 a.m. I told him he had not made an appointment and that my lunch was at 12.00 and my solicitor was coming at 12.30. He said he thought I could forgo my lunch as he wouldn't be having any, and I told him I had to have my lunch so I went and had it. He was elderly and deaf and wanted to go back over my history, which I found tedious in the extreme. I told him I felt low and unstable. My solicitor didn't arrive until 1.20 p.m. so there was no time to go over anything with him since he brought the lengthy report of Dr Sashidharan and the update of Graham' s report and Jo' s.

I got though the ordeal, which lasted nearly two hours, and everyone said I did it brilliantly.

When the tribunal doctor told them how fussy I'd been about having my meal I told them what did they expect, since I was obviously institutionalised. That made them laugh. It was very good having a friend, Margaret Harrison, sitting next to me and she gave a heart-felt plea for my release from the Section. The chair, a lawyer, was a man called Howe and the lay person was called Mrs Start. She was by far the most with-it member of the panel and her questions were very probing but intelligent. I feel absolutely knackered. I do not as yet know the outcome but have to be informed within seven days.

Afterwards, Graham gave me a slip of paper from the pharmacy on drugs and one of the points on it was 'Take your pills standing up and wash them down with water.' Well really!

19 May

I received a letter this morning saying I would not be discharged from the Section. I feel very miserable and powerless and trapped. I think my father is influencing the staff and Graham, and he will kill me through Graham.

20 May

Not winning the discharge of the Section has cut me deep. I feel aggrieved that the solicitor was so poor and I'm angry with that. The only thing I asked him to do was to prevent me making out my case first. In a criminal trial, the defendant always goes last and a Mental Health Review Tribunal should be at least as fair as that. With the solicitor being an hour late, we didn't have a chance to go through Graham's report and squash some of his arguments. Having a tribunal is deeply upsetting. So many negative things about me were made public – or at least laid open before the many people in the room.

Label Removed, but Scar Remains

JOHN BELL

There is a saying that goes, 'Sticks and stones may break my bones but names will never hurt me.' Yet there is one name that has caused me more pain and unhappiness that goes beyond imagination. And not only the name but all that went with it. The name in question is 'schizophrenic'.

Three days before Christmas 1968, my father died from cancer. Five weeks later, my mother followed him. In a very short space of time I had gone from being a happy, carefree schoolboy to an orphan. I had only just turned 14 at the time. I went to stay with an uncle until arrangements could be made for me to be fostered or adopted.

Unfortunately, it never got to that stage. On the way home from school one day I was knocked off my pushbike by a car. As a result, I was admitted to hospital with severe concussion. After a week I was discharged. I then started to get attacks of anxiety. This, I have been told, is quite common after having concussion.

My GP did not think so at the time and so passed me over to a psychiatrist. After a long talk with the psychiatrist. he said that I would be safer in hospital. When he told me which hospital, I refused point blank. This was the place that my mother had referred to as Cotford Lunatic Asylum, the place they put people who were mad or insane. I knew the place as Tone Vale Mental Hospital.

Anyway, the psychiatrist issued me with some drugs which he said would help me. In fact, they did the opposite. The effects of these drugs were quite horrific and as a result I ended up in another hospital where some tests, including a lumber puncture, were carried out.

In September 1969 I was taken to Tone Vale and the only reason I was given was that they wished to discharge me from the hospital and I had no place to go except Tone Vale. The truth of it is that the psychiatrist had told my uncle that he suspected I had schizophrenia and that I would be safer in Tone Vale.

This was the start of events which have devastated my life.

At Tone Vale there is a special unit called Merryfield. Because of my age I should have gone to that unit. Instead, I was placed in the main hospital, which, I can tell you, was a very terrifying experience. I knew that there was nothing wrong with me, that I did not need to be in a mental hospital, but I'm afraid I was the only one who saw it that way.

For the next seven months I went through hell. It was no use trying to talk to the nurses as all they did was mock me. My uncle took the trouble to visit me now and again, but they always knew when he was coming and so the dose of Largactil was upped to a level that I was unable to stand up.

On more than one occasion I was beaten up by nurses. They actually enjoyed doing it. And when they used to tell me that nobody would believe me, they were right. Like the charge nurse once said to me, 'Who is going to believe anyone in a mental hospital. We just put it down to you being ill. Tell people if you want but they are not going to take any notice.' I tried to tell my uncle what they did to me once, but the charge nurse was right, he didn't believe a word of it. And as a result, I was given a shot of Paraldehyde.

The worst thing that I suffered in that first seven months is something that I have done my best to hide all these years. I was sexually abused by another patient one night. And when he had finished, he threw me onto the floor and kicked the living hell out of me. And a nurse just stood there and laughed.

My lucky break came when the Chief Medical Superintendent went on holiday. The doctor who stood in for him called me into the office one day. She told me that a mental hospital was no place for a boy of my age and as she could see nothing wrong with me, she discharged me there and then.

What I thought was the end of it all was just a break. A social worker was called in to take me back to my uncle's house. When I showed up he was horrified. He made it clear he wasn't prepared to have a schizophrenic in his house. Everybody else shared the same view. Not one single person wanted to know me.

My mind could take no more and so I stole a motorbike and rode it straight into a brick wall. I just wanted to die. There was nothing left to live for. I was alone in a big, cruel world and with the threat of having to return to Tone Vale. How I survived I am told is a miracle. I made a right mess of myself. I really wish I had not survived – it would have saved me from what was to come next.

I was taken back to Tone Vale under Section 25 of the Mental Health Act 1959. Before the end of the twenty-eight days were up I was handed a piece of paper stating that I was being detained under Section 26 and the diagnosis was 'schizophrenia'. I was then taken to the back of the hospital and placed on a locked ward. It was put to me by the charge nurse of this ward that the only way I would leave it was when they transferred me to the geriatric ward below or in a coffin.

There were seventy patients on this ward and it was impossible to talk to any of them. Their minds had been destroyed. I saw some of those poor buggers get ECT neat. No doctor present either. I fell victim to it twice. Hardly a day went by when I didn't get beaten by a nurse. But that's it. They weren't nurses. They were keepers. Some of the things that went on are unbelievable.

One day, I was taken down to see the Chief Medical Superintendent in his office. He told me that my condition was worsening and that they were considering giving me a small operation which he assured me would make me feel a lot better. On the way back to the ward my escort of two nurses delighted in showing me the operating room where he would 'fix' my brain.

It's fair to say that the RSPCA treats stray dogs better than I was treated by the nurses on Hood Ward. After two years I was released from Tone Vale. It would take far too long to say how, but I can tell you that it was by the skin of my teeth.

The fact that I had been labelled a schizophrenic has destroyed my life ever since. Everything that I have ever wanted to do has been ruined by that one word and the fact that I was detained in a mental hospital as a youngster. Employment, for example – people are reluctant to work with you when they find out; they feel threatened.

What happened to me years ago did a lot of damage – damage that can never be repaired or reversed. They took everything away from me. My youth. My rights as a human being. My dignity and self-respect. But the one thing that I did manage to hang onto was my mind, which is why for the past eighteen years I have fought so hard to prove that I was wronged. I fought so hard that come the finish I could take no more and became very ill – so ill, that in June 1990 I was once more admitted to Tone Vale, the place I swore I would never end up in again. Back to the scene of the crime, as one nurse put it.

But it was worth going back. Why? Because the answers that I had been searching for, for so long, I got in the one place on this earth I never dreamed of – the place responsible in the first place. I was amazed at how much the place had changed over the past eighteen years. The building is still the same, but the methods of nursing have changed, and for the better I am glad to say.

The ward that I was on years ago is closed and boarded up now. What did surprise me is that they went to the trouble of getting it opened for a short while so that I could go up with the hope of laying some ghosts to rest. If nothing else, it certainly stirred up my emotions. It filled me with anger to think that so many lives were ruined on that ward.

My other major surprise was that during a meeting with my psychiatrist, Dr Hunt, he told me that he could find no evidence that l was schizophrenic, that the diagnosis of schizophrenia was made in error and that he would give me a letter to this effect. All the staff were amazed, as they told me there is no way that Dr Hunt would do this, but he did. I have been told by numerous people in the medical profession that this is a first. It means so much to me, because I no longer have to prove that I never suffered from schizophrenia. But it still doesn't justify what happened and how it has ruined my life ever since. Nobody can give me back what I have lost.

While I was in Tone Vale last year, it was suggested that I write a book which I am in the process of doing. I need to write this book – not just for myself but for all those others who can't tell their story, how they were destroyed, how they never got a chance. Getting it published is my only problem. I don't know how to go about it. I intend to carry on fighting as well – fighting for better conditions for those diagnosed 'mentally ill'. It's like my key worker, Staff Nurse Chris Parker, said to me: 'Psychiatry has come a long way since you left Tone Vale in 1972, but it still has a long way to go.'

To finish on a happier note – I shared a joke with Chris when I was in Tone Vale last. He said that having a key worker must seem strange to me. It's a pretty new thing at Tone Vale. I replied, 'No. They had them here in '69. They unlocked the doors to let you in and then locked them to keep you in. '

Part four

MOVING INTO THE COMMUNITY

Introduction

The articles in this section suggest different standpoints on what it means to make the transition from being in hospital to life outside. The previous section contained some disturbing accounts of in-patient treatment, yet it is too simple to depict what happened in the past in hospitals as 'bad' and community care as automatically 'good'. These accounts give a more rounded picture of the variety of experiences of long- and short-stay hospital life, as well as the kinds of resources people can muster in changed circumstances.

'I Want to Become Part of My Family Again' was recounted to researcher Christine McCourt Perring, and puts across vividly the fact that for Jane her experience of hospital and the projected move are just small pieces of the jigsaw that makes up her life. Jane was born in London in the 1920s and left Friern Hospital for a group home in 1987. She felt abandoned by her family during her hospital stay, and divorced her husband on leaving hospital. The move was an opportunity for Jane to take charge of her relationships, to reconnect with her daughter and grandchildren and to find new independence.

'Paying the Penalty' by A.N. is the first of four articles, grouped together here, by residents of 'The Pastures' psychiatric hospital in Derbyshire. The articles were written as part of a project to describe contrasting experiences inside and outside a psychiatric institution, as the hospital was on the brink of closure. The first author refers to her own damaging family background. When she left hospital her adult children blamed her for their lives spent in care. She continues to pay the penalty.

Wendy Lindsay evokes poignantly in 'Treading on Eggshells' the uncertainty and tension experienced by her family while all were emotionally vulnerable when she left hospital. Her role as a parent was seriously disrupted as her children tried to protect her from the strain they were feeling. These accounts by women demonstrate some of the expectations held of motherhood, and the difficulties that inability to fulfil these expectations can present for women struggling to maintain their close relationships.

Miranda, in 'I Don't Feel it's Right' shows the stresses of adapting to group home life among strangers. Terry, in 'I Can Get About', has a happier experience of excitement and fulfilment after forty-one years in hospital since the age of thirteen.

Martin Henderson's poem,'The Sanctuary in North London', gives a graphic picture of a shabby yet relaxing spot where there is a rare sense of caring. Perhaps this is the sort of place that Joan Tugwell, given 'A Second Chance for Life', would have appreciated. Joan Tugwell battles with the vicissitudes of first no electricity, then overwhelming bills, and insufficient money for food. She nevertheless conveys the joys of simple activities, such as having a cup of tea with a friend, or being trusted enough to look after a neighbour's cat and house.

In his oral account 'I've Got Memories Here' Clive takes the reader on a guided tour of St Mary's Hospital in Herefordshire, and his memories of it. For Clive this was a place where he felt safe, and was 'looked after with no worries'. His piece acts as a reminder that people had no choice about leaving hospitals which were closing.

Jim Read's article, 'Nutter to Normal', suggests that even a relatively short stay in hospital can leave a lasting imprint on the shape of a person's life. Jim Read writes positively about his initial struggles on leaving hospital more than twenty years ago, and subsequent success in building a new life.

Jenni Meredith's poem 'Alienation' deals with an issue which all the authors in this section will have faced: the stigma of a 'mental illness' history, and the difficulty of knowing whether, when and how to tell colleagues or friends.

Peter Good's article 'A Comparative Study of Application Forms for Housing Benefit and an American Express Card' is not directly about hospitalisation or life post-hospital. He writes about the context of marginalisation (shared with anyone dependent on state benefits) which is starkly conveyed in the language of forms designed to sift the deserving from the undeserving. Sadly, recipients of community care more often encounter the condemning tone of state benefit forms than the warm blandishments used in invitations to use a credit card.

I Want to Become Part of My Family Again

JANE

My mother was an exceptional woman. For a long time she was alone with my brother, but she married again. She married partly because it was so hard for a woman to keep a family alone. We didn't suffer the conditions that some of them did, as working-class children, because of her strength. She was a foundling, brought up by the nuns. I had polio as an infant, though I didn't know it till late on. I don't think it affected my parents' relation to me. Mum was protective to me and Johnny alike.

My first school was St Joseph's. Holy Jo's they called it. I hated it. Me and my brother were very clingy to my mother and she didn't really want us to go. Johnny didn't go until he was seven and got caught by the school board. When I first went, the nuns told her they didn't cane the children, but I was even caned for being late. When she found out she took me away, particularly because they had lied to her about it. I went instead to the convent a bit further away, where she had lived as a child. I was happier there, but I didn't really like school. I did want to find out about things. I was bright as a child, but it just wasn't like that in school. I went to the local secondary, but didn't go very much, partly due to the outbreak of war.

I think my literacy problems were inborn; I couldn't have taken courses because I just couldn't spell. I was brought up as a Catholic but I've lapsed now.

At the outbreak of war, my father lost his job by chance and because he was sixty-five had to go on a pension. My brother was called up. He was nineteen. The pension didn't account for dependants, so we all had to live off a single old-age pension, which was very difficult. My mum couldn't work because she was a very sick woman. We lived in Inner London, but

111

after a land mine landed near our house we moved further out to get away from it all. I was twelve then and was evacuated to Somerset, so I effectively left school at twelve. My mother came with me and we were taken in by a local family. The wife offered to take us in because she had two boys and her husband had always wanted a daughter. Their marriage was very shaky and possibly she hoped this would patch it up. I was to be the daughter he never had. At first he made a real fuss of me and was very affectionate. I was already physically matured and soon he started to want more than affection from me. Eventually he tried to rape me. I told my mum and she didn't call the police because she didn't want to cause trouble for them, but we left. I was just glad I'd had my mother there. A lot of children were evacuated alone.

When we went back to London, I was a teenager and used to go out to the dances and everything. The US forces made a big impact on us. They were so different from the British men. Not only wealthier, but more interested in women themselves. I went out with some men in the forces. I couldn't understand a young woman not wanting to. When I was sixteen I got a job. Factory work, just for the money. We all did it, but only enjoyed it if the company was good. My mother died when I was sixteen. She had been ill for a long time.

Women in my day were brought up to have ideals of marrying a dream man, but my husband certainly didn't live up to it. I probably didn't know him well enough when we were married – only six months when we got engaged and I usually only saw him one day a week because he worked in a pub. He was a very old-fashioned man, who wouldn't lift a cup or cook. The type you'd have to stir the sugar for. He expected me to do everything for him. I really enjoy cooking now, because it isn't a routine thing I have to do everyday, like it was when I was married. I think lack of a career or alternative means of support did trap women in unhappy situations. I thought of divorce earlier on, but I stayed on to keep my daughter. Once you've been in mental hospital, it's extremely difficult to get custody of a child if it is disputed – the hospital doctor told me this. My family also tried to persuade me to stay married at that time.

I think the literacy problems put a blight on my marriage right from the start. He wanted me to help with the business, but I was very nervous about my writing. I didn't tell him when we were courting and when he found out he tried to teach me, but we didn't make much progress. I even tried an adult literacy teacher, but didn't get very far with it. I first became depressed in my twenties. My GP was interested in helping and didn't like Friern, so he sent me to see a psychiatrist at the Free. He offered me a full psychoanalysis and explained it would mean seeing him for an hour, once a week for five years. He said I would have to lie down on the couch and would have to tell him if I thought his nose was a funny shape! He said if I committed myself to the full five years, he could cure me. At the time, it seemed like such a long time and I hadn't realised how serious the problems could become. I wish I'd gone through with it now, after everything. I wonder if I had done it, if things might have been different.

Ron was the manager of a pub and we lived over the premises for the first few years. He was a drinker, so I worked part-time to pay the bills. Then, after a stocktake showed a large discrepancy, he was sacked without notice. We had nowhere to go, so we went back to live with my father, even though it was a tiny basement flat. He worked on and off, sometimes living in on the premises and we still had to live in those difficult conditions. I worked to keep us. At first we had nothing because he wasn't entitled to National Assistance after being sacked, and then when he got a job his wages had to go to paying back the money which had gone. I was worried about my daughter, Karen, living in such a place and sent her for short-term fostering. She was so distressed by the separation that I soon took her back again and she went to a childminder while I worked. A few years later, Ron got another publican's job, through my father, and we had somewhere to live again, but he was sacked after a few years for the same reason. We were sent off on holiday while they investigated and we couldn't even get back in to claim our furniture. We were forced to move back to my father's.

After this I became very stressed and depressed. I was sent by the GP to a rich man's hospital. It was lovely there, more like a hotel, so much so that you could get to like it too much. They had a time limit of one year. You could take children under five with you, but Karen was over five so she had to go into a home and this upset me. Unlike hospital, everyone had to help in the running – three people would cook the evening meal every night and everyone had to take their share of work, because it was part of the treatment, even if you were paying. I reckon it helped me to some extent, but when I came out I went back to the flat and didn't go out and saw no-one for four years! I went back to Ron and tried to be the good little wife, but it didn't work out. I'm frightened of the idea of living alone now because of the experience of being lonely all that time.

I was suffering from depression, Ron had a bad heart and then my father had a stroke and lived for several years afterwards, with me caring for him. He could walk around a bit but he was incontinent. Ron used to go out drinking, but I couldn't get out, not even to work. The GP told me I must get a job if I was to get over the depression and I found one in a school canteen, but then dad got worse, falling over. The doctor said he couldn't put him in hospital, then a few days later a woman doctor came and agreed to admit him, so that I could keep my job. He died the next week. I felt guilty because he'd cursed me for having him put in hospital, even though I felt it was the only thing to do. I know he would have died anyway. He was 95 and very ill. I suppose my life was ended at that time in a way.

I can't believe how naïve some professionals could be! Like the GP telling me to have another child, that this would make Ron be a better husband and make me feel less depressed, when we were desperate for somewhere decent and large enough to live. Some time after this I learnt that a wealthy cousin had recently died and included me in his will. As I was desperate for somewhere decent to live I used it to buy a place and that was how we came to live in my flat. I lived there with Ron and Karen from that time until I went in to hospital to stay.

It was years later, when Karen was grown up, that I went in. The GP gave into circumstances and allowed me to go to Friern. I'd been on tranquillisers for fourteen years. Before going into Friern I'd been carrying on with my life and managing pretty much as normal, still going out, doing the housework, part-time work in factories. I was upset by Karen leaving home and worried about it, but there's nothing else I know of that sparked it off. It was just like this – one morning, I woke up shaking and unable to control it. There was only one drug that I think helped me. I'd sort of managed the drugs myself for years, cutting down when I didn't feel so much need, but I could never do without just one. I had been prescribed all these drugs but at the time I was admitted, it was the trend for taking people off them. The consultant told me I was over-drugged and took me off medication completely. I went barmy and was very ill as a result. I can't understand why, after all that time, they'd made such a dramatic change. I think it's down to lack of agreement about psychiatry. I was in such a terrible state, they searched the medicine cabinet for something to give me!

I got into art, quite by accident, while I was in hospital. I'd never been taught how to draw or paint. I could have spent all day painting if they'd let me. I went to writing classes too, though I still can't spell.

My husband and daughter stopped coming to see me. I don't know why but I wonder about it. He said that on the first visit I wouldn't see him, and on the second I wouldn't speak to him, then apparently he got upset by seeing me on a ward with people in such a terrible state and didn't like coming.

It doesn't have to be like it was for me – my father had been mentally ill, but he was never put in hospital. My mum had always stuck by him. He had support from my mother and managed to carry on a normal life. My solicitor said he couldn't understand why I'd been in hospital all this time. I can't understand myself why a lot of the patients were there for so long. My husband has been to see me once in the house already. I think my ownership of the flat is what brought him, now I've left, because he's living there. Otherwise, why hadn't he been to see me in all that time? He used to go drinking in a pub near the hospital and he could have arranged to meet me there, since there weren't restrictions on me going out. Some patients used to go home for weekends. I was allowed, but they never came and I never saw my grandchildren. I suppose Karen was worried about taking them into that place. Then Ron came to see me in hospital again a couple of years ago, saying he wanted me to sell the flat and buy a family home out of London. Karen was unhappy and wanted to move out with the kids and was hoping I could buy somewhere big enough for all of us. They started to ask if I could come home for the weekend, after years of not bothering.

I didn't see my brother for years either, though he did write. He rarely came to London. It's taken me a long time to build up the courage to phone him. When I did, he said I should have done it [a divorce] years ago! He didn't talk much, but he's always been like that. His mate was very friendly and he rings me for a chat now, every so often. After all those years in hospital, not seeing him for eight years, Ron expected me to go back to him and be the good wife! Even when I said I was divorcing him, he didn't really give up. He isn't Catholic, but he tried to tell me this was a reason for not divorcing him! Only when I said I was leaving hospital and going to live somewhere else, not going back to him, did he accept the fact. I've sworn my affidavit now. I was surprised how little it came to, after all those years. It seemed to take very little to sum it all up, just a few paragraphs once the solicitor had condensed it.

I think a lot about my daughter. I've suddenly noticed that she's going grey and seems almost middle-aged – that's the result of not seeing her for years. I felt outside of everything at first, not seeing the kids grow up. I feel like I want to treat them, do things for them, become part of my family again.

Paying the Penalty

A. N.

My youngest spent his first birthday at Beech House (part of the Pastures). That was when I'd really cracked up. The other children were in foster homes because I couldn't cope. And my divorce was going through. I was on electric shock for a long, long time, three times a week. I came home for weekend leave without the baby but my husband was alcoholic and he didn't want us, and we'd got an eviction over us head. Without the doctor's support I don't think I'd have ever got the children back at all.

My family didn't back me up – I've never been wanted by my mum and stepfather and I had to do everything on me own, only the social workers it was that kept an eye on me. When I went in The Pastures the children went in foster homes. When I came out they came back gradually. My daughter wouldn't accept me. She was in care up to the age of seventeen she wouldn't behave herself (absconding, drugs). My youngest son's turned on me now, saying I didn't want them, blaming me for them being in care, I'm to blame for him being in prison.

They say, 'As regards being a mum, you're dead. We've not got a mum.' That's what I've got now.

My youngest son's got a baby. I can't go to the house. I can't see the baby. I knit him a baby outfit and sent it and they sent it back. I can't see the daughter's two either. I've got a lad twenty-six but I don't think he's friends with me now, because he's not wrote back, he stood by me but I think now he's turning. They're ganging up against me. I'm serving the penalty, if you understand; if I'd done a murder I couldn't be no worse off. They're making it as if I've been a bad mum and I'm still paying the penalty.

I feel angry. Because when I was seventeen me stepfather got hold of me, he didn't touch me internally but he got hold of me. Me mum

116

wouldn't believe. They said to me, 'Oh, you're backward, you're mental deficient.'

I can't forgive them. My brothers are all intelligent, managing directors. I don't fit in.

The doctor says to me, 'What are your family trying to do to you, because I can't think of a word to describe them?' He says 'How do you feel?'

I says, 'I just feel like jumping in the lake 'cause I can't swim, so I know that I'd drown.'

He says, 'You don't want to be so stupid – don't do it.' But he knows.

He says, 'Forget the past.'

But how can you forget forty-three years?

Treading on Eggshells

WENDY LINDSAY

After I ran away from hospital, my husband discharged me. I felt much less of a risk being at home than in the control of hospital staff. But I still felt unable to understand all the fears inside myself or how to begin to cope with all the problems at home which I had not been able to deal with before. I knew that to stay in bed, as before, was no longer an option. I started to keep busy. There was plenty to do and doing it led my family to believe I was fine, in many ways I was, but I still felt vulnerable – emotionally – and even more vulnerable about saying so. I was expected to take over my family without help, as if I had just been away for a holiday. Those early weeks back at home were some of the hardest times I had known, terrified of going back into hospital and at the same time half wanting to go back so I could give up on the struggle to cope. Not knowing what to say or what to do, afraid of hurting people, upsetting them, especially my children who were also very unsure and very wary. We were all treading on eggshells.

One moment everyone was trying to be so helpful, making drinks, being so loving and then the next moment something small would happen, maybe a disagreement with the children or even a small accident, a spilt drink, and it would explode out of all proportion. It took months to really settle down to be together again.

The small children would come home from school and if I wasn't in sight they would run from room to room calling in frightened little voices, 'Mummy, mummy, where are you, we're home!' Their anxious faces would light up when I appeared and I realised just how my going into hospital had affected my adorable, loving children.

I remembered their little, anxious faces at the hospital, bewildered at what was happening. No one explaining anything to them; the reasons why their mother was going in and out of this strange and disturbing place, remained a mystery left to their own imaginations. I tried to explain

118

it was because I was unhappy and sad, not because I didn't love them, but this took years for them to believe or understand. I could see them straining in their efforts to be well behaved when I was home as if somehow it was all their fault.

'Don't go back,' the youngest would say, 'I'll be a good boy.' And he would try so hard to stay good, but of course young children can't sustain under the pressure of 'good behaviour'. I listened to them tell me how afraid they were when I went into hospital, and how they hated visiting me but did so because they loved me. They were so confused by the people in hospital with me and were afraid I was crazy and would do some of the 'mad' things other patients were doing. They told me they felt ashamed I was in a mental hospital and didn't want their friends to know. It felt to them that this was too awful to talk about, so they kept all these feelings bottled up inside themselves and they didn't even talk about it to each other. They pretended everything was all right.

Other children had teased them, saying 'Your mum's mad,' 'Your mum's a loony', so when they should have been crying with the hurt of that they were steeling themselves inside and shouting back 'No she's not!', or inventing other reasons why I was in hospital. My daughter found it particularly distressing to hear teachers, shopkeepers, neighbours, talking about me in front of her, or within earshot, as though she was invisible. Worse still was the cruelty of children at school teasing them with, 'You're crazy – just like your mummy!' The idea that 'it runs in the family' terrified them; they felt tarnished by my and other relatives' mental history.

On one occasion when I arrived home the house seemed empty and quiet, then as I sat drinking a cup of coffee I heard a noise upstairs. I jumped out of my chair and as I got closer to the noise could hear it was vomiting. I rushed into the room, it was dark with the curtains drawn, hanging over the side of the bed was my teenage son with his head almost in a bucket, retching.

I went over to him. He looked up and said, 'I'm all right mum. Are you staying? Are you home for good? I'm all right, just another bad headache.' He was trying to make me feel better; he was worried about me! My heart almost broke and I was steeling myself not to break down. I had been so preoccupied with my own pain and the small children that I had lost sight of my eldest child. He had been so good, and because he had made no demands I had missed his hurt. I had no idea he was struggling so hard.

'How long have you been like this?' 'A week . . . ' he replied, vomiting, unable to say more. 'Darling, why didn't you ask for help'?' 'Everyone was so busy.' He fell back on his pillow.

I ran for a cool wet cloth to wipe his hot forehead and then called a doctor. He had a severe migraine.

When we were able to talk more my son told me how hard it was for him at school. He didn't want 'anyone' to know his mother was in and out of a mental hospital.

Mark rarely came to see me in hospital – it upset him too much – nor did he ever want to talk about it. He coped by saying nothing. He buried his fears and hurt, it was the only way he could cope, but it left me feeling totally helpless and hopeless despairing of ever being able to reach him, he seemed so far away.

Dr Allen was my main strength. He helped by arranging for Mark to change school – where no one knew me or the family. Over the next few months the headaches got less and less. Even today, fifteen years on, Mark is not able to share his feelings. He just doesn't want me to know.

It is painful knowing my mental illness has cost me a close relationship with my first-born child, who I love with all my heart.

I was filled with guilt at what I had done to my children by not being able to cope with my own pain. The bitter legacy which I was passing to them. One day they may have forms to fill out which ask, 'Is there mental illness in the family?' Will they be penalised for telling the truth? For some jobs, certainly. It seems totally unjust for my children to be labelled by something that is to do with my past. What do I do? Stay silent and not speak of my experience for fear of the prejudice and stigma which follow?

I tried to overcompensate and I would do anything to try and make up for what had happened, but of course we never can, and in trying I just became exhausted and at risk of ending up back in hospital. At the same time I could see them straining in their efforts to make everything all right and still know that I would end up back in hospital; it felt that I was betraying them.

In the morning when the small children awoke they would jump out of bed and I could hear them running to my room to check if I was still there or if I was all right. When they saw me they would jump on the bed with excitement and then we would all get up and make breakfast.

It was obvious they didn't want me out of their sight ever again. The two days which the youngest had experienced in care had been emotionally devastating. My small son had enormous problems not wanting to go to school. He would cry and protest and even run away from school once I had got him there. Eventually he was allowed to stay at home with a tutor and he was happy to learn that way as long as I stayed in the house, where he could hear me pottering about. I was shattered to learn that my emotional illness had caused my children so much pain and I was at a loss as how to help them with it. The only option I had was to give the children as much opportunity to talk and cry about it as possible, but often anger was the way they expressed everything. I would feel helpless but learned that to allow the children to express what they felt with me, helped them. I also learned there are things they couldn't say to me, the feeling among them that 'We mustn't worry mummy' not confiding in me because, 'I didn't want to upset you' – all in case they put me back in hospital. So if they became upset I would ask them if they wanted to talk to someone else. I never, ever asked the children to tell me what they had said to other people. I felt that this was their privacy.

I'm sure my children have endured much that I don't know about, but I am happy and secure in the knowledge that if they ever do want to tell me, they will, *when they are ready*. There is so much I have not told them and will only ever do so if they *ask*.

So much of the time they felt lost and alone with no mummy and too much to cope with in a hostile world. How I wish I could have gathered them in my arms and loved them. Why couldn't anyone do that for me while I was not able to help in any way myself?

In spite of our experience we are doing so well as a family and hold our hope for the future. All of this has taken years and on the way many tears, a lot of anger and patience. It has been a long, long road, with many twists and turns, never knowing what was around the corner, and it is not over yet. There are things from my past which still upset me but I can cope now in a way I couldn't before, and I have a wonderful, supportive family, loving each other no matter what, always .

I Don't Feel it's Right

MIRANDA

When I left hospital I went to my parents for a while. We did have a few arguments and that but I think I needed to be with my parents because I did rely on them very much. They did everything for me; I mean I didn't do anything, they looked after me. But as they were going to Australia I had to move away, and they live right in the middle of nowhere. The hospital accommodation found me '65' and I moved in.

I didn't like it at all. There was between six to nine residents. That place was a bit like a hospital, they were all hospital people. I didn't like having my tea at four o'clock and all the meals provided and the way they treated you like children. I tried to get on with them, I felt I did, I mean R. didn't start on me 'til my parents went – well he did a bit, swearing at me. Then it all just started going wrong. They'd just get at me for anything. I used to go to the pub and that and come back a couple of times a bit drunk and I did play music but only a couple of times. and that old bloke, R., was always swearing at me, muttering about me to himself, ever since I refused to go to bed with him, he's had it in for me. He tells me to f . . . off all the time, and kicks me and shouts in his room about me, calling me, 'A black-haired cow, black-haired bitch!' He's been there for years, so they're all cliquey. I told the cook about it and she had a word with him and the landlord did, but he just carried on. They just used to start on me for no reason. The girl who did the cooking tried to help a bit, but they all ganged up on me. I don't even know what happened.

Then the landlord came in and he said, 'You've got a week's notice.' Just like that.

I said, 'Why?'

'Not getting on with the people in the house and playing music.'

I said, 'Look, okay, I'll calm down.'

He said, 'Okay, you can stay.'

The next night I went out to the pub; I got a bit drunk, but I just came in and went to bed. Then the next night that bloke, R., started swearing at me and I just swore back at him. On the Friday the landlord came in and said again, 'You've got a week's notice,' and didn't even say why or anything.

When he'd left I went mad, I said to this R. 'You've got me into trouble, you've got me thrown out for nothing!'

And they just said, 'You've brought it all on yourself.' 'Don't be so stupid.' I said.

The landlord came back, saying, 'You've got to go now, you've got to go now! You're causing trouble. If you don't go I'm going to ring the police, get you sectioned, put you back into hospital, there's nothing you can do!'

I tried to get hold of my community nurse but as it was a bank holiday weekend she wasn't working and the accommodation officer at The Pastures didn't want to know – I was discharged from hospital.

Luckily the same morning I'd got the paper and I'd rung up and arranged to see this place at six o'clock, they said I could move in there and then.

I feel really pissed off, really low and really depressed. I don't feel it's right, I don't think I'd done anything that bad to justify them kicking me out, apart from getting drunk a couple of times. The landlord was absolutely despicable – I mean he said to me, 'If you don't go to this place, it's too bad, you'll have to go to those hostels or something, or get out on the streets, you're not coming back tonight.'

I didn't even have my parents, I had nobody. I supposed I'd have to ring up my cousins but that was the last thing I wanted to do. I don't think that landlord should be allowed to get away with what he did, but what can I do?

My community nurse came today, she thinks in the long run I'm probably better off out of there. I'd like my own flat, I'd probably like to share with someone, because I like company.

I Can Get About

TERRY

When I first heard I was going to live outside I was really excited but a little bit nervous. I went into hospital when I was thirteen years old, because I suffer from epilepsy, and I was there forty-one years. How would I be able to cope? Would I be lonely? These were the thoughts which came to mind. In spite of these concerns I couldn't wait to leave as I'd got more and more bored and frustrated over the years.

I'm in a house now with two others, Freddy and Neville. We have a landlord and landlady to help look after things, and they drop down every day.

The landlord offered to do the cooking. 'Alright,' I said, 'do it.' They do the washing as well, but they don't live here. It's our home. We share the jobs like hoovering and washing dishes. Neville does the gardening at the landlord's and I go up weeding and I do his windows sometimes. I learned to do windows at the hospital; I can do a better job than the window cleaners. I use a clean rag and clean water – I could make a lot of money.

I've had a hip replacement since I left the hospital, so I can get about a lot more. In the day I go up to the Rosehill Club, which is just at the top of the road. We go bowling or to the cinema or on day trips, and I've made a lot of new friends. We've been to Butlin's once and we're going again in October. We save up over the year. At Butlin's, Jane said we shouldn't drink in the day – but we all go out in the night, which is better really. We have a good time there.

I love going for walks at the weekend and I go visit family, my sister, and friends. I've still got somebody, but Freddy's got nobody.

The Sanctuary in North London

MARTIN HENDERSON

Walter Cranmer, always available
Opens the door,
He owns this place
And has made it a refuge,
Those who come here are here,
Ostensibly
For cups of tea.
There are many refugees
From psychiatry, recent policies,
And conversation ranges widely –
Shabbiness reigns
Yet there are few enough
Places like this
In this time of 'community care'.

I meet here a woman
(Currently in hospital)
Fragile, illogical, sweet
A tender annual running to seed.
The muscular self-reliant
Stay for weeks.
The radio is always on,
Playing classical music.

There is a sense of caring
Rare except in hospital,
Perhaps at war.

People can relax, talk here
In this queer setting I unwind
Myself and leave
Happier than I came.

A Second Chance for Life

JOAN TUGWELL

After spending thirty-three years in psychiatric hospitals I was asked if I would like to live outside in the community, and I said 'yes'. I was very excited. I thought, oh, to live in a house on my own, to have peace and quiet, to be able to cook my own meals, do what I liked and go where I wanted.

But alas, on my first day in a one-room flat I found I had no electricity. I phoned the electricity board, Seeboard, and was told they would turn it on on the Wednesday. I said I wanted it on that day, Monday, so they came and turned it on.

I had nothing to cook on and if I had not brought my kettle, I would not have been able to make a cup or tea. I had hardly any furniture and no carpets. I felt lonely and depressed. I just sat down and had a good cry.

When some resettlement money came through, I bought an electric stove and a carpet, and gradually I managed to buy the other things I needed.

I had my budgies Billy and Sammy with me. Being an animal lover I find them a great comfort. I do not keep the budgies in their cage, and they have a great time up on the window ledge watching the wild birds outside.

After I'd been in my flat for three months the electricity bills started to come through – over £100 each time. On Christmas Eve of my first Christmas out of hospital I received a letter to say they were going to cut off the electricity. I was left numb and was so upset I felt like ending my life there and then. Over a period of 14 months my bills came to a total of £564. I was unable to buy much food and there were times I had nothing to eat.

I had a social worker who tried to help me by complaining to Seeboard,

126

but she did not get far, so l decided to do something myself. I wrote to the secretary of Seeboard at Tunbridge Wells and I told them if they did not do anything about the high bills, I would take the matter still higher. I am having checks done on the meter, so l hope to have some of the money repaid to me.

I am hoping to be able to do a part-time job at home. I will be able to earn up to £24 a week. I am slightly disabled in my hands and arms due to previously self inflicted wounds, so l am only able to do easy work.

There are some people living next door to me who are handicapped, and I try to help them when I can. I also give them advice on how to look after their budgie. One of the women cooks food for them all, but I think they should have a little help as sometimes they do not cook the chicken properly and this could lead to food poisoning.

The neighbours are a mixed bunch. Some are friendly. Jean, who lives next door, is a very good friend. I don't know what I would have done without her. We go into each other's flats to have cups of tea and we often take turns to cook a Sunday dinner for both of us. Another neighbour, Win, gives Jean and me a lift into town in her car on a Friday and we all do our shopping then go back to Win's house and have a cup of tea, a cake and a good chat.

I felt very honoured when another neighbour, Mrs Cox, asked me if I would look after her cat for a week and she gave me a key to her house. I thought that it was very nice of her to trust me, considering I had been a patient for over thirty-three years.

Nearly every day I take another lady's dog, Foxy for a walk. At other times I also go with Jean and her dog, Sunnie. Foxy and Sunnie get on very well together and sometimes we let them both off their leads when we go into a big field.

I have three cats that come into my flat. I have to close the living room doors so they cannot get to the budgies, as they are free to fly around. sometime the cats will have a sleep on the chair in the kitchen.

It is nice to be able to go to the shops and buy food, and to do my own cooking. No more locked doors, or being locked in a tiny room. I do babysitting on three afternoons and a Saturday evening. Although the children are a bit noisy, I love them. The two eldest stay up with me until their parents come home. The two younger children used to fight and argue when I first went, but I put my foot down by telling them if they did not stop they would have to go to bed.

We have a little shop near us called the Arlington Stores. Rita and Tony, the people who run it, are nice. If I am broke they let me get some things on tick and pay them back when I get my money.

I hope if I am successful with the electricity board my bills will be a lot less and I can enjoy life the same way as other people do and have regular meals.

My one great regret is that my mother, who was excited about me getting out, died of cancer six months before I was released. I miss her so very much.

I've Got Memories Here

CLIVE

It's a lovely old building, beautiful. Ahhh – I wouldn't like it if they knocked it down: I've got memories here. It's like a part of me, this place. I wouldn't like to see it destroyed. I think a lot of people have the same feelings about this place as me. Where I'm living now there are several people who are there who've been up here for a long time. They seem happy enough – they don't talk about it, but they were here.

My bed was in the corner here. That partition wasn't there, nor this cupboard; a wardrobe was in the corner and my bed was there.

I used to be in one of these cubicles when I was first admitted. There was a dartboard, I remember that, blinking dartboard on the wall . . . that brings back memories. I was just looking at the dartboard and this voice said to me, it said: 'Look around you.' And I looked around.

'You'll never get out of here.'

'Don't want to bloody go!' I said. Crazy. I went back into my cubicle there and lay on my bed. Just lying on the bed I was – night time. I shut my eyes tight. I could see the car coming up. Two of them, the mafia, coming up to see me. There they were – they were obviously going to torture me and murder me eventually. I just lay on my bed and I tried to force that car off the road in my mind. In my mind I forced that steering wheel off the road. I destroyed the car, like. That gave me a bit of peace. I drove the car off and I went to sleep.

This was the nurses' office through there and this used to be a blind up here. Looking through this glass at night in that bed across there I could see the desk. The light was on. It was a dim light and there was something on the desk and it looked like something weird. I remember now what it was, but it looked strange to me.

If you had a nightmare you'd get up and go into the nurses' office and they would reassure you and you'd go back to bed, or you'd have a cup

129

of tea and cigarette. You couldn't smoke in here – but go into the nurses' office where the night staff was on.

I thought I could stay here for the rest of my life; some did. Some were here for years and years and years. Better than the flat. In the flat I was hearing voices and everything else and having feelings in my mind and nobody to talk to. The worst thing was the loneliness. You're by yourself, struggling there – cooking your meals, washing your clothes. And then you come here and everything is done for you. There were no worries, no bills to find – just great. The nurses were so nice and the doctors, and they were all smartly dressed and they treated you well. I was treated well, anyway, by all of them. You can get well in an environment like that. It was the company you see, the companionship.

Nutter to Normal

JIM READ

Loony, depressive, failure, one of the mentally ill. One day I was and the next day I wasn't. One day, to reach my front door I passed a sign saying The Cassel Hospital for Functional Nervous Disorders and the next day I just pushed open the gate to an ordinary house in a suburban street. Nutter to normal, just like that. My three-year stint as a mental patient was over.

After dropping out of university I was an out-patient on medication and drifted into becoming a day patient at my local bin. Everything about the way I was treated there encouraged dependency and, after a few weeks, I had almost completely accepted the role as a long-term hopeless case. It took the threat of ECT to stir me into action. I discharged myself, came off my medication and went to live at the Cassel which, despite its intimidating name, was (and still is) a therapeutic community. After eight months, I was only a little wiser about myself but had at least regained some of the confidence that had been shattered by traditional psychiatric treatment. It was 1973; 1 was twenty-two years old and ready to have another go at ordinary life.

The process of transition began when I started looking for my new home. I soon found a room to rent in a flat that I would share with two friendly young men. All was going smoothly until one of them kindly offered to pick up my belongings in his car. He would only have to see the sign outside the Cassel to fuel any prejudice or fear he may have had about sharing his home with a newly discharged mental patient. I mumbled something about letting him know and fled back to the Cassel wondering what on earth to do.

A nurse helped me to decide that attempting to keep my past a secret from people I was going to share a home with was an even more intolerable option than telling them. And so a couple of days later, trying to steady my nerves by chewing gum and puffing at a cigarette at the same time, I told them. And they were fine; completely relaxed about it. No problem. Phew!

I vividly recall the day I moved in, helped by Joanna, a fellow patient. I was terrified of her leaving me – not because I was having an emotional crisis about being left alone in the big, wide world – but because I had reached the age of twenty-two without being able to cook anything other than a boiled egg. Only when Joanna pointed out that packets of frozen food had cooking instructions printed on them did I feel able to let her leave.

Having achieved social acceptance and learned how to cook fish fingers, my next challenge was employment. This was a scary one for me. After less than a year as an out-patient, I had been turned down for a job on medical grounds. A couple of years later, with a more impressive psychiatric history, what chance did I have? But this time I was lucky. In London, where I was living, there was plenty of temporary clerical work available through job agencies, and they weren't too bothered about checking up on me. And so I was immediately dispatched to my first job. It was in a psychiatric hospital. I was the first person they had sent there who stayed more than a day. They never did find out why I was so relaxed about it! There was no office space for me and I worked wherever I could find a quiet corner. Once I sat in a temporarily vacant psychiatrist's office, and a patient tapped on the door and asked 'Can I have a word with you doctor?' I glimpsed an opportunity to transcend my personal history in one fell swoop, but the moment passed.

So I had made a good start, but there was an almighty snag. I was still lumbered with all the emotional baggage that had taken me in to the psychiatric system. It was all too apparent that life was going to carry on being a big struggle for me unless 1 could get some help.

The answer – I hoped – was to be weekly group therapy at the Maudsley Hospital in South London. It was a bitter disappointment – not so much a disaster, more a non-event. Nothing useful happened at all. I kept going because, as far as I could see, if I gave up I would never sort out my problems.

Meanwhile, I continued to reach various staging posts in my progress towards becoming a competent human being. I cooked Joanna spaghetti bolognaise. I bought some clothes that fitted me properly. I even had my unkempt and unflattering long hair shorn off, and emerged from Scissors in Kensington with a sharp-looking David Bowie cut (without the orange dye). I got involved in local politics and joined a yoga class – a valuable and regular calming influence on my jagged nerves.

I had friends. Some people who knew me before my mental patient days were still around and pleased to have me back in circulation; there were my former Cassel colleagues and, in a big city, plenty of new people to meet who also acted weird from time to time and wondered what life was all about.

I was so pleased to be joining in with normal life that I could be blissfully happy doing the most ordinary things, such as sitting on a bus, smoking a fag on the way to my mundane and low-paid job. (By then I was working as a local government clerk, having first proved myself as a temp.)

Once, after going to a concert with a friend, I was exhilarated, not only by Stravinsky's *The Rite of Spring*, but by my success in queuing and ordering drinks at the bar without becoming a quivering wreck. Travelling home, I sat in a train that didn't move for ages, and then there was an announcement telling us to get on another one. The faces of the other passengers set in the look of resigned despair familiar to users of public transport. I grinned at them and said 'It doesn't really matter though, does it?' They probably thought I was mad.

On other occasions I would be as low as I had ever been. I would experience a minor setback – a rejection at a party, perhaps, making a mistake at work or feeling unwell. My carefully rebuilt confidence would be shattered and in no time at all I would be overwhelmed by fear and despair. Then I would lie in bed ringing casualty departments saying I was an ex-mental patient and needed Valium, only to be defeated by their insistence that I should turn up and talk to somebody.

Friendships were okay but more intimate relationships were not so easy. They never had been for me. And that was before the inevitable invitation to 'tell me all about yourself' was so panic-inducing. I never did figure out whether to share my mental health history with a new love before or after our first night together.

Once the novelty had worn off, work became a struggle. I've always been easily bored. Clerical work was deadly. But, trapped by a dodgy CV and my own fragile confidence, I could see no way out.

I still needed help, but from where?

The turning point came when I found a co-counselling class. Here was everything I had hoped to find in group therapy. For the first time ever, I was given a model for what people are like, how we get hurt, how that makes us feel and behave, and what we can do to recover. It made sense to me. And there were practical methods we could learn and practise with each other. I liked being in a group that wasn't for 'the mentally ill' or 'neurotic' but simply for people who wanted to make their lives better.

Co-counselling didn't provide easy solutions, but it did offer the tools to assist me to struggle in a profitable direction. Before, I had been like someone who was trying to cross a mountain range without a map or a compass. I didn't know where I was and couldn't find any clues to help me. Now I had the equipment. If I could work out how to use it, and be systematic and disciplined in acting on the information it gave me, I would get to the other side. I was determined to do so.

I began to see that I had choices in life. I had been coping, hanging on, getting by. But I could think about the future, make plans and begin to put them into practice.

I wanted work that would give me the opportunity to use and develop my talents, and put my strongly-held political beliefs into practice. I wanted to put a stop to the disabling bouts of depression and anxiety that I was still slipping into. I wanted a lover. I wanted to change attitudes towards mental distress, in and out of the psychiatric system.

That was twenty years ago. I haven't done badly.

My big breakthrough with work came when I got a job with Friends of the Earth. I had spent two years working part-time and on the dole, while setting up and running a local group, and they were more interested in my proven commitment and ability than formal qualifications. It was brilliant to join a team of such committed and skilled campaigners, and a tremendous opportunity to learn about political organising and lobbying, and develop skills as a writer, editor and public speaker. Later, it turned sour and I was ousted for organising the staff into a trade union. But even that was an enriching, maturing and sometimes hilarious experience.

The depression lessened as my life got better. I discarded enormous amounts of fear in my co-counselling sessions. I got better at pushing aside the negative thoughts that still pulled at my attention.

Relationships have been difficult. But they are for most people I know of my generation. It's great that men and women are trying to find new ways of being together, but it isn't easy. I used to observe other people's struggles. Now I'm at least involved in my own. That's progress.

I did get to do something about the mental health system. It wasn't until ten years after I had left the Cassel that I felt I had the ability and the opportunity. I started by proposing to the Workers' Education Association that I teach classes on the politics of mental health. These became great learning experiences for me as I spent days reading up about the history of psychiatry, medication or the Mental Health Act before teaching a class.

Now I earn a living as a mental health consultant – creating opportunities for people with more recent experience of psychiatric treatment than myself to put their views to service providers. In the last year I have had the opportunity to meet with psychiatric survivors from all over the world. We are becoming an international community of which I'm proud to be a member.

Three years as a mental patient had a profound effect on the course of my life. It is not an experience that I would recommend; neither is it one I regret.

Alienation

JENNI MEREDITH

WhAt will she think

If I mention the eLectric shock treatment?

Casually plug It

Into the conv$E$rsation?

How will she adjust her perceptio$N$s

The epilepsy wAs a challenge

(Had To be confessed; I'm a non-driver).

So how wIll she

Handle the fact that she's wOrking

Alo$N$gside a survivor?

A Comparative Study of Application Forms for Housing Benefit and an American Express Card

PETER GOOD

A characteristic of our times is the marked separation of apparent ends of opposites – human/animal, male/female, sane/insane, high/low. Power is vested in the dominant half of a given opposition and progress is comfortably assumed to be the pursuit of the 'positive' arm of a duality. Too easily, the more the 'rational' aspect becomes shored up the more its 'irrational' partner becomes diminished and distant. However, the positive may only be defined by reference to its negative, and, in its interests to secure this imbalance, the positive must be constantly vigilant to protect itself from its 'low' and 'vulgar' opposite.

Thus 'high' (church, education, arts) must constantly define 'low' (entertainment, income, fashion) in order to confirm itself as 'high'. The ordering of Western culture through the control of this high/low duality can be illustrated in a variety of everyday interactions.

If you add up all the words contained in the instructions and questions on an application form for an American Express Card you reach a total of 128. There are a maximum number of 44 possible answer boxes that you are required to respond to.

On a Kirklees Metropolitan Council Directorate of Health and Housing application form for housing benefit there are a total of 1134 words that make up direct instruction and question. Contained within this document are 396 possible answer boxes that you may be required to answer.

While I consider myself to be no smarter than the average bear (I'm certainly no dumber) I had enormous difficulty in attempting completion of the housing benefit form. It required of me some two hours work at the kitchen table with a small mountain of official papers dug up from various cubby-holes. I am also required to provide proof of income for up to 34 possible other sources of monetary gain. The task was wearying and unpleasant.

Both these organisations are established institutions, both are offering some form of credit and both wish to make comprehensive investigation into each applicant's financial standing. From this point similarities between the two start to fade. American Express is granting credit amounting to thousands of pounds to an applicant. Kirklees Housing is talking in terms of single figures, at best tens of pounds.

Conveniently, American Express's application form turns itself into a pre-franked, ready-addressed envelope that just needs popping into a postbox. The very size of the housing form would prove costly in postage. The only instruction available requests that the completed document be 'returned' to the District Housing Manager. I think most folk are expected to return the form by hand. There was a tray full of unstamped, completed ones by the side of the housing receptionist anyway.

The image each organisation has of its potential clients is clearly reflected in the language used on their respective forms. Note (a) on the Housing Benefit form reads:

'If you are living with relatives or friends as part of their family IT IS NOT NECESSARY FOR YOU TO COMPLETE THIS FORM as you are NOT ENTITLED TO HOUSING BENEFIT.'

Responding to the melody of this language we may pick up instantly on the weariness of long-suffering benefit clerks who can spot instant administrative anomalies from the briefest of inspection. The words upped in capitals are being SHOUTED, much in the manner of an exasperated tourist who shouts louder the more they are not being understood. This first note is to set the weighting of a high/low duality throughout the document.

In contrast it becomes much more comfortable to feel the language of the American Express form. Here the instructions on how to fill in the form amounts to 12 user-friendly words:

'Please use block capitals in ball point or felt tip.'

Immediately I am made to feel that my name is important:

'Please spell out your name as you wish it to appear on your card using no more than 20 letters or spaces.'

It is not only in words that American Express gets its message across. There is much use of colour and differing type faces. The form itself feels physically correct and businesslike. It even seems to fold itself. Should I have any doubts as to what I imagine American Express imagines I look like there is a flattering photograph displaying two attractive people. One casually holding a card and the other a briefcase. Handsome, sensitive and very cool. It is as if we are two people, both finding ourselves placed on the higher rungs of life, and we are simply speaking to each other.

Approaches from the low to the high for assistance follow similar patterns across a wide range of agencies. The considerable time spent in waiting and processing. The very extent of the questioning and requirements of an almost confessional honesty all seem to congeal into an inevitably dehumanising malaise. Vigilance is required in observing the subtleties that take place in the process of how the powerful take care of the powerless. The clues are always to be found in the language used. My application form required a great deal of time for its completion. A visit to the Housing Office and securing a place in a queue ate up much time. Even that time was about to be restricted. Several large, badly stencilled notices were Sellotaped to the walls and doors:

PLEASE NOTE. FROM THE 21.1.88 THE HOUSING BENEFIT/ REBATE COUNTER WILL ONLY BE OPEN BETWEEN THE FOLLOWING HOURS. MONDAY – FRIDAY 9.00 AM – 2.30 PM.

The endless questions contained in the form required me to bare my material life structure before an anonymous administrative complex. Its very detail seemed to weary me, slowly pull me down, and always the sense, expressed frequently in capital letters, that I am being SPOKEN DOWN to. Thus I surrendered my trust into the hands of the Council and began a period of waiting for notification.

Hilda lives alone in a set of flats purpose built for the elderly on the outskirts of Huddersfield. With help from a neighbour she had completed an application for Housing Benefit. Once submitted she had become utterly devastated by this entry:

'I understand that a person who dishonestly obtains housing benefit by any deception will, on conviction, be liable to imprisonment for a term not exceeding five years under the Theft Act 1978. WARNING – GIVING FALSE INFORMATION COULD LEAD TO PROSECUTION.'

The thinking processes of the elderly living alone may well be different from an administrator working from an office. Hilda's life gradually became taken over by a belief that her application contained a misrepresentation concerning a couple of building society accounts she held. Each hour she expected the police to arrive and arrest her. Her pain was compounded by the horrifying realisation that her trial and subsequent imprisonment would ruin the reputation of her son living in Southampton. As she sat for most of the day in a chair by the window awaiting the arrival of the police, her images grew and twisted themselves into all sorts of monsters. The fear and the panic spiralled. In desperation she decided to confess all to the building society manager, and it was he who subsequently contacted the hospital to say that an elderly lady in his office could not be stopped from weeping.

We see things differently from different positions on a high/low perspective. Another's language can be received in such a way that its original meaning can get itself lost and occasionally tragically warped. To begin again and attempt a reconstruction of the housing benefit form would require a major refocusing of how we as strangers care for other strangers.

Attempting to talk to each other in a language that identifies us both as fellow citizens may well be a start. For many it will be a rare therapeutic experience. Identification of the age-old positioning of the high against the low is a process so ingrained within ourselves that we come to take it for granted and fail even to notice it. American Express cards and housing rebates seem utterly incompatible. They are. I got neither.

Part five

THERAPY AND SELF-HELP

Introduction

The resources referred to in this section tend not to be easily available to users of psychiatric services. Often service users do not get the choice or even know of the existence of different forms of help. We have grouped these approaches (often dubbed 'alternative') together in the hope that they will inspire people with a wider range of possibilities to be explored.

Alternatives are not necessarily more effective than more mainstream approaches. Rosalind Caplin acknowledges in her account of her eating distress, 'Time, Faith and Encouragement', that 'alternative treatments are not the panacea for all ills'. Her efforts to control her eating and the brutal psychiatric treatment she receives spiral her into starvation. The qualities referred to in the title of Rosalind Caplin's article were important for her, and the sense of acceptance she encountered from a counsellor and alternative therapist was a breakthrough in her slow recovery.

Rosalind Caplin found that 'feeding' of her creativity countered her eating distress. Creativity comes into other accounts too. For Colin Hambrook, 'Healing Through Creativity' was to be found in writing and performing poetry, with support and encouragement from the organisation Survivors' Poetry. This unlocked possibilities of self-discovery and self-expression. His poem 'Dreaming the Absurd' demonstrates how poetry can convey the inexplicable. Maureen Sangster in 'I Have Found Ways Out of Fear' has learnt to use any activity 'where the surprising occurs' to break her patterns of obsessional behaviour. She draws motifs, such as a mandala, or a tree, to offset the world of her mental distress. David Wigoder gives a painfully funny description of his experience of group psychotherapy as an in-patient at a psychiatric hospital in 'Neurotics at War: Art Therapy'. A harmonious group venture turns to a sticky mess in his bid for domination of the group mural. David Wigoder's account shows how such group processes can reflect the individual's inner life as well as his or her patterns of social interaction.

Brian Taylor in 'Reflections on Therapy' weighs up the case for and against psychotherapy, referring to Jeffrey Masson's critique. He emphasises the importance of friendship networks in helping people through times of despair. In reviewing his own experience of timely help from a therapist when he was bereaved, Brian Taylor concludes that therapy can be of value, provided it is rooted within appropriate values.

Friends are not always available, or able give the help that is needed, and this is an important reason for turning to professionals. 'Building Relationships', Jill Reynolds's account of humanistic therapy, demonstrates the difficulty of assessing forms of help that are broad in their intent and offered over a long period of time. Her conclusion is ambivalent. While she was helped at a difficult time, she did not feel liked or understood, and wonders where the responsibility lay for her sense that the therapist found fault with her.

Louise Pembroke writes in 'It Helped that Someone Believed Me' of the help that she found from other survivors. She has her own feelings and experiences validated in this way, particularly by a supportive partner. Louise Pembroke has been able to take ownership of her experiences of voices and entities, and find her own meaning. Perhaps this is the most valuable possibility that any therapy or treatment has to offer. It can nevertheless prove elusive in many well-intentioned approaches.

Time, Faith and Encouragement

ROSALIND CAPLIN

My struggle for survival began at fourteen. As a child I felt I lived in a world of strangers, and however hard I tried, I never seemed to fit in with what others expected of me. I felt guilty and blamed, repressed both emotionally and creatively. My traditional religious upbringing did nothing to touch the deeper spiritual yearning I always had. I felt an outsider, embarrassingly inadequate within my peer group and family, with nothing to offer.

I tried desperately to do what I imagined others wanted, just to be accepted, but I failed miserably. I felt that I had to take control over my life. Inwardly I was starving for love and acceptance; outwardly I could no longer swallow what I was being 'fed' with – my body silently screamed no, and I thus projected all my distress onto one area of my life I still could control – food.

Denying myself enough food was paradoxically both an attempt to fit into a stereotype ideal, and a search to define my individuality and true purpose in life. At the same time I was denying myself the right to exist at all. Very soon this quest became my entire purpose for living. If anyone attempted to take that control away from me I fought tooth and nail. I had invested everything in my relationship with food – it was all I had. For once I felt I was achieving something for myself, and as I lost weight so this determination to succeed increased.

However, silently I was crying 'As you cannot see my deep distress, I am forced to "bare my very bones" so that at last you may notice and help.' But no one saw beyond my shrinking physical form, and my deeper emotional and spiritual starvation continued to be denied. I was medicalised and carted off to a psychiatrist, whose only answer was immediate hospital admission, heralding a seven-year cycle of increasingly frightening episodes. I was given a psychiatric label, one that regards 'anorexic' women as spoilt little girls who refuse to grow up,

142

dislike their mothers, are afraid of sex and wilfully refuse to eat. This amounts, in their words to 'attention seeking'.

Treatment concentrated solely upon trying to fatten me up so that I would look 'normal', but it did not work. Once, when subjected to a behavioural therapy regime, I gained two and a half stones in five weeks. I was not allowed visitors nor to visit the bathroom unattended until I had reached this defined 'target weight'. I felt deep disgust and loathing for my body, and abject powerlessness. The worst of it was that my real feelings continued to go unheard, so I screamed inwardly, silently and alone.

During subsequent admissions I refused to comply so easily, even though I knew the consequences of this would mean greater suffering. But I desperately needed to hold firm to my truthline. Each mealtime became a battle, with several members of staff brutally holding me down whilst mechanically stuffing vast amounts of food into my mouth, as I fought for breath. Afterwards I would lie, exhausted and covered with bruises, aching all over. On one occasion my nose was also held as whole chips were forced down me – the more I panicked the harder they held, till I felt myself beginning to lose consciousness – eventually they stopped.

I felt forced to cut myself off from the frightening outside world. Although never religious I filled my diary with anguished pleas to God to release me from all this torment. But he never seemed to hear and I became driven by fear for my very survival. In my anger against the whole regime I started smashing plates and banging my head against the wall. This was considered to be 'acting out' and I was accordingly punished with seclusion. In sheer desperation I turned my justified rage inwards, cutting my wrists and arms in an attempt to release my emotional angst. The psychiatric answers were to double my dose of major tranquillisers to keep me quiet.

From then I experienced feelings of paranoia and of being trapped. As a last resort, at only sixteen years, I was given fifteen ECTs. Nothing had meaning any more, and each time I was discharged from hospital, I lost all the weight and more. Paradoxically, it seemed my only means of emotional survival. This cycle continued for a number of years, until I became physically very ill. The thought that many years of self-destruction would sooner or later present consequences had never crossed my mind, but I had reached a precarious threshold.

The turning point came while I was in hospital, with a collapsed lung and weighing just three and a half stone. Too weak to lift a teacup without using both hands, I suddenly realised my fight for life had driven me to the point of death. In that deep moment of crisis I knew I had to surrender my soul; there was nothing else I could do. I was the passive victim of these two archetypes of mortality – life and death. Then suddenly I experienced a surge of energy shoot right through me. I sat up, grabbed a pen and wrote. When finished, I lay back, exhausted but knowing I had chosen life.

This was only the beginning of a long and arduous struggle towards recovery, but the support I received from the hospital staff was invaluable. For once I was mercifully blessed with a doctor (not a psychiatrist) whose approach was infinitely more aware and holistic than any I had hitherto experienced. With his encouragement I began to draw and paint again. I started to write and read. My creative efforts were rewarded with interest and acknowledgement. Through this experience I realised how creatively blocked my life had become, and I was able to reconnect with my inner world. I sensed too that these pursuits reached a deep part of me and fed me, as no amount of physical feeding could do.

Furthermore my dietary choices were thoroughly acknowledged and respected. Cottage cheese salads, omelettes and wholemeal bread were supplied by the dietician. I never had to be force-fed or drugged. I was treated throughout with dignity and respect – such a different experience to those of the past.

I spent a year there, gradually beginning to engage with the outside world. When I was eventually discharged, I was to many still underweight, and physically and emotionally traumatised by previous abuse, but I have never needed to return.

However, wounds take many years to heal and the heavy psychiatric legacy was an interminable burden. I was also extremely institutionalised, had lost many friends and felt 'disconnected' and 'unreal'. For several years I lived in this 'twilight' zone, struggling to find work and accommodation, but I was unable to socialise and lived as a virtual recluse.

Then, through one of those unexpected twists of fortune, I began to see a counsellor and alternative therapist, with whom I began a long and trusted relationship. Through this came my interest and awareness of alternatives and their different approach to health and healing. This man was probably the first person who understood where my distress was coming from. As his wife had 'anorexia', he was aware of some of the deeper meanings; and thus neither criticised nor judged me. He could also sense the more spiritual dimensions within me and awakened these. Here was an ally, no longer did I feel so totally alone, as for an hour each week I would feel accepted and nurtured as a whole person, and not seen purely in physical terms. That was a major breakthrough.

However, my energy was extremely low and at times I was deeply depressed. Not only had years of damage caused by the drugs and ECT affected my thought processes, but I had consequent liver and kidney damage. I also suffered extreme blood sugar problems, food allergies and colitis, which only worsened my mental and emotional functioning, and were continually accentuated by my disturbed eating habits. Though I received much support from my counsellor, my body was still suffering dreadfully, and at his recommendation I decided to see a homeopath. I continued the homeopathic treatment for many years, finding my energy and vitality gradually increasing, as did my self-confidence.

My experiences with the homeopath were similar to that of my counsellor – time and space to talk, respect and acknowledgment. My label was not considered in the remedy – which was given on the basis of my overall personal makeup, my emotional, physical and energy states at the time. I was treated as an individual – a response far removed from the psychiatric one, which still considered me to be abnormal.

Over subsequent years I have resorted to many different forms of alternative methods, from colour healing, flower remedies and herbs to art therapy and cranial osteopathy. At various stages in the long process of recovery each have offered longlasting benefits, and I have grown from the experience. What was perhaps more significant was that I began to start respecting and listening to my body more, which had previously been so blocked off. I began to see that the interconnectedness of mind, spirit, emotions and the physical was the essential journey towards healing. Subsequently I trained and qualified as a herbalist, and later as a counsellor and nutritional therapist and naturopath. I am finding the strength to challenge my own outworn dietary habits, and start putting knowledge into practice. It is very hard, painful often, having to acknowledge the damage and scars inflicted upon my body that are ever present, and that I am partially responsible for. But my creative work is a constant joy, as is the work I do in facilitating groups and seeing individual clients.

Alternative treatments are not the panacea for all ills – there are no quick fixes nor magical cures to eating distress. It takes time, faith and encouragement. I am still uncovering painful wounds, but the healing of each one is a learning process that in itself feeds me with strength and even greater determination to live.

Healing Through Creativity

COLIN HAMBROOK

I returned to London in November 1991, homeless and in a state of acute mental and emotional crisis. The only support I was offered by the psychiatric services was a course of antidepressant medication which I knew could only lead me further down a path of dependency and then addiction. This was one of the pitfalls I was battling to avoid. Fortunately for me a friend had been involved in setting up Survivors' Poetry and encouraged me to attend its workshops and performances.

Although I have never been a patient in a psychiatric hospital, I have lived my life on the edge of mental breakdown always seeming to be moving from one crisis to another. My mother was diagnosed and treated as a paranoid schizophrenic when I was ten years old.

The fear which ruled her life had been steadily increasing from the time of my birth when religious indoctrination by the Jehovah's Witnesses created an emotional and ontological stranglehold from which she was never able to free herself.

From a young age, I was painfully aware that the behaviour patterns which set the tone of my family life were not those considered 'normal'. And along with that discovery came the realisation that it was dangerous to talk about such experiences .

While in my teens I began writing literally to save my life! Scraps of poetry and prose were scribbled feverishly on the backs of envelopes and suchlike. Some of these followed me around in my pockets; the rest lay discarded.

Survivors' Poetry provided a focus for my writing and the chance to value it.

While in a fine art course I had been determined to express feelings and intuitions around the issues of mental and emotional distress which had affected my life so profoundly. These were very personal artistic statements which it took a lot of courage to produce but which aroused little interest in any of the tutors or fellow students. Occasionally, they appeared threatened by them . As a result I became very isolated and by the time the degree course was over I felt mentally and emotionally bankrupt. Without really knowing what I was doing I plunged myself into some very demanding care work at a time when my energies were already sorely depleted. Alongside coping with grief over my mother's death I developed health problems and was thrown out of several places of accommodation. As a result, I left the job and wandered around Ireland for a while before returning to London in a lost and bewildered state.

My motivations were unclear. Everything I had put myself through in order to achieve the degree suddenly seemed pointless as my life was once again thrown to the wind through circumstances beyond my control. I was reduced to sleeping on floors always uncertain of when a friend's hospitality would run out. I attended a day centre for the homeless in the city knowing that if the worst came to the worst I might get a bed in a hostel.

My options were few but eventually I found a room in a squat through friends and managed to save the £500 necessary to move into rented accommodation by doing odd jobs gardening and working as a pizza dispatch rider.

All the while my *raison d'être* was very much centred on the hopes and aspirations afforded me by Survivors' Poetry. It was a new and vital experience to have the opportunity to share with others who are also struggling to find some meaning in lives which the world looks on at best as failed and at worst as a burden to society. To find the courage to express with honesty the fears and shattered dreams which have kept you continually falling down the bottomless pit of impossible and disempowering situations. To find that your words aren't greeted with a dismissive silence or patronising advice. To find instead people who recognise and appreciate the pain behind your experience; people who value your expression as poetry and who are prepared to encourage you to refine it.

I had been close to suicide once again but my self-respect returned. I was still feeling pain but had enough of a sense of worth to cope with it. Slowly I gained the confidence to stand up in front of an audience and perform the poetry and songs I had taken to the group for review and comment. At first I performed to the fairly safe audiences at the Survivors' Poetry performances, but soon found myself doing floor spots at numerous poetry and music venues throughout London. As Survivors' Poetry gained momentum opportunities were made available to perform for a whole variety of recipient groups and organisations.

Survivors' Poetry is a purely arts-based venture. Its brief is in no sense meant to provide a space for therapy as such. Although discussing content is a major part of what happens, there is an emphasis on improving poetic form in the facilitation of the workshops. It gave me the chance to break through my sense of isolation in the process. Having that human contact without the involvement of professionals made the experience much more meaningful.

The group's anthology *Survivors' Poetry: from dark to light* is, I think, a testament to the sensitivity, honesty and integrity which underpins the struggles of many people who find themselves caught up in the psychiatric system.

The value of Survivors' Poetry is that it offers our experience a valid vehicle for expression. It gives people the chance to claim back some of the dignity and self-respect taken from them.

Confronting and overcoming my fear of schizophrenia has been a major task. I don't believe that the voices and hallucinations from which I've suffered in my life have merely been the result of a 'biochemical imbalance', but have reflected a need from deep within myself to find myself. Survivors' Poetry has helped me to validate this achievement.

Reference

Survivors' Poetry: from dark to light, Survivors' Press, London, 1992.

Dreaming the Absurd

COLIN HAMBROOK

And I wonder if I'll ever be sane
dressed from head to toe
In a madman's frame.
And I wonder if I'll ever be whole
For to be myself
Is to be a fool

I am dancing,
I am a spinning tree,
Whispering an ancient melody:
But there is a bureaucrat
In the toilet of my mind.
He's counting the faeces
I've left behind.

And I wonder just who I am;
swimming through the air
on a leg and on an arm;
and I wonder how it can be
that humans put a price on this life.

I am flying,
I am a cunning man;
Questioning this meaningless sham
But there's an autocrat
in the attic of my mind.
He says that I'm important
but I don't know just what he means.

And I wonder just what's going on,
for my atoms are dust
and I am a memory
laughing, I am a weird bird,
soft and dark,
dreaming the absurd.

I Have Found Ways Out of Fear

MAUREEN SANGSTER

One day in March 1981 I began giving myself electric shocks off the electric heater. I put myself into hospital. The world was full of electricity and fear.

This electrical obsession was later replaced by other obsessions. I would get cancer, go blind, become deaf. Each obsession was accompanied by compulsions – actions I felt I had to repeat such as irritating a mole on my neck because it might become malignant; staring directly at the sun a certain number of times; poking my ear infection. . . .

It is what the psychology books call obsessional neurosis, always involving rituals of touching, counting and checking. These can last for weeks – six in the case of my mole compulsion.

During these compulsive states I panic and feel powerless. I fight myself. One part of me urges, 'Touch the plug with your wet hand. It might be dangerous,' while the other part thinks, 'Be careful round electricity.' The conflict is about self-control. It feels like a fight between a child and its parent – a vortex with no constructive way out.

Yet since my breakdown in 1981, my compulsive periods are fewer. I can now recognise the beginning of an obsession and take preventive action. This means I have found ways out of fear.

Art therapy is a way out, writing with my left hand, any activity where the surprising occurs, where feelings are expressed, where you can pour out onto paper what you need to know.

Take a roll of old wallpaper, for example, or newsprint and tear off a piece as tall as yourself. Paint on this, using different brush strokes, enjoying colour and textures. The physicality and sheer size of the painting gives a sense of power. In one such art therapy session I painted a huge mother figure crushing her children underfoot. Once such an

150

image is outside you, it is much easier to deal with the pain of a difficult mother–daughter relationship such as I have.

My compulsions/obsessions are energy misdirected against myself. Attention-seeking, they are a bizarre means of self-assertion.

I had to find other ways of building up a sense of self. I started to paint a mandala a day and this was very helpful. The idea is Jungian: draw a circle and paint whatever comes to mind within the safety of that shape. It contains any pain. I prize my notebooks full of small – just $2\frac{1}{2}$ inches in diameter – mandalas. In them I find hints I am a person. I realise, 'This is me. I like trees, fish, cats, churches,' because I keep on drawing these. These repeated motifs of happiness have offset the world of my mental distress where switches, plugs and sockets dominate.

A compulsion is often triggered by the sight of something dangerous such as a worn flex, a loose connection in a plug. I feel I have to touch it. Then I become frightened of my own mind because I can't justify avoiding danger. I question what is a sensible fear of electricity and crouch, breathing rapidly, over the object.

My way out is to take deep breaths, continuously repeat something like 'Let it pass,' and move slowly – so as to lower my adrenalin – towards a chair. If sitting down isn't enough, I draw.

Drawing refocuses my energy. I learnt to interrupt my compulsions in this way through behavioural and cognitive therapy on the NHS for a year. My compulsion then was to check all the switches were off before leaving my flat. I'd go round the flat four times, increase this to seven and then think each individual switch should be checked four times, seven times, twenty-one times! It took ages to leave the flat.

I had to make myself sit down and draw when the compulsions began. Though it was difficult, I eventually grew proud of my ability to choose between my compulsions and another activity. My drawings and the comments I wrote beside them broke open the compulsive pattern and showed the strong hidden feelings behind my rituals – feelings of frustration, loneliness, rage and sexual fears about being a woman in this society, 'sockets wait – poked – women murmuring behind their holes'.

Another way out of the fatalism of having to complete harmful compulsive patterns is through visualisation. Eyes closed, imagine a television screen. Who is on it? What is happening? I have seen horrible images: my mother's head being severed, black vomit pouring from her mouth. Though upsetting, when framed, these images are helpful. I see on the television screen what I am anxious about and a state of anxiety usually precedes my compulsions.

Diary-keeping is a safer ritual than any compulsion. I prefer to use a blank paged book into which I put not only words but pictures torn from magazines, even a dried rose. I record dreams alongside events and feelings. Diary-keeping is about making connections in a free-flowing way – not in the probing dissecting way of my obsessions.

I do not want to use the exhausting, complicated, symbolic system of my compulsions/obsessions to say what I think, what I feel, to draw attention to my need to touch and my need to feel that I am a unique person. Instead I have discovered that I can refocus my energy in a way which is not only creative, but healing as well.

Neurotics at War: Art Therapy

DAVID WIGODER

By the middle of September 1981, I had survived five of the most remarkable weeks in my life, as a resident member of a psychotherapy unit administered by a major psychiatric hospital in southern England. During that period I had lived with a group of people who amazed, horrified, infuriated and, occasionally, soothed me. Few, if any, of us understood the unrelenting distrust we felt towards most people: one of the unit's functions was to make us aware of this. Our lives had become intolerable weights of insecurity and fear, manacled by emotional disorders which scarred us with suspicions about ourselves and each other. Together, we attempted to share our experiences, and we tried to do this in ways which were new and confusing. We were introduced to several types of therapy, verbal and non-verbal. They were all frightening.

On Wednesday afternoons we assembled in the hospital's art room. Art therapy began with us sitting on orange plastic seats, forming a circle, where we proposed, and decided by a majority vote, which feeling or subject we wanted to express. Then we moved to separate, upright easels, and, in silence, created our work. An hour later we returned to the circle, to explain our paintings, discuss them – or ignore them.

Usually, the subjects proposed, whether by staff or residents, were predictable, often suggested as a direct result of recent confrontations in the group. Typical suggestions from residents related to people – *parents, family or children*, for example; and feelings, such as *love, hate, anger or rejection*. It made little difference to me what we agreed upon for the week's subject: whatever it was, my paintings were always abstract and

153

violent, daubed with thick brush strokes in scarlet, purple, black and orange. Staff members some times supplied us with unexpected ammunition – *silence* proved lethal, I remember; but not as lethal as the dynamite which exploded during my fifth session.

Stuart, the senior staff member, a short, dark-haired, bearded Welshman, suggested something familiar to him, and novel to the residents. 'We could try a group mural,' he said casually, explaining, in response to our quizzical looks, precisely what a group mural was. Other subjects were proposed, but the mural sounded original, challenging, and, its most attractive feature, harmless fun. I willingly voted for it, having no conception of the catastrophe which lay ahead.

The hospital's art room reminded me of school. I was surrounded by familiar, old and battered wooden stools, glass jars for water, unrinsed brushes stained with age, shelves stacked with paper, crayons, palettes, and sticks of charcoal; and the heady aroma of paint, turpentine and accumulated dust seeped into my nostrils.

To prepare for the mural, we selected a colour, our unique colour, for the duration of the session. I chose a vivid scarlet, and equipped myself with a large, new pot of the stuff. As soon as the subject had been agreed, I rushed to the paint shelves, determined that nobody should reach that glorious colour before me. I also selected two broad, heavy brushes and filled two jars with cold water. Then we organised the working surface. We were allocated our own 'territory', a sheet of white A2 cartridge paper. The ten sheets were spread on the floor and joined with Sellotape on the under-surface, five sheets in two rows, forming a great white rectangle at our feet. We hovered by our blank mural, while Stuart repeated the game-rules.

'We choose a personal symbol,' he said, 'and paint it on our own sheet of paper. When we've finished, we can do anything, and go anywhere, on the mural.' We agreed to paint for forty-five minutes. From that moment talking ceased.

Excited by this new venture, I wanted to participate in creating an original and unified picture, to prove that I was an important part of the group. My symbol was a large, six pointed star, which I carefully centred on my sheet of paper. Other members chose geometric shapes, 'stick' figures and a house: someone wrote their name. When the symbols were completed, Stuart nodded for the second stage to begin.

Loading my brush, I painted free-style lines, moving clockwise from my star, linking it with the other symbols. I noted with satisfaction that my 'territory' was occupied by all the other colours. The mural grew into a colourful mass of bright, attractive, interweaving designs. I felt exhilarated and energetic, and decided that my next incursion round the mural should be different and inventive. Rapidly I added arcs, dots and circles to contrast with my original solid lines. My scarlet touched and merged with other colours. I no longer wanted to move in an orderly route, but darted between the other artists, dabbing paint where I could, filling in empty spaces, enjoying the image of my colour glistening brilliantly from the floor. It seemed unimportant that my fingers and clothes were spotted with paint, as I bent down or knelt on the floor, making quicker and larger scarlet patches This is wonderful, I thought, proud of the fascinating designs flowing into each other as the mural developed.

Afterwards, I could not decide when friendship turned to enmity, but the later realisation that such a spontaneous and unexpected change was possible left an awful and unforgetable memory which still haunts me. I began to resent the other colours. They took up too much space, and, even worse, abused my scarlet by covering it up. The empty white areas were disappearing, leaving me too little space to do what I wanted. I painted aggressively over other colours, splashing thicker and thicker layers of paint, so that scarlet, and not green, or blue, or yellow, could be seen as the dominant colour. I forced other brushes away with my own gleefully stabbing the paper, delighted with the large scarlet mass which spread across the mural. In places, I saw, the scarlet no longer looked attractive, because other colours had watered it down or changed its tone; but I continued, withdrawing briefly to rush to a nearby shelf and grab another pot of paint.

Twenty minutes had passed when I looked at the clock. I became worried that I might not have enough time to do all that I wanted; but, at the same time, I was uncertain of what I was trying to achieve. The more effort I put into my painting, the less attractive the mural became. I noticed that some members had stopped painting and returned to their seats. Good! The prettiness and the colours of the mural ceased to be important. I was concerned now, not with colours, but with people. I had to show them all that I was in charge.

One male resident, Jim, had chosen yellow. I pursued him, determined to obliterate his colour, consciously intending to inflict pain, remembering how persistently he infuriated me in the group. I understood and enjoyed his fury when he realised what I was doing; but the harder he tried to regain his place on the mural, the more determined I became to eliminate him as a competitor. A few minutes later he walked away, defeated. Marvellous! I was winning.

The mural had become a liquid mass of disorderly colour, a great expanse of mixed and unrecognisable tints, a vast, purplish quagmire. Undeterred, I continued my assault, rushing along each side of the rectangle, unstoppable. Part of me understood that what was happening was dangerous and wrong; but a wilder, uncontrollable force proved more powerful. A distant, inner voice was trying to say something to me.

I knew that the rest of the group were incapable of understanding the purpose of the mural: where they had failed I would succeed. Reloading my brush with deadly paint, I stretched across to the centre of the paper and introduced a new symbol, a small red circle. That'll show them, I thought, that I want this group to be united. What better than a nice, red sun in the middle of this wasteland. But I could not stop. I enlarged the circle, from a diameter of six inches, to twelve, to twenty. Then I encountered a new problem; the others who were still painting appeared unwilling to help develop my new plan. Didn't they understand what I wanted to achieve? As my sun expanded they got in the way, them and their interfering paint. There was one exception: blue. Cathy had chosen blue, and I liked Cathy, so for a time we circled together, her blue bordering my red. We smiled at each other, both understanding our mutual feeling of power. But quickly the partnership dissolved; despite wanting her with me, she kept clouding over the advancing sun.

I looked at the picture and was upset to see that no matter how much scarlet I splashed on the drenched paper, it became inexorably uglier: from purple it had become a barren dirty-brown. I continued throwing paint wildly at the mural, desperate to eradicate the ghastly colour, my brush spearing the image in front of me. When Cathy stood up, and threw her remaining blue paint into my sun, I felt hurt, but strangely peaceful, too. I was alone. The mural was mine. - Everyone had bowed to my scarlet power. Forty minutes had elapsed as quickly as forty seconds. Five more minutes remained; but having routed the enemy, there was no need to continue. My colour, bruised and fatigued, covered the whole, literally the whole, mural: there was not a square centimetre which I had not bludgeoned with my brush. I had won. Exhausted and elated, I rejoined the group.

Then, when I surveyed the monstrous, horrible mess on the floor, I realised that something had gone terribly wrong 'How did it happen?' and 'What have I done!' I kept repeating silently to myself, as I understood the awfulness of my destruction. It was too late to change anything: the damage was complete and unalterable. What I most desperately wanted at that moment was to escape. Val, the female staff nurse, shattered the growing tension, and my hope of escape. 'Isn't it ugly?' she said, sounding bored. Her words were more powerful than bullets as they ripped into my feelings. I sweated with shame and humiliation. 'I didn't enjoy that. I felt threatened,' said Jim, not without some pleasure, I thought, as he quickly agreed with the woman who constantly terrified him. 'I couldn't continue,' he added. I thought that he must hate me more than ever, for we both knew that I had made him retreat.

My stomach churned. My mouth felt dry. My cheeks burned. My hands shook. Cathy, my friend Cathy, complained loudly, 'I thought we were supposed to work together,' and gave me a vicious stare. If anything else was said, I didn't hear it; my thoughts and feelings had retreated into history. I saw, through the mural, the repetition of numerous events in my life, when from hope had come disaster. I related the destruction on the floor to all that I had destroyed in other places and at other times. I did not know what to do with my shame and rage. Terrified of further recriminations, and the memories invading my mind, I rushed from the room, into the cool, damp afternoon. I did not want them; and I believed that they would want nothing to do with a power which could only destroy.

I walked hurriedly through the spacious hospital gardens, furious that I was in such a place, feeling guilty and ashamed. I had no alternative: I had to leave the unit, I decided. But it had become the only refuge where I could talk about, and share, some of my despair with others who were experiencing similar emotional chaos. Bitter tears streamed across my cheeks. A light drizzle cooled my face as I continued walking away from the unit, towards the nearby town. At the end of the hospital's main tree-lined roadway, I hesitated. Ahead of me was the fearful reality of a town, bustling with people among whom I felt hopeless. Behind, presumably happy at my departure, was another group, no less terrifying. I can't return, I thought bitterly, not after what I've done. I sat on rain-soaked benches or meandered through the chilly grounds for five hours, straining to make a decision. To leave the unit meant losing the only hope I had; to remain, I would have to humble myself before a group of people I despised and resented. Desperate to exhibit strength and power, I felt weak and useless. 'If only someone would come and help me,' my distant, inner voice pleaded. They didn't. I had to go to them.

Not knowing where else to go, I returned to the unit, expecting accusations, and intending to apologise. The battles which awaited me there felt less frightening than the false peace I had fantasised about when I thought of leaving.

Reflections on Therapy

BRIAN TAYLOR

I went to Mind's Annual Conference in Blackpool feeling rather wobbly. Along the sea front there was a gale too fierce to walk against. Inside the aptly named Winter Gardens the menu was equally powerful and purging! Brave people speaking out about experiences of sexual abuse by helping professionals and harrowing accounts of the devastating consequences of psychiatric treatments – in particular electroconvulsive 'therapy' (ECT).

Then there was Jeffrey Masson. He proved to be a fine speaker sweeping his audience along in an almost evangelical wave. It felt frustrating that he only had a twenty-minute slot. He had so much to say. In a hall of several hundred delegates not one voice was raised in defence of therapy. There was even talk of abolition which took me by surprise since I've yet to hear anyone at a Mind conference calling for the abolition of psychiatry.

I also found it quite disturbing since at the time I was getting very good support from a therapist. This article is then something of a delayed response to what was going on in the conference hall from a beneficiary of therapy. I am in no hurry, though, to make up my mind, particularly on the vital and as yet unanswered question of safeguards.

Therapists have often told us that we need an expert to help us see round the unconscious blocks that bar our way to healing. Maybe there are times when this is helpful but Masson has shown that psychoanalysis has itself been constructed around Freud's own blocking out of his early discovery that childhood abuse lies at the root of so much suffering (see also Miller 1990).

In his book *Final Analysis* (1990, 1992) Masson describes his appalling experiences as a trainee analyst. He concludes that therapy is inherently corrupting and should be abolished. In *Against Therapy* (1988, 1990) he excavates the field and turns up a lot of muck. What is most disturbing is the degree to which abusive behaviour by therapists has been flaunted by them and accepted by their peers. One therapist, John Rosen whose methods would not have looked out of place in a torturer's interrogation manual received the following compliment from none other than Carl Rogers of 'client-centred therapy' fame: 'We owe a real debt to such therapists . . . [for] . . . provoking a relationship where no desire for a therapeutic relationship exists initially.'

Accounts in *Against Therapy* and elsewhere clearly demonstrate that therapists have a long track record of abuse in relation to people experiencing mental distress.

Masson allies himself with survivors of the mental health system and is now being subjected to highly personalised attacks from therapists. His demolition work has been of great value and I have no wish to arm such critics, but I find myself struggling with his sweeping conclusions.

Against Therapy deals mainly with psychoanalysis or the use of talking or behavioural treatments in institutional settings – in other words, with the elitist conservative and medicalising end of the field. While it's vital to look at why such therapy can go wrong, nothing in the book remotely resembles the therapy that I've experienced and that other people I know have found helpful.

Some years ago I also benefited tremendously from co-counselling. This he dismisses in a footnote as a 'faddish therapy' despite it having been around since the 1950s. It offers a pretty democratic system of structured mutual support which has been helpful to many survivors.

Masson makes statements such as 'the tyranny of judging another person's life to be inadequate was and is the very wellspring of psychotherapy', which go way over the top and hardly help his case. The image of the privileged male therapist attending international conferences and working in wealthy suburbs with his duly labelled 'hysterical' women 'patients' may be true of elitist therapy, but it's only a part of the story.

The therapists I know are mainly women, are financially struggling, perhaps having to take poorly paid part-time work to subsidise work they do with people who can't pay much. Often they have had their considerable skills and experience belittled by medical and other professionals. Masson seems largely unaware of this grassroots end of the market where some therapists and counsellors do help their clients come to their own understanding of their distress in a respectful and loving way.

Do we then accept Masson's view that some people remain decent despite their training as therapists? Or can we find some core of values and skills that can ensure good simple human qualities in a therapist and screen out most abuse?

I think of real therapy as having its roots not in psychoanalysis but much further back in shamanism and in the folk wisdom of the witches and old wives. Such wisdom can't be readily incorporated into the apparatus of social control; nor can it be readily quantified by researchers and accountants.

The word 'therapy' derives from a Greek root meaning to give attention. Certainly much of what is called therapy today goes far beyond this original meaning, which excludes analysis and interpretation. My feeling is that analysis and interpretation should be left out of the therapist's repertoire, except where offering the the humblest and most careful manner.

You've no doubt heard of crop circles. Well, I'd like to turn briefly to the subject of crisis circles. Call them support circles or human circles or what you will. They form in a manner no doubt mysterious to experts around a person in despair. I hoax not. Sometimes the shape of the circle is so strange that people at one end don't even know about the people at the other. They are perhaps diametrically opposite to the better known 'case conferences' which seem to revolve around the professionals' agenda.

Over the last twenty years I have seen such circles form around a number of people. I was one of the beneficiaries of this form of ordinary human magic. People contribute to crisis support in various ways using little-publicised techniques such as taking the person for a meal, making them cups of tea, listening to them, letting them know someone cares and perhaps letting them scream or cry – sometimes for rather a long time, and often for much longer than a 'fifty-minute hour'. Many people I know today have a long track record in co-counselling self-help therapy, healing or other forms of what might be called 'inner work'. This can greatly enrich the quality of support and healing that takes place in the circle.

About twelve years ago I co-counselled with a man whose previous experience had contrasted sharply with my own. In his twenties (back in the early 1970s) he found himself living in London and went, on recommendation, to a well-known therapist in Hampstead.

After a couple of months she got him to repeat his description of an early traumatic memory over and over again in ever more detail. On that fateful day she pushed him to go deeper and deeper until something snapped. He found himself screaming his head off, his body frozen into an all-engulfing scream. He was 'primalling', and to make matters worse, the person in the flat below started to bang loudly on their ceiling with a broom. The hour ran out and he had to go back to the flat where he lived on his own The effect of this experience was traumatic and lasting. It plunged him into several years of psychiatric treatment. He is unemployed and on invalidity benefit twenty years later.

My friend has not ruled out the possibility of going back to a therapist, but says that if he ever gets enough money to afford it, he would insist on a written contract. This would specify that the therapist must respect his process, making very little intervention, if any. This is after all one of the choices made routinely in co-counselling. It would almost completely rule out interpretation, since any realisation about what's going on has to come from the client. He still values co-counselling for its accessibility and its relative safety from abuses of power.

In my twenties, at about the same time, my emotional distress reached crisis pitch. In my case friends were amazingly tolerant. I was able to go on and on and on. Not an hour in the hands of a professional but many weeks held by a small human circle. In the end I managed to piece things together, without using the kind of professional 'services' that had so badly hurt another of my friends.

At that stage I would have found the idea of going to a therapist or counsellor highly intimidating. How far that was a reflection of cultural values is hard to say. It wasn't the done thing for a young man to ask for help, but I doubt there was any professional help available that I would have regarded as safe.

Our two experiences make an interesting comparison and show that in difficult and sensitive circumstances, ordinary people sometimes do a far better job than professionals. I wouldn't wish to leap to any grand generalisations however. My friend's therapy was neither client-centred nor client-paced, and I may have been lucky with my friends. Many people in crisis experience heightened psychic sensitivity or paranormal states. Ordinary people can often cope with such phenomena, while professional structures, not least the therapist's hour, can't.

Despite the above, professional help of the right sort that really is clientcentred, can be invaluable in the work of prevention. It can be a valuable part of inner work, along with meditation, tai-chi, relaxation, healing, artistic creativity, gardening, chopping wood and the like. Too many people simply don't have a confiding friendship.

The professional may also be very helpful during the long process of repair, when even the best circles of friends become stressed, and people simply need to get on with their own lives. Last year, I went through a very complicated and prolonged bereavement. It became clear that leaning on friends for a long time was going to put important relationships under too much strain.

It was a relief going to a therapist who had an impartial view of the situation. He provided insightful suggestions in a very careful and gentle way, never imposing an interpretation or invading my 'process.' His support was, quite simply, invaluable. It is certainly not a service I should like to see banned.

Many people put a lot of energy into caring for others, whether it be children, sick relatives or in a work situation. I think there's a strong argument for them having the chance to use a therapist or counsellor to help them sort out their own personal issues. That was certainly another of my reasons for going to a therapist instead of resuming co-counselling.

Another positive argument for therapy is the part it can play in helping people survive mistreatment and oppression. Such therapy needs to be firmly rooted within appropriate values, of course. No one should be surprised if elitist and conservative therapy subverts social change that threatens its power base.

Therapists have clarified a number of simple but powerful packages of survival skills, to help us listen or assert ourselves more effectively. These can be of enormous benefit and are increasingly finding their way into general use as part of our 'emotional education'. Feminist therapy is supported by staunch critics of psychiatry such as Phyllis Chesler (1990), though some survivors have criticised a tendency to retain both medical diagnoses of distress, and power structures inherent in therapy.

Therapy may be even more valuable for men wishing to change. Men often crack up partly because of having neither the permission nor the language for dealing with the accumulation of everyday distress. If many of women's problems stem from men's inability to form intimate relationships, then therapy and co-counselling for men may well benefit partners and families.

I still see a strong link between what I think of as therapy skills and positive cultural change. I don't see how you can get very far in helping heterosexual men to deal with intimacy, for example, unless their underlying distress is worked through. It simply can't be done with the head alone! I've seen a number of friends greatly helped by therapy in their long years of struggle out of emotional paralysis, often caused by abuse of one kind or another.

Then there is the whole question of the massive over-medicalisation of distress. Prescriptions of harmful and toxic psychoactive drugs still run into the millions. I'd have thought this gives us the most pressing reason of all to get the matter of safeguards sorted out rather than abandoning counselling and therapy altogether.

References

Chesler, P. (1990) 'Twenty Years Since *Women and Madness*: Towards a Feminist Institute of Mental Health and Healing', in 'Challenging the Therapeutic State: Critical Perspectives on Psychiatry and the Mental Health System', special issue of *Journal of Mind and Behavior*, vol. 11 (3/4) pp. 313–22.

Masson, J. (1988, 1990) *Against Therapy*, Fontana Collins, London.

Masson, J. (1990, 1992) *Final Analysis: the Making and Unmaking of a Psychoanalyst*, Fontana, London.

Miller, A. (1990) *Banished Knowledge – Facing Childhood Injuries*, Virago, London.

Building Relationships

JILL REYNOLDS

Probably the loneliest period in my life was when I started work for the Open University. I had some idea of what 'distance learning' involved, and the importance of finding ways to support students who were struggling to study, often in the margins of their time, and without the stimulation of an academic community to keep them going. I hadn't fully recognised that I was opting for a version of 'distance earning' which would make me feel very vulnerable. I lived over a hundred miles from my office base, didn't want to move, and aimed to work at home, going into the office for essential meetings only.

How do you get to know your new colleagues when you don't meet at work? Most of the time I struggled at home on my word processor, trying to produce something that might pass for a piece of academic writing. I went through all the time-wasting strategies that I could – must clean my house before I start, need to read another book on this subject, perhaps I'll feel more like it if I go for a walk first. Others seemed to produce course texts much more easily.

No one but me appeared to want more feedback and encouragement on how they were doing. When I suggested that we talk more about how we were working together as a team, a colleague pointed out that many had chosen this work because it protected them from the demands of day-to-day communication, and the normal working environment. As I prepared course material on 'getting support for yourself' and strategies for sharing problems and getting help, tears were streaming down my face. It all sounded sensible stuff – but who was there to give me support?

My two closest friends were going through crises in their relationships with their partners. I always seemed to be listening to interpersonal problems, and my own worries were too boring to bother anyone with. I felt jealous as a friend unfolded the latest drama concerning her partner. At least she'd had a relationship that had lasted ten years. I didn't have a partner to complain of! I hadn't had a sexual relationship for years. This was all the more poignant for me as the course I was working on was

163

essentially about relationships. Here I was, in my forties, with no relationships worth speaking of, and about to be exposed as incompetent at my job.

I had to do something about it. I had tried co-counselling, but always had the feeling that if I really let rip with my feelings, my co-counsellors wouldn't be able to cope – after all, they were doing this because they needed help themselves weren't they? I chose June, an older woman therapist, on the recommendation of a feminist friend. I thought she would be wise, and that she would understand what life is like for a single middle-aged woman.

So each Monday morning would find me, armed with a large supply of paper hankies, staring at the gas fire in a small front room. I explained that I was rather low on friends at the moment, that I needed some support, and also encouragement to help me make more friends. I hoped to look at what I wanted from relationships and how I went about them. This all sounds rather brisk and straightforward as I write it down. I was surprised at how humiliated I felt in asking for help in this way.

June told me that she was a humanistic therapist. I never found out if she was a feminist. She seemed more interested in finding links with my early experiences than exploring the wider context of my life now. By the end of our first session June said that she thought I was trying to avoid feeling pain. I had never seen myself as someone who blocked off her feelings. It's rather easy to get me to cry. In fact tearfulness was one of the problems that emerged as the therapy got under way.

Something might happen, often in a formal meeting at work, where I would feel overwhelmed and exposed. My efforts to keep tears at bay and not draw attention to myself were generally unsuccessful and my body would eventually convulse with tears. The cause was often quite trivial, but this only made things worse, as I thought others would assume something terrible had upset me. Once I started crying it was hard for me to stop. Layer on layer accumulated of what I thought people must be thinking of me. I would imagine how I might explain myself to those present, and to my therapist. The scenario I played out in my head of seeing myself out of control felt uncontainable.

June provided the containment which allowed me to talk about what I experienced. One of her goals was to get me to express what I felt, and be more immediate about it. She helped me to see that my tears were often unacknowledged anger. But having therapy seemed to involve dealing not only with my problems, but also aspects of my personality that I was rather attached to. I find it difficult to give immediate responses. It takes me time to think about things and work out my reaction. People often seem to appreciate this – colleagues expect to get a considered opinion from me – friends can trust me not to go off the deep end.

We never really cracked this being immediate business. To me it felt as though I'd need a complete personality transplant. And expressing my feelings didn't seem to get any easier. We settled for the more modest goal that I notice for myself what I felt, so that at least I could decide what, if anything, I wanted to do about it.

Another thing that June seemed to want me to change was my way of trying to be entertaining. I have a dry sense of humour. I learnt it from my father, and it's one of the few remaining things I have of him. June wanted to rob me of my way of having fun! She would point out that I was making light of something that I actually felt rather deeply about. I soon found that there was no point in trying to make my therapist laugh.

I did not like feeling vulnerable. The paper hankies that I continued to bring with me illustrate the point. June asked why I was not making use of the pack placed by my chair. Mine were larger. To my astonishment, she expressed willingness to provide the kind I liked! I had got used to taking care of all my own needs. It seemed odd that someone was willing to help out with this.

I did want to do my therapy well, but my efforts were often counter-productive. I would anticipate what June might be thinking, and try to justify myself before she could find any fault. This involved me in rather long explanations. Sometimes June would tell me she was experiencing a feeling of sleepiness, or boredom, and she thought this was due to something that was going on for me, rather than an original feeling of her own. Back to me not letting myself acknowledge my feelings. This would all get a bit convoluted, as I would feel criticised. When I expressed my annoyance June seemed angry and upset herself rather than grateful that at last I was saying something honest.

June often insisted that our exchanges in these sessions, and my feelings about her, paralleled in some way what went on in the rest of my life. Time and again, I would start to deny that she had that kind of impact or importance in my life. Then I would wonder whether implying that someone wasn't that important to me was what I did with other people, as a way of protecting myself.

Communication was a problem – and I had always thought that I was an excellent communicator. June complained that I was never prepared to express myself in a way that was clear to her. She said that I expected her to make all the effort when we were at cross purposes. She leapt on the information that I related (almost in parentheses) about an unpleasant incident when I was eight years, as though I had been deliberately keeping it back. Perhaps I did leave a lot out, but there didn't seem any point in explaining things that I already knew about.

As I began to stand up for myself, instead of simply feeling crushed by negative interpretations, our relationship seemed to get more competitive. At one point, apparently feeling put down by me, June told me that she had six years of higher education herself. There was always the nagging feeling that perhaps other people also found me arrogant and controlling.

I never really felt that June liked me. But I did feel that she cared about me and took my concerns seriously. I did a number of things that I enjoyed: learnt to rock and roll, went on cycling expeditions, organised a tennis group, sang in harmony at music workshops. Perhaps I would have done these things anyway, but June helped me to notice my own efforts, to recognise successes and to value the things that gave me pleasure.

When I started a significant relationship I was able to understand more about what it was that I wanted from a man. I met him at dancing classes, he was working away from home. He wasn't free, he loved his family life – oddly this suited me too. I wasn't at risk of total loss and disappointment, and he wasn't always around making a nuisance of himself. It was an experience of feeling liked, admired, and cared for, and I was able to accept this. June gave me encouragement while trying to help me to protect myself.

June thought I made most progress at the times when I was feeling worst about myself. A low time was when I broke my wrist in a cycling accident. None of my normal coping strategies were available. My friend's work contract had finished and he had gone back to his home town. I couldn't cycle, dance, swim. I couldn't even open a tin without going round to my neighbour with the tin-opener. All my anxieties about dependency were to the fore, but I had to let someone help me, and June relished the opportunity. While I did learn some things about myself from this period of being at a low ebb, I couldn't see this as a time of progress. I was only too glad when my wrist recovered and my optimism returned. Perhaps I just didn't want to explore my deeper fears about myself in the way that June thought was needed.

Therapy lasted nearly three years. June called it two, and I got the impression she thought we had hardly started. My suggestions that I would like to have an end point to aim for were ignored, and eventually I said I wanted to stop in four weeks. What decided me was a creative writing workshop I had attended. I could see the potential and the pleasure, in turning my observations into something fictional, rather than hanging onto them as something to work on in therapy. I was also increasingly finding myself mentally rehearsing arguments with June in between sessions. I would try to elicit friends' support and sympathy over my disagreements with June. This didn't seem the right use of therapy or my friends' time.

June revealed that she was planning to retire in six months and wanted me to continue therapy until then. I wanted to use the energy and excitement the thought of creative writing generated in me. Those last few weeks were hard. I began to lose confidence as June kept telling me that I could change my mind, and offered me a follow-up appointment.

Was the experience worth the investment of time I put into it? Would I have got more out of it if I had invested longer, or more of myself? Although I am quite critical of our therapeutic relationship, I did get some support at a time when I needed it. I also learnt (usually painfully) something about my impact on others. But I wonder how much you can do in therapy without a feeling of being liked and understood? I felt June often found fault with me. Was that my problem, hers, or something we constructed together?

It Helped that Someone Believed Me

LOUISE PEMBROKE

I always had a lot of spiritual activity in my life. That has always been quite important to me. I need spiritual contact. I remember when I was about ten years old, I had a year of continual dreams, like a serial. I could tune into it each night. In this dream I was indestructible, and the person who was persecuting me was also indestructible. Between the two of us, it was a question of who could terrify the other more. I always took the same physical forms – that of a crucifix or of a metal box.

Around that same time, I began to feel a spiritual presence outside my bedroom door. Fortunately, it felt as if there was something in the door stopping it from passing through and getting in. But I knew that if this spirit could get in, it was going to be harmful to me. I would just feel it pressing on the door. I could actually see the door sometimes bending under the pressure. It stayed there for seven years, day and night. I didn't think anybody would believe me, so I never told anybody about it for those seven years.

When I was seventeen I came into contact with a spiritual healer. I met him literally by chance. I did not seek him out. He was a friend of a friend who had noticed that I was very distressed; increasingly distressed from the age of about fourteen. This friend suggested that the spiritual healer might give me a hand. When I saw the man, I told him about the spirit outside the door. He said 'Why don't you talk to it?', so I did. I talked to the spirit, and it went away. Then one day I woke up and felt as though my own spirit had died. This was devastating. I felt like an empty vessel. I thought that if my spirit had died, my body might as well follow. So I tried to kill myself.

When I recovered, everything took a new shape. I noticed that another

168

spirit had got into my body to take the place of my own. I felt that this entity was very evil and bad; my body felt contaminated. It was as if there was something rotting inside me. I wanted to get rid of it, so I went to a priest and had an exorcism performed on me. As with the spiritual healer, a friend of a friend said: 'Well, I know this priest. Why don't you go to see him?', and I did. I told him about the entity in me, and he performed the exorcism. I didn't realise he happened to be the Church of England's top exorcist. I was okay for a while, but then the entity came back. I now know why it came back. I have a hole in my aura, and it is located in my chest. I know the exact point. I have learned to recognise when that hole opens. So now, when it opens, it is very simple to cover it with my hands, or my partner covers it. If I do this, entities cannot get in. I can stop them. It is so simple.

Back to when I was nineteen. So I had that bad entity inside me, but I also had another spirit beside me that would be following me around. It was a male spirit, and he told me his name was Fred. He told me that he was the devil's advocate, and I could always feel him beside me by my right shoulder.

Over the next couple of years, everything was quite a blur. It is hard to remember some of what was happening during that time. I don't know if Fred had any connection with the entity inside me. Very rarely did he order to me to do things. His comments about me were persecutory, continually putting me down. Fred didn't tell me why he had come, but he would just tell me that I was shit, fat, ugly or stupid. He would tell me what he thought of me, and the single words would drop into my head. It was almost like my head was a cup and you could drop an object into it. That object would bang at the bottom.

I didn't talk about him to anyone for quite a while. At times he would do something which was absolutely terrifying. He would send out snakes to attack me, and this was when I became very freaked out. It was at times like this that I would become so-called catatonic because I was just terrified. He would send the snakes out in a specific pattern. He would let me know by saying: 'I send them. They are coming.' Fred would also tell me their colour. Then I would sit down and think: 'Oh shit, what am I going to do?' Then I would hear the thumping of the snakes' heads against the door. They would come in from under the bottom. Sometimes I would literally see them whizzing up and down the room. I could not see them in a way that I can see this chair and this table. It's hard to explain how I could see them, because it is not that kind of literal vision. It was more like I know their dimension, their shape and their size. It is a different type of vision.

Sometimes there would just be a couple of little ones, and they would get into my drink. When I started to swallow, I would realise there was a snake in my stomach. They would bite my inside and then dissolve.

Sometimes they would go over my legs, and occasionally one would bite my neck or wrist and would just stay there. Then I would be immobilised, terrified and unable to speak. I would sometimes see the snake go into the gas fire and be burned. I could smell it burning. The noise is overwhelming; their actual hissing. When there were a lot of them, the sound would be deafening. While all this was happening, it was very difficult to tell other people what was going on. So I felt helpless, because I really did not know what to do.

I came into contact with psychiatry at seventeen. I was talking to them about eating and throwing up, so I started off with an eating disorder label. When I started to talk about an exorcist, they were not too sure. It didn't quite fit in with how they had got me categorised. Then I made the mistake of telling my consultant about Fred and the snakes, and he said: 'Oh, this is very interesting, I know what you are talking about', and he labelled me as schizophrenic. He informed my parents, but I didn't realise this at that time. I remember him saying: 'You have got an underlying illness', but I did not understand what he meant.

For five years, until I was twenty-one, my life was in such a mess. During that time I was going in and out of hospital. As an in-patient, as an out-patient, and through casualty, as I was continually harming myself. Fred was there most of the time. The evil spirit was still in the place of my spirit. I felt as if I was dead. How could I be alive if I did not have my own spirit in my body? I did not exist. I started self-harming because I felt powerless. It was a reaction to the treatment I was receiving. I would cut myself up as a way of expressing my pain and anger. Also out of sheer frustration, as a way of dealing with all the things that went on, including Fred and the snakes. I was never instructed by the spirit or Fred to do it. That was something I did of my own free will.

Around this time, I would also hear a female voice screaming. The sound was by my ears; outside my head. It was like two female heads screaming in. Now, I think that was a metaphor for my own screaming. At times, I could not cry or scream. Certainly in a hospital you can't do that, but even outside of the hospital I felt I couldn't do it. So I think I would hear my own screaming and I would cut myself instead of crying. Because when the blood ran away, it felt like tears. The injury was doing the crying for me.

Obviously, psychiatry wasn't very helpful. When I became frozen and rigid when the perceptual differences were very intense, they would just prod my body. I was subjected to behaviour modification and drugs. It was very difficult being told what to do and having no control in my life. But I would try to behave in the way that was expected of me. As I was being treated like a child, then I would behave like a child. It was expected of me, so I would live up to their expectations.

When I came out of hospital and went to the day hospital, they tried to blackmail me into taking injections of tranquillisers. Then I said: *'no'*. It was the first time I actually took a stand. The first time I was assertive. Then I made the decision to escape psychiatry.

When I came into contact with other survivors, it was the turning-point of my life. That was when I could start to look at what the hell had been going on. It was not until I got out of psychiatry, was not drugged, was not controlled, that I could look at what had happened. When I came into contact with other survivors, I had a chance to talk about the anger, and have those feelings validated. I felt safe to talk about my experiences without fear of being judged or told that I was stupid or sick. It was such a relief. I then gained a couple of friends who accepted me as I was. If I could feel the snakes coming in, I did not have to rush off. I could stay.

I think that when my understanding grew of what was happening, that was when Fred left me. It was not as if one day I woke up and realised Fred was not there. Very gradually, his presence became less and less. The snakes have always stayed. Fred does not send them out, so I don't know why they still try to trouble me, but how I deal with it now is very different.

At first, I would not be able to say what was happening till it had finished. But gradually, when it started I alerted someone; I could actually say 'The snakes are in the room' to another person. One of my friends would even talk to the snakes and say 'Go away, leave Louise alone.' It helped that someone believed me. Somebody was taking me seriously and doing something. It did not necessarily help the snakes to disappear, but I didn't feel totally alone. It does not help to tell me they are not real, because they are. There is no point in denying what is happening to me.

What has been quite liberating is that my partner is particularly good in helping me deal with the snakes. If there is one attached to my body, I can actually say to him: 'There is one on my hand'. I can tell him how big it is, and he will help to pull it off me; physically pull the snake off and throw it right out of the front door. He can dispose of it for me. I am not yet able to do that for myself.

However, my ability to deal with the snakes is developing. It is very rare that I am completely incapacitated. If I am, it is only for a few hours. I know that they will go away eventually, and it helps when I am assertive with them. The other week, they were all over the bed and I said: 'Just fuck off, go away.' When I get angry with them they will go away, even if it takes all night.

My own spirit has come back. It is hard to pinpoint the exact time when it returned. But it was definitely at some point when I was escaping psychiatry. My spirit periodically leaves me, but that is not so much of a catastrophe any more. I do not feel the need to kill myself every time my spirit leaves me. I feel very depressed if it is not with me, but I know at some point it will return. I learnt a lot from my partner, because he has had much experience with voices and entities himself. It is so easy to talk to him about it: that makes a major difference. I have taken ownership of my experiences and found my own meaning.

Part six

WORKING FOR CHANGE

Introduction

Since the mid-1980s there has been a significant change in the relationship between users and providers of mental health services. For the first time, service users have achieved credibility as people who have something valid to say about the treatment and care they are given or compelled to receive.

An impressive array of schemes designed to include service users in the planning, provision and evaluation of mental health projects has been developed. At the same time, there has been a growth of independent organisations of people who have been diagnosed and treated as mentally ill, and other organisations that are 'user-led' but also include their relatives, friends and allies.

In this section, people who have been involved in these activities share their experiences and the lessons they have learned from them.

We start with two articles about how service users/recipients want mental health services to change. In 'What We Want From Mental Health Services' Jim Read gives an overview. Peter Campbell focuses on 'What We Want From Crisis Services'. They draw on the body of experience and knowledge that has been developed within the movement of service users and people who regard themselves as survivors of the mental health system. Both may be accused of being unrepresentative of the majority of people using mental health services. In 'Who do *You* Represent?' David Crepaz-Keay defends the legitimacy of the views of people who, by their very involvement in debates about mental health services, are untypical of service users as a whole.

Vivien Lindow and Jan Wallcraft offer mental health workers new challenges. In 'What We Want From Community Psychiatric Nurses' Vivien Lindow invites them to become expert in supporting their patients to deal with the adverse effects of treatment, such as the trauma of being locked up under the Mental Health Act; to back people up who resist psychiatric treatments such as ECT and become knowledgeable about the effects of medication and strategies for coming off it.

In 'Becoming Fully Ourselves' Jan Wallcraft takes a look at what can go wrong when people attempt to empower themselves through collective action, why, and what can be done about it. Drawing on her own experience, she suggests how mental health workers can be effective allies for service users who are working for change.

The next two articles are about projects that have run into difficulties, but both writers have learned and gained strength from their involvement in them. Sue King had a frustrating time as a member representative on the management committee of a drop-in, but, in 'We Can Still Find a Way to be Heard' she is able to say that 'both disappointment and achievement inspired me to fight for what I know is right'. In 'Listening in the Asylum' Mary Nettle reports on how she and a colleague were commissioned as 'user-researchers' to investigate the living conditions of long-stay patients. Their report was never published, but the experience has inspired them to draw up some guidelines to ensure that the same mistakes are not repeated.

Continuing the theme of doubts and hopes about 'user involvement', in 'Shaking Hands with the Devil' Edna Conlan offers a sceptical view of her involvement with decision-making bodies. But, like the previous writers, she does not dismiss this activity as a waste of time. She concludes that 'even when the most we can do is to be there and bear witness to what is going on, it seems to me to be well worth doing'.

We conclude with two articles that perhaps point the way to the future. Peter Beresford, Gloria Gifford and Chris Harrison make links between the mistreatment and discrimination experienced by people who are treated by the psychiatric system and by people with physical impairments in 'What Has Disability Got to do with Psychiatric Survivors?' They have joined forces with organisations of disabled people and found common ground in campaigns for civil rights.

In 'Beyond Rage' Terry Simpson shows how self-help and working for change can go hand in hand. It was through a support group that he was able to deal with his rage about the mental health system. By doing so, he felt more empowered to take action to change it. The continuing support of his group has enabled him to find the most effective ways of doing so.

What We Want from Mental Health Services

JIM READ

In the last few years, there has been a growth of advocacy projects, patients' councils, local forums and national networks of people who are recipients of psychiatric treatment. There have been surveys and research projects to find out service users' views, and publications and videos produced by people who – to use one memorable phrase – have experienced services from wrong side of the drugs trolley.

With all this activity, which has never occurred before on anything like the same scale, a picture is beginning to emerge of what service users want from mental health services. Those involved in self-advocacy have very different views from each other about basic issues, such as, is there such a thing as mental illness, is there a role for medication, can compulsory detention in psychiatric hospitals ever be justified? But, despite these fundamental differences of opinion it seems comparatively easy for us to agree the principles on which a mental health service should be based. These can be grouped under the headings: information, choice, accessibility, advocacy, equal opportunities, income and employment, self-help and self-organisation.

Information

More than anything else, service users want to know about the effects of medication. One extensive survey found that 68 per cent of people who have been prescribed major tranquillisers were not informed about the expected effects (Rogers *et al.*, 1993). Having been told about these effects, most of us will want to know about the alternatives to medication. Users want information about the range of services available, particularly on discharge from hospital into the community. This is easy to say and it is easy to agree to, but the action rarely happens. I recently spoke to some people being discharged from a day hospital who didn't know what a community psychiatric nurse is or that there was a drop-in centre a hundred yards away. It is crucially important we know our rights, both to received and refuse treatment.

Choice

Everyone is different and not everyone wants the same treatment. Someone who can't sleep may benefit from yoga, sleeping pills, meditation or counselling, but which of those do mental health workers offer? Someone who is freaking out may well welcome an admission to an acute ward, but for someone else it may be what they most fear. Is there a crisis house which relies less on medication, and what about intensive support to stay at home? Above all, time and time again, people say that the choice that is missing is someone to talk to.

Accessibility

Service users do want services that are near their homes and we want them to be open when we need them. Mental health crises do not conveniently occur between 9.00 and 5.00, and for us Christmas can be the loneliest time. Service users want somewhere other than an Accident and Emergency Department, a place we can simply turn up to say: 'Help, I'm in a mess'. The more hoops that users have to jump through to access a particular service and the longer we have to wait, the more sure you can be that use of that service will be determined more by social status and assertiveness than by need.

Advocacy

Generally, service users are scared of mental health workers. Professionals might not feel very intimidating but there's something about the relationship that we have with you, especially if you're a doctor, which means that we're scared of you. Obviously the powers under the Mental Health Act have a lot to do with this. It's not easy for us to say, or even think, what we want in a situation such as a ward round or review, especially if we fear that what we want to say is not what the mental health workers want to hear. Service users need access to independent, funded advocacy services, to support them to put their views across.

Equal opportunities

Service users want a service that takes account of the whole range of attitudes to emotional distress or mental illness. Is it more rational, for example, to believe that there is a mind but not to believe that there's a soul? No one has the monopoly on the truth when it comes to mental health. We need to recognise that racism and sexism, even Majorism, can drive you mad. People who, for example, are working class or who are mothers, who are perhaps gay or lesbian, want workers who they trust to understand their experiences, and that means fair promotion opportunities in the services for people from a range of different backgrounds, and it means the kind of training for mental health workers that currently they rarely get.

Services need to offer privacy, security and freedom from harassment, from staff and other users. Don't assume that its not an issue in your hospital or mental health project. One study of residents in a psychiatric hospital found that 71 per cent had been threatened with physical violence; 38 per cent had been sexually assaulted and 27 per cent had been sexually assaulted by staff (Nibert *et al.*, 1989). Certainly I know of a number of day centres in London that have been taken over by men in such a way that women actually feel unable to use them. In a US study, 15 per cent of male therapists actually admitted to sexual contact with clients, 92 per cent of them women (Bonhoustos *et al.*, 1983). Here are some quotes from some research into the experience of Black psychiatric patients in Leicester (Leicester Black Mental Health Group, 1989). From a woman patient: 'They would call you names and say you were a mad Black woman. There was one nurse and I really didn't like her. She would say how mad all Black people are.' And from a male patient: 'I found the patients even more racist than the staff. One of them had the habit of calling me 'Sambo'. I couldn't believe it – even the mad people hate us. I told the nurse and she told me I was imagining it all.' And later talking about the staff: 'I became very wary of all the white people and the only Black people I saw were the cleaners.' Service providers must implement good equal opportunities policies and programmes.

Income and employment

Please do close down the big institutions but don't dump us in special needs ghettos where we go to day centres not to meet our emotional needs but because otherwise we can't afford to eat and to keep ourselves warm. Professionals can't do much about the recession and welfare benefits cutbacks, but you can set up housing and employment schemes that give us some money to spend, and training schemes to give us the skills to compete for jobs; and you can recognise that we may be able to make positive use of our experiences by working for your mental health services.

Self-help

This is not about mental health services on the cheap – it's about unleashing our desires and abilities to support one another, and to come up with new and imaginative solutions. The Hearing Voices Network, is a fine example of this, to quote from their information leaflet: 'The network has been set up to assist voice hearers to find their own ways of coming to terms with their voices, by showing that there are various explanations for the experience of hearing voices which have been shown to empower voice hearers, enabling them to live with the experience in a positive way. There are people who find ways of coping with their voices other than the use of drugs and who have found alternative explanations for their voices outside of the psychiatric model, which has assisted people in coping with their voice experience. The knowledge gained by people who can cope with their voices can be beneficially shared. People who hear voices can be assisted in developing ways of coping with their voices by participating in self-help groups in which they can share experiences, explanations and methods of coping, and benefit from mutual support. People who hear voices, their families and friends, can gain great benefit from de-stigmatising the experience, leading to greater tolerance and understanding. This can be achieved through promoting more positive explanations which give people a framework for developing their own ways of coping and by raising awareness about the experience in society as a whole' (Hearing Voices Network, u.d.).

Self-organisation

Service users have a lot to contribute to the design and implementation of services, but our experience knowledge and abilities remain locked away unless we have opportunities to meet together to find common ground, and to think about what we really want and how to go about getting it. For that, properly funded and supported patients' councils, local service users' forums and national networks are needed.

Any local group of service users will have a lot of practical details to add. They will be experts on which services and staff are doing their jobs well and which are falling down. They will know what is missing and have constructive proposals for filling the gaps. They may even disagree with the principles I have outlined here.

Having a general idea of what service users want is not, of course, a reason for failing to involve local people in the planning and development of your services. But this is necessarily a slow process. Start it now if you have not already done so, but do not feel you have to wait for the perfect consultation procedure to be in place before beginning to change your services to better meet people's needs and expectations.

References

Rogers, A., Pilgrim, D. and Lacey, R. *Experiencing Psychiatry: Users' Views of Services*, Macmillan, Basingstoke (1993).

Nibert, D., Copper, S. and Crowmaker, M. (1989) 'Assaults against residents of a psychiatric institution: residents' history of abuse', *Journal of Interpersonal Violence*, vol. 4, no. 3, pp. 342–9.

Bouhoustos, J., Holroyd, J., Lerman, H., Forer, B. and Greenberg, M. (1983) 'Sexual intimacies between psychotherapists and patients', *Professional: Research and Practice*, vol. 14, no. 2, pp. 185–96.

Leicester Black Mental Health Group, *Sadness in my Heart: Racism and Mental Health*, University of Leicester, 1989.

Hearing Voices Network (undated) Information leaflet, Hearing Voices Network, c/o Creative Support, Fourways House, 16, Tariff Street, Manchester M1. Tel: 0161 228 3896.

What We Want from Crisis Services

PETER CAMPBELL

This article outlines some of the things some or perhaps many mental health service users/survivors want from crisis services. It is influenced by my own experience of receiving mental health services over the last twenty-eight years (sixteen admissions onto acute wards) and by my involvement in the user/survivor movement in the last ten years, It is also particularly informed by the following facts: I am a man; I am white; my crises would usually be described by most experts in terms of psychotic episodes.

I am not able to address precise definitions of mental health crisis here, but the reality that a proportion of those who are deemed to be having a mental health crisis resist such an attribution must be openly acknowledged. Numerous recipients of crisis services are not just unwilling recipients but are compelled recipients. Such disagreements have traditionally been explained through the lack of insight within the distressed persons, their inability to know what is really going on and what is in their best interests. While this approach has been very convenient in justifying control of unco-operative people, it is not the most encouraging starting-point for responses sensitive to individual wants and needs. A more sophisticated appreciation of insight and a willingness to address the range of reasons why people may deny they are in a mental health crisis would be most helpful. It is certainly possible that these denials are not so much because people do not think they are in difficulty as because they object to their problems being characterised as mental illness ones or dislike the interventions being offered.

Although the manifestations of mental health crises have a wide range and may be strongly contrasted, the basic wants and needs of people in crises of this kind are probably very similar. I have regularly asked groups of survivors, groups of mental health workers and mixed groups to do an exercise imagining themselves in a mental health crisis and then drawing up lists of wants and not wants. Overall the lists are always very much the same, although people who have been through services usually have a sharper idea of what they do not want. The fact that people in crisis may have difficulty communicating or talk of worlds, concepts and perceptions with which mental health workers have limited natural sympathy should not lead to assumptions that their wants and needs are extraordinary or esoteric or that there is inevitably a gulf between what people say they want and what they really need.

On the other hand, individual wants and needs do conflict and compete. How can you reconcile someone's desire for space with someone else's desire for a feeling of physical limitation and safety in the same location and with extreme limitations on the number and flexibility of staff? It is hard to see how the traditional acute ward, wherever located, can possibly provide a sensitive response to crisis within its contradictory imperatives for supervision and privacy, containment and renewal, peace and quiet and restimulation. The widespread demand for alternative approaches and different destinations is rooted in personal experience of the barren, ordered chaos of the acute ward. When mental health service users talk about their crises, several strong themes tend to emerge and these have a vital relevance to crisis provision.

People want more control, particularly more of their own control over crisis situations. Given that many of us are unlikely to be contemplating a future where we never have another mental health crisis, the fact that we gain confidence that further crises will not destroy us is of the greatest significance. Existing services, no matter how insensitive, do often offer that reassurance. From then onwards, the desire to increase our own control in our loss of control becomes central. Recently there have been encouraging signs of a move away from approaches seeing people with a mental illness diagnosis as uncomprehending victims of outbreaks of inscrutable illnesses, towards responses asserting our essential competence and capacity to moderate our crises. Examples of this (coming perhaps from rather different perspectives) are: *Inside Out – A Guide to Self-management of Manic Depression* (Manic Depression Fellowship, 1995) and work on intervention in the preliminary (prodromal) phases of psychotic episodes (Bradshaw and Everitt, 1995).

People want to gain understanding of and from their crises. We want to learn from our crises things that are relevant to the rest of our lives. We want to integrate these experiences into the weave of all our other experience and not to carry them around with us as some separate and unsightly garment. In this regard I feel crisis services, indeed mental health services as a whole, remain clearly deficient. I remember the frequent use of the phrase 'Och, it's not the real you' to limit and circumvent aspects of my concerns when going through crisis in acute wards. Sadly, I am convinced that for many mental health workers it remains true that they do not think the content of our crises, particularly those they define as psychotic, are real, relevant or of anything but negative value. It is ironic that while increasing numbers of people in the user/survivor movement are seeking new meanings in their most vivid personal experiences, so many mental health workers continue to look the other way.

People want to be treated with respect and dignity. Clearly there are many levels to this demand. For myself, the lack of respect I now perceive is related to concerns expressed in the previous paragraph. For others the denial of respect may be far more blatant. In particular, I often wonder how different my journey through the crisis services would have been if instead of being a six-foot-four-inch white, Protestant Scotsman, I had been a six-foot-four-inch Black Rastafarian man.

No one would deny the very real difficulties of always providing a sensitive response to people in crisis. Nevertheless we should also not overlook the fact that crisis responses are still occurring that are quite obviously going to increase the trauma of those experiencing them. How is it still possible for someone in crisis picked up under section 136 of the Mental Health Act 1983 to be kept in solitary confinement for a period of hours in a police station cell while awaiting assessment?

How can anyone with a caring imagination possibly think such destinations are places of safety? It is also important that the quality of crisis care being given to people who go through Accident and Emergency Departments continues to be scrutinised. Evidence of the mistreatment of people who self-harm (including the sort of misunderstanding of people who self-harm without suicidal intent that can involve endless waiting at the bottom of the queue and being stitched up without an anaesthetic) suggests that the scope for re-education is very large.

People, particularly people involved in the user/survivor movement, want twenty-four-hour non-medical crisis services. This remains a key issue for the future of crisis services in the United Kingdom. For, although in the last ten years the demand for twenty-four hour services has gradually gained acceptance, the demand for non-medical provision has stayed very much at the margins. This may be partly due to the refusal of psychiatrists to consider approaches challenging their reliance on medication. (It is interesting how the medical establishment's clarion cry of 'Anti-psychiatry' so quickly paralyses the faculty of rational consideration.) But is also due to a failure to define more carefully what people mean by non-medical services. Does this mean absolutely no use of medication? Does it mean not using medication as the standard first resort? Does it mean having medical and complementary approaches? Does it mean having staff teams that are not led by psychiatrists? Does it mean an open employment of the expertise of local users/survivors?

At the moment, debate on these questions does not seem to be very open and it is not easy to discover what progress has been made in different localities. Although there is evidence from other countries that it is possible to support people through crises without using neuroleptics (Mosher and Burti, 1994; Podvoll, 1990), our NHS system seems reluctant to innovate. As it stands, using the expertise of survivors and not using medication appear to be the most likely elements to be dropped from new crisis services.

I conclude on a personal note. My first crisis admission was not a medical event. For me, it was a moral event, a moral failure. All my subsequent admissions have contained shadows of that first failure. None of the important implications have been medical ones. In my view, the crucial questions about mental health crisis services are to do not with locations and technology but with understandings.

References

Manic Depression Fellowship (1995) *Inside Out. A Guide to Self-Management of Manic Depression*, Manic Depression Fellowship, Kingston upon Thames.
Bradshaw, T. and Everitt, J. (1995) 'Early Intervention to Prevent Psychotic Relapse', *Mental Health Nursing*, vol. 15 no. 6., pp. 22–5.
Mosher, L. and Burti, L. (1994) *Community Mental Health – A Practical Guide*, Norton, London.
Podvoll, E. M. (1990), *Seduction of Madness – A Revolutionary Approach to Recovery at Home*, Century, London.

Who do You *Represent?*

DAVID CREPAZ-KEAY

'But you're not like *my* clients.' If I had a crisp tenner every time that 'argument' was used to counter my entire presentation on increasing the participation of people who use mental health services in the planning and provision of services, I would probably be better paid than those who level the charge. 'Who do *you* represent?' That's my other favourite. A similar financial deal on that one and I'd be in the league of a National Health Service Trust director.

I enjoy a well-reasoned argument. I admire the professional who can construct a defence of their service, or who can constructively criticise my ideas. I am open-minded enough to learn from such exchanges. The type of professional who argues in this way will usually benefit from the discussion. But why is so much valuable time and energy wasted on what is little more than a personal attack, the first defence of a frightened traditionalist who hasn't bothered to listen to a word of the twenty-minute presentation that invariably precedes the charges?

'But you're not like *my* clients': the 'articulate user' syndrome. The first difference between me and his – for it is invariably a man – clients is that I have a platform, an opportunity to have my say, a genuine prospect of being heard. He is the type of professional who sees the professional – client roles as rigidly defined. I have been treated by professionals like that type. He is not interested in what his client has to say anyway.

His clients are probably disempowered by months or years of not being listened to. Then they are disempowered by being asked to get involved, probably by sitting on a committee, and being ignored by a wider range of people. That sort of thing would sap anyone's confidence. My confidence has grown over years of increasing involvement, with tremendous support from friends and colleagues in the survivor movement who knew what I was facing every step of the way.

His clients are probably drugged up to the eyeballs. People who have known me on depot injections, on cocktails of uppers, downers and mood stabilisers; people who have supported me through eighteen months of withdrawal against medical advice; people who've been through it themselves will understand. The drugs used in psychiatry can make it very difficult to articulate anything. The effects drugs can have on memory, on concentration, even the mechanics of standing and speaking, make it very difficult to contribute with confidence. There was a time when I was on depot injections – it lasted two years – when I just wanted to stay in bed. I had precious little energy for day-to-day life. Participating in anything more demanding than making lunch would have been impossible. If I stood up to quickly, I would fall over. Not too impressive at the start of a speech!

'Who do *you* represent?' I know that committees, meetings, conferences and planning teams are packed full of 'representatives'. I know that the culture into which we are drawn likes to see itself as 'democratic', but how representative or democratic are they? I have had this challenge cast at me in a meeting in which I was the only individual who had actually been elected!

I cannot hope to represent the 'user/survivor movement'. Being chair of Survivors Speak Out does not entitle me to wield a trade union style block vote. It does give me the chance to air views that do not get heard either often enough or at a high enough level. While the views I express are predominantly my own, I believe they do reflect widely held concerns. I spend most of my life with survivors and current and ex-service users. They are my friends, my colleagues, my lifeline. To most of the professionals I deal with they are clients, consumers, people with a mental illness, or worse.

It is this different relationship that entitles us to speak without feeling the need to be representative. We are a diverse bunch. We cut across the boundaries of class and gender and culture that still grip the 'mental health' professionals, particularly at the higher levels. I do not claim that the survivor movement is a perfect model, but I would ask people to look carefully at their own glasshouse before they throw their 'who do *you* represent' stones in my direction.

What We Want from Community Psychiatric Nurses

VIVIEN LINDOW

One of the most persistent complaints among service users is 'They never listen.' But diagnosis and the effects of psychoanalysis get in the way of listening. The medically inclined listen to the words of service users in order to diagnose: 'Is she psychotic?' This robs our words of their meaning. The analytically inclined listen to demonstrate their skill in gaining insights. This again robs our words of their meaning. If we disagree with our clever analyst (or even therapist or counsellor) it demonstrates denial, projection, transference or one of the other 'mechanisms' that stop what we are communicating being heard.

This means that many of us who have experienced a lot of psychiatry approach new relationships with mental health workers with an expectation that you will not hear what we say and that we have to convey our needs through other behaviour. This is unfortunate if you do want a straightforward relationship, but it is just one form of damage that those of us who have been in the system for some time may have sustained especially if we have been in hospital.

Having mental and emotional distress described as an illness has some advantages, including relieving feelings of guilt, and getting support. However, my experience of multiple admissions to hospital was that the harm far outweighed the good. Teaching me that I was ill led me to give responsibility for a 'cure' to medical experts. If they were not attempting to cure me, why put me in hospital? I was certain that the next pharmaceutical breakthrough would put me right; why otherwise did they keep changing and adding to the drugs I took?

The idea that doctors and nurses now best persists, despite a century of abuse of and damage to mad people in the name of medicine. The paternalism of the system loses view of us as self-determining adults. The motives of workers are never suspect: ours are constantly being put down as 'manipulative' or 'acting out'; our behaviour is to be prevented rather than understood.

The other major disadvantage of the illness framework is the pessimism it promotes about outcome for severely distressed people, especially those with recurring psychotic experiences. Yet we know that the deterioration in the past was due to institutionalisation: that the deterioration in the present is due to damage from long-term use and abuse (by doctors) of powerful psychoactive drugs, and to social exclusion.

I will return to drug damage, but there are other areas of harm that mental health nurses might explore with people who have already received treatment, and hospital admission in particular.

For many years 1 was deeply ashamed of having had ECT, regarding it as a punishment for getting married, leaving my closest friend to get killed alone on holiday. On my case record ECT had been a success, in that I experienced the euphoria that brain shock victims get. The euphoria was short-term; I suffered deep psychological damage. In addition to feeling punished, I thought that it indicated what a 'bad case' I was: that I could never get better. I had consented to the treatment, no-one had told me about adverse effects, and I believed that if I wanted the doctors to help me I must co-operate with them.

My husband regarded ECT with revulsion, and said 'If you're going to let them treat you like an animal, I'm leaving.' I felt deeply betrayed by him in an hour of great need. It is very frightening treatment. I permanently lost much memory of the year preceding the ECT (though not the period immediately before the ECT, which came back within two years). It is deeply damaging to one's sense of well-being to have complete strangers greet you in the street, avowing that they know you well from some recent activity. For my own satisfaction, with the help of others, I have pieced together a sketch of that year.

If people are angry or fearful about ECT, back them up. Put them in touch with literature that is critical of ECT, and get yourself informed (Johnstone, 1990; Frank, 1990). By far the most helpful thing for me in my long recovery from ECT was reading of other people's anger at this barbaric 'treatment'. It legitimised my own horror and helped the healing.

I feel angrier about ECT than about being sectioned under the Mental Health Act. There is less pretence that taking away someone's freedom is therapeutic. However 'necessary' a sectioning might be, and that is a separate discussion, depriving someone of their liberty is bound to do psychological damage. Never again will I regard my fellow humans with the same trust now I know that legally they can lock me up when I have done nothing wrong.

Hostages are rightly regarded as having been traumatised by their experience. Locking someone up under the Mental Health Act is regarded as routine. I have never heard of a mental health professional willing to tackle the emotional issues involved for someone who has been deprived of their liberty. Within the system, you soon learn that the way to get out is to show gratitude and promise to obey orders in the future. The damaging effects of the experience are never mentioned in hospital. CPNs can help by making it clear that you are willing to discuss this with people after discharge.

Learning from past crises, CPNs and other mental health professionals could work out a way to respect the person's wishes should a similar crisis recur. I carry a 'crisis card' (available from Survivors Speak Out) that tells people whom to contact and my wishes should I not be able to communicate these during a mental health emergency. Many of us would like a non-medical place of safety for such occasions. If there is a move locally to set up such provision, please give it all the encouragement and backing you can: the powerful psychiatric establishment is almost certain to oppose it.

Another form of emotional and mental damage that I haven't experienced, but many people in hospital still do, is seclusion. This is solitary confinement with sensory deprivation, used in prisons for punishment and torture. Peter Campbell (1991) writes:

> For me it is horrifying (literally) that at the deepest point of my distress I can be locked into a small room with only inanimate objects to relate to. . . . Over the years, I have never received support or counselling after periods of seclusion.

Like the other violent procedures I have listed, seclusion is never mentioned afterwards. Those of us whose behaviour is frightening or even dangerous are usually well able to talk about ways of preventing us from doing harm, even the necessity for restraint at times. The wall of silence makes it much more likely that we will become more alienated from the system and likely to resist restraint in the future. There are good reasons for non-compliance with a system that so many of us experience as coercive.

Many people come to CPNs with drug dosages set by the hospital psychiatrist. Have they been informed of the adverse effects? Are you fully aware of the tong-term effects of many of the major tranquillisers? There is some evidence that most ward nurses are unable to recognise the signs of tardive dyskinesia (Breggin, 1993). I wonder how different this is for CPNs.

Are you willing to explore with people the major interferences with quality of life that these drugs can bring? Would you be willing to live permanently with a drug that made you impotent, or interfered with your libido? This is only one of the major health problems caused by psychoactive drugs: a disorder for which non-psychiatric patients are treated at great expense by other specialists. The one I found most difficult was permanent mental confusion: how was I to now that this was a drug side effect, not a symptom of my illness? I only found that out when, against all medical advice, I stopped taking the prescribed drugs.

Do you inform someone who is on a combination of drugs into which no trials have been run? Derek Russell Davis (1991), a retired professor of psychiatry, points out the inadequacy of drug trials for all the major groups of drugs prescribed by psychiatrists when taken singly. He adds that 'there have been virtually no clinical trials of combinations of drugs; the adverse effects have not been evaluated'. He adds revealingly;

> Some psychiatrists are unduly dependent on prescribing drugs because they lack the simple skills that would enable them to talk with the patient and foster a therapeutic partnership.

I know that most workers find it difficult to take responsibility when a person decides not to continue medication. The thought that it is anyone's responsibility but the patient's is rank paternalism. Responsibility lies with mental health workers to try to help undo the damage done by the system.

Failure to recognise drug dependence is a frequent form of medical denial. I know many women who have struggled off antidepressants. What is difficult to let go of is the sedative effect, not the antidepressant effect. If someone is taking them for a year, they haven't worked. What many people long for is the immediate buzz and relaxation, not for the longer-term effect. This may not be true of all anti-depressant takers, but it is certainly true of many people I have met in self-help groups.

Ignorance of the withdrawal effects of psychoactive medication, particularly the major tranquillisers, is commonplace among doctors. In all these areas, since most doctors are unwilling to learn from their patients, we depend on other professionals both to inform the medical profession and to learn from our experiences. If you haven't read psychiatrist Peter Breggin's *Toxic Psychiatry* yet, please do.

Psychoactive drugs foul up our nervous system. Whatever line you have been spun, they are not acting on known chemical imbalances of the brain. Coming off them is very stressful and a long-term process. People who have done it (I am one of them) talk of two years or more before the system readjusts. During that time we need a great deal of support. Peer group support can be helpful if properly resourced; professional support may suit other people better, or be an essential additional support to self-help groups. Because withdrawal is so stressful, the behaviour and feelings ('symptoms') that caused us to go on the drugs in the first place often recur. If these are treated as withdrawal signs and people supported through them, they frequently go away, never to recur.

Many of us need help to find new ways to deal with our distress. What helps will differ from person to person. We need access to a range of alternatives. I am highly suspicious of anyone who wants to replace bio-psychiatry with some new orthodoxy. We simply don't know enough. I needed to mourn the death of my friend. Many prescribed drug years after her death I felt as though she had died yesterday. I was only able to mourn when I came off all medication.

I meet so many workers who are not content with what is going on in the mental health system. There is little CPNs can do about the psychiatrist-dominated hospital scene, but by acting together as responsible professionals surely CPNs could form alliances with service users to bring about a more healing and helpful service in the community?

It is not enough to keep practising to undo the damage done by others. More CPNs could try to stop the damage in the first place, by being confident that what you have to offer is, above all, humanity and respect for your fellow citizens.

Notes

Breggin, P. (1993) *Toxic Psychiatry: Drugs and Electroconvulsive Therapy: The Truth and Better Alternatives*, Fontana, London.

Campbell, P. (1991) 'In Times of Crisis', *Openmind*, no. 52, p. 15.

Frank, L. (1990) 'Electroshock: Death, Brain Damage, Memory Loss, and Brainwashing', In Cohen, D. *Challenging the Therapeutic State: Crucial Perspectives on Psychiatry and the Mental Health System*, Journal of Mind and Behaviour, New York.

Johnstone, L. (1990) *Users and Abusers of Psychiatry*, Routledge & Kegan Paul, London.

Russell Davis, D. (1991) 'The Debate on Drugs: A Personal View', *Openmind*, no. 49, pp. 10–11.

Survivors Speak Out, 34 Osnaburgh Street, London NW1 3ND.

Becoming Fully Ourselves

JAN WALLCRAFT

Marx said that the motor for change was class struggle. Though the term 'class' seems to be out of fashion, the axiom can be updated: the motor for change is the struggle of oppressed people for dignity, empowerment and self-determination.

In the second half of this century we have seen many such struggles take place, on a worldwide scale: the Black power movement; women's liberation; the liberation struggles of people in third world and communist countries; the fight to end apartheid; gay and lesbian pride, and people with disabilities fighting for rights, not charity. In the 1980s it was the turn of one of the most oppressed groups; people labelled 'mentally ill'. For centuries we have been silenced by denial of our human rights, the shame of the stigma of madness, routine invalidation as self-determining human beings, the fear of punitive and damaging treatment, and the effects of treatment itself.

For the past ten years or so we have been finding a voice; coming together and realising that, although our life stories are all very different, there are common threads in our experiences of having been misheard, devalued, written off and damaged because of other people's fear of madness. Sharing our stories finally gave us the courage to believe that we are not mad: we are angry; that what we are saying is not all the result of deluded thinking; distressing things really have happened to us, and our distress and anger is often a reasonable and comprehensible response to real-life situations which have robbed us of our power and taught us helplessness.

I date my own loss of power back to my first encounters with authority. I will never forget the terror I felt at the age of four, being left at the school gates. School was a nightmare for me. I was bullied by an infant mafia

191

who demanded my school bus money and left me to walk home. I lost my self-confidence, and even gave up speaking at all, withdrawing into a shell as a kind of last defence, like playing dead. I hoped that if they couldn't see they were hurting me, they would leave me alone. There was nothing else I could do. My beloved father used to take me to school on his bike on his way to work. and would look sadly at me when I begged him not to leave me, but would leave me anyway. If even he could not prevent this awful fate happening to me, I realised there was no use my fighting it. Inside, part of me froze and stopped growing.

Nobody at school seemed to care what happened to me. Before starting school my world had been familiar, and sometimes beautiful and exciting. Here, I was small, unimportant and in danger. My fear increased with my isolation, and my isolation with my fear. When I was taken by one of the class teachers to the head teacher to be smacked for using a path that we had been told not to use, I knew that even the powerful adults were not on my side. I would not have deliberately disobeyed, but I was too young and too distressed to keep an instruction in my head all day, even if I had taken it in and understood it properly in the first place.

My work in mental health for the past ten years convinces me that most of us, whether or not we have been psychiatrised, have learned to feel powerless in similar ways. As children, our self-confidence was trampled on, our feelings were hurt and our protests silenced. Adult society is frequently unthinkingly cruel to children, without realising it. We do what has always been done, and justify ourselves by repeating that 'It is for their own good'; 'Life is not a bed of roses'; 'You have to learn the hard way', and other such platitudes.

As Alice Miller, that most enlightened of psychoanalysts, says, (1987) 'Society's invisible walls totally block off any awareness of the suffering of the humiliated and manipulated child.' Her books explore the way that child-rearing practices throughout history have recommended repression of the child's individuality as early as possible. Though child-rearing fashions change, the view that 'sparing the rod spoils the child' and that children's willfulness must be conquered as early as possible still seems to underlie much child rearing and schooling. As more empowering educational ideals flounder because of poor resourcing and large class sizes, we are driven back again to reactionary educational goals of discipline and rote learning. Schooling, in any case, cannot compensate for social deprivation and the destruction of communities.

I believe that self-advocacy and empowerment in mental health must be seen in the context of the struggles that all of us have to become fully ourselves, fully human, respected, loved, valued and fulfilled. The self-advocacy movement, at its best, represents a flowering of the potential of a group of people whose humanity has been denied for centuries.

The first self-advocacy project in which I was involved was a women and mental health project. We started as an informal support group of women, some of us former mental patients and some not, but all of us committed to changing the mental health services because of our own personal experiences of being distressed and not finding the right kind of help.

We applied for a grant, in that exciting period of the early 1980s when grants to community groups were relatively easy to come by. I found myself agreeing to be chair, just as a formality, so it would appear that we has a proper committee, although until we applied for the money we had studiously avoided anything so rigid, hierarchical and bureaucratic as conventional committee structures. Our application was successful, and overnight we were the management committee of a funded project. We had the support of some local community development workers, which was vital because we were plunged into writing constitutions and job descriptions, and advertising for and recruiting a worker.

A key founder member became ill and went into a psychiatric hospital, missing much of this process. When she returned the worker was in post and we were no longer an informal group of women enjoying the luxury of talking about our own oppression and disempowerment and identifying how the system needed changing. We were busy trying to learn how to be responsible employers. Already we had accepted a number of compromises. The worker considered that our plans to create a network of volunteer support to help distressed women stay out of hospital were impossible to achieve overnight. She had come up with some more modest and achievable short-term goals. Bogged down with PAYE and insurance, and with other organisational tasks such as buying equipment for the office, we were in no position to argue; in any case we saw her point. We had no time ourselves to do much more than administer the project, and we could not expect her to achieve miracles.

When the founder member returned, she was deeply disturbed by the new situation. It was not at all what she had envisaged. Soon she was at loggerheads with the worker, and it seemed that the whole project would blow apart. We tried everything – committee meetings, talking to both parties; we tried desperately to unravel the disagreements, but it had all gone too far. The tensions forced some of the original committee members to drop out. Suddenly our community support workers were nowhere; they melted away, making encouraging noises from a distance, but basically leaving us to resolve the mess by ourselves.

I realised that being chair was no longer a nominal role. I had to take some decisive action. I will never know if what I did was right. It had been impressed upon us that we had a responsibility as a management committee to support the worker, and I felt she had not had time to settle in and find her way before all this controversy blew up. I called an emergency general meeting and had the founder member removed from the committee, despite in principle sharing many of her concerns about where the project was going.

The project survived, but I had had enough. I could no longer bear to be in that room where we had endured so many tense, painful meetings. Within a short while there was no one left from the original committee and the project passed into new hands. Though it continued and did valuable work, it had become something totally different from the network of informal support we had idealistically conceived when we used to meet in each others' houses. The women's group no longer met at all; we had been too deeply affected by all that had happened. I am sure that each of us learned a great deal from the experience, and certainly in retrospect it was a major step in my own empowerment, but at the time it was extremely distressing and confusing, and I could not think rationally about it for some years.

Similar things have happened with other women's projects set up with enormous enthusiasm and radical ideals. But these failures – if failures they are – are so hard to talk about, because of all the hurt feelings involved, that we have not learned as much from them as we might have done. Such problems are not, of course, confined to women's projects. Informally, mental health system survivors support each other well; but when we try to set up committees and constitutions, get money and employ workers, things can start to go badly wrong. To get the resources we are forced to compromise our aims and objectives, accept rigid structures which may not suit us, and spend a lot of time organising meetings, doing book-keeping, and dealing with all the bureaucracy and administration involved in a more formal project.

We seem to lose sight of our original purposes; people drop out, feeling the group has become too bureaucratic. As in any committee, often a few people end up doing most of the work. If these people are still working through their own distress at having been devalued and oppressed, they may feel a need to prove themselves, and then may experience an extreme sense of personal failure if they become exhausted, depressed or ill and have to take time out. Some people are not good at working collectively. They like to feel indispensable; they take on too much, monopolising all the power, and then complain that others are leaving everything to them. Idealism does not protect against the temptations of power.

When things go seriously wrong and the group or project falls apart we can become very bitter and disillusioned. Instead of learning and growing, we may be left feeling cynically that we can trust no one when even our own friends and colleagues seem to let us down. Undoubtedly these problems are not specific to mental health self-advocacy groups; they are common in any kind of voluntary organisation, but it is important to be aware of what can happen and to try to set things up with a reasonable chance of success. Although we can learn a lot from failure, it can be a blow to our self-confidence and leave some people feeling very damaged.

However, though some survivor projects have not worked as planned, others – like Survivors Speak Out, the national mental health self-advocacy network – have grown and flourished. SSO began in 1986 as a mixed group of survivors and allies, but as the survivors has grown in confidence and experience, the role of allies has been gradually reduced until now only survivors can vote and be on the co-ordinating group. This decision was not reached without some anger and hurt feelings, but on the whole I think that SSO has provided a good example of how allies can give crucial practical and moral support at the early stages; by being around for as long as they are needed, then gradually taking a back seat as survivors develop the confidence and ability to take on more responsibility.

SSO has kept the respect and friendship of most of its allies and has maintained a high profile without ever selling out its principles of commitment to self-advocacy. It has allowed itself to develop gradually, at a pace that did not outstrip the resources available. The fact that SSO no longer needs non-survivor allies to be centrally involved is a credit and a compliment to the empowering nature of the help that they gave.

When training workers in empowerment and user involvement, I am sometimes asked what should be done if the users won't get involved and don't seem to want to be empowered. If you encounter this problem, look at your own agenda. What are you trying to do, and why? Who are you doing it for? Are you doing it to make your service look good, even though nothing is meant to change drastically? Is user involvement just an added extra, a kind of window-dressing? If users are not interested in what you are offering, your agenda may be different form theirs and you may be trying to impose your own ideas of empowerment.

As Edna Conlan, of the UK Advocacy Network, has said, 'Users don't need to be told how to be empowered, any more than how to breathe.' The key to empowerment is self-determination. It is about finding out what you want to do and what you want to be.

Workers need first to look at the ways they actually prevent empowerment, and to stop doing those things. The second step is to actually lend a hand and facilitate empowerment. Look at what you do that may be actually preventing self-determination and empowerment:

- Do you categorise people and make assumptions about them based on limited information, rather than seeing each person as an individual with a unique life-story? (I hope that one day it will be recognised that psychiatric stereotyping labels such as 'manic' and 'schizoid' are every bit as damaging and dehumanising as racist and gender stereotyping.)

- Do you see yourself in a permanently parental role to the people using the services you provide?
- Do you hang onto your role as a way of feeling superior, indispensable; do you hide your own vulnerability by appearing not to have needs?
- Do you assume that, if users disagree with workers, the users must be wrong because they are sick?
- Do you 'protect' people from the truth, for example by not giving them full information or giving disinformation?
- Do you talk incomprehensible jargon and talk over people's heads?

Power comes from within. You can facilitate it, but you can't make ti happen. There are a number of ways in which professionals can facilitate empowerment:

- You can find out about the national self-advocacy movement and pass on that information to local service users.
- You can give people the money to pay their fares to meetings and give them space in which to meet.
- You can offer your assistance in a number of practical ways, such as arranging training in the skills people in the group identify that they need: for example, committee skills, fund-raising, understanding the structures of the health and social services, how to make meetings work, speaking in public, or how to run training workshops.

But don't go in with a mental blueprint of what empowerment looks like: it looks different for every individual. For some people, empowerment may mean having a place on the management committee or the local joint care planning team. Some people may feel empowered by beginning to write poetry or by setting up a self-help group to reduce their dependence on drugs. For some it means getting a good job, going back to college or making new relationships. For others empowerment means ceasing to try to meet the expectations of society, and simply living life in their own way at last.

Each person using psychiatric services is on an individual journey; a journey which has often been crudely interrupted by the intervention of psychiatric treatments designed to impede thought and action. Allowing someone to restart their own journey is risky, but if we don't allow people to take risks they cannot learn and grow. Empowerment is risky, but it is our right as human beings.

Reference

Miller, A. (1987) *For Our Own Good*, Virago, London.

We Can Still Find a Way to be Heard

SUE KING

The Mary Seacole House (MSH) is a drop-in day centre for those suffering from mental health problems. It is the only centre on Merseyside that caters for the needs of Black service users. Its management committee, Granby Mental Health Group, has a majority of Black members on it. These members know how much harder everything gets when racism is a daily occurrence. The committee is made up of individuals from a wide range of backgrounds: university lecturers, writers, social workers and therapists. It also has representatives from housing co-operatives, doctors' practices and hospitals, together with a whole range of support links in the community. It was set up to provide a different approach to the care of service users.

The committee is made up of dedicated, well-meaning individuals, whose collective impact has greatly benefited many mental health care users, and helped turn dreams into reality by establishing and overseeing the MSH. Yet, as wide as their vision is, they cannot see the MSH – and mental health care in general – through the eyes of a service user unless they themselves are or have been one.

I first joined the MSH in September 1991, and through its unique setup, it catered for me, a Black women whose world had fallen apart. It offered me the right kind of support and understanding to enable me to get through my crisis and face the world again as a stronger, more confident woman. However, many service users' needs are not met, many good ideas are never heard, and far too many decisions taken with the perspective of those affected being totally negated.

Service users and ex-service users need to have a more dominant position on management committees. Early attempts to recruit members to attend the MSH management committee meetings were unsuccessful. Members were not prepared for the formal structure of the meetings, and those that went seemed unwilling to participate. Although the idea was

197

to have two member representatives, it was hard to get even one. A problem with member participation is that it requires a sensitivity to many different styles of communication. This can be time consuming and hinder the smooth running of the committee.

I became the only member representative of the management committee in November 1992. No one told me what was expected of me in this role, or about procedures, subcommittees, criteria and so on. I was given no guidance or training. In fact my role on the committee was never defined. I was told I would be 'an equal voting member', yet I was denied access to certain meetings and it became clear that matters involving staff and recruitment were *not* considered my area and that some members of the management committee were more equal than others.

I saw my role as a voice for the members who used the MSH. I started holding regular members' meetings, where ideas were discussed, experiences shared, and opinions heard. Then at committee meetings I reported back the ideas of fundraising by and for members, money raised to be spent on better outings, arts and crafts or anything members agreed to spend it on. Members' fundraising ideas included holding a jumble sale, candle-making and other crafts to sell; a newsletter with adverts, a poetry competition and a tuck shop. I raised members' concerns about the complaints procedure as it was complex and intimidating. Further concerns were about low staffing levels, the need to get volunteers in place and the members' willingness to rally round and help keep the house open. Yet on each one of these points the committee failed to act, or they would take so long getting round to taking any action that members lost interest and faith.

After many months of attending management committee meetings, I found that service users' views were undervalued, and no interest was shown in expanding service user participation in the running of the MSH. The committee were more interested in getting members away from the pool tables, and into the classroom. Basic computing, English and maths were introduced to members. Although they attracted initial support, numbers soon dwindled.

The committee were both surprised and worried by the low take-up. They were unaware that a one-year basic computer course, once a week, in a classroom for a year could be intimidating, unsuitable, uninteresting and not wanted by the members; or that the underlying cause of lack of interest and participation is that the activities do not cater for the needs of the members. This situation caused me to write the report 'I Hear What You're Saying But . . . ' which was presented before the management committee 3 May 1994. The report acknowledged the low-take up of activities, and went on to say:

There are several reasons for this apparent lack of interest.

Firstly ideas that are brought by the members often cause an immediate surge of enthusiasm. This, however, is often whittled down by the fact that there is an extremely long time between ideas being tabled and their fruition.

Members find this factor extremely frustrating. This is more often than not added to by the lack of explanation as to how their ideas have been received and little or no clarification as to the processing of those ideas. In other words members are not privy to information on who decides what, how that decision is arrived at and when, if ever, it is likely to happen. When they hear nothing they make the natural assumption that their project will not be going ahead. The result of this is that members lose interest.

There seems to be a general feeling that communication is lacking at many levels at MSH. What seems to irritate members is that they are treated firstly as service users and secondly as people.

The management committee were critical of members spending too much time playing pool, and not enough learning a skill or getting a qualification. Again I quote from the same report:

Some members of the management committee have expressed concern about the different types of activities on offer to the members. As you will no doubt be aware, most of the activities on offer at the MSH are designed to build confidence and self esteem, so that individuals can go on to develop interpersonal skills which will help them to relate to society as a whole. This may well be in the form of academic skills, developing a craft or a trade or skills that will help them to lead a 'normal' life. Looking at it from this angle shows that pool, for example, can give not only confidence to participate but a whole wealth of other skills and techniques that are needed to cope with society. Participants have to learn the rules and *play by them*.

They have to develop co-ordination skills and think several moves ahead of play. Players of different calibre often play against each other and it is amazing to see how eager they are to pass on the skills that they have learnt. (Pupil becomes teacher.) Players learn how to win and how to lose. Pool can be a way for many to relax, spend time with their friends, get to know new members, share experiences, counsel each other, develop team work skills; all this while they are having fun. Although pool by itself will not teach people to live in the outside world it is definitely a step in the right direction for many people at the house. Never underestimate the value of non-conventional forms of learning as these form the basis of the whole ideology of the MSH. It is the need to *learn* rather than to be *taught* that should be a lesson to us all. We should focus on more activities that teach skills, that are fun to do and are a learning experience rather than getting caught up with the stagnant classroom environment.

My research into the problems of communication revealed that rigid procedures and protocol only inhibited development, yet with good communication, flexibility and partnership we could move mountains. It is unrealistic to attempt to fit service-user participation into the existing structure. What is needed is to look at that structure and reorganise the whole hierarchy to involve service users effectively. To attain a real voice there must be opportunity for change at each and every level. This would mean members having the option to be involved at each stage. How can you plan a service and effectively introduce it without the full participation of those who are to receive that service? It is clear to me that there needs to be an overall move towards empowerment and partnership.

After reading my report the management committee agreed that a special meeting was needed. Although this meeting did take place, little was achieved. The committee thought the meeting would give everyone the opportunity to speak out, and that would solve the participation problem. They didn't know that their very presence intimidated members, as did the thought of speaking at a public meeting.

The approach of the management committee had not changed, they were still blissfully unaware of the changes they would need to make. Until the management start respecting service users and learn the importance of genuinely listening to and valuing what service users have to say then neither service users nor carers will ever reach their full potential.

It is hard to contend with society judging, labelling and condemning us as 'loonies', not worthy of equal respect, rights and status. Is it too much to expect that the body set up to protect and care for us, should take notice of our opinions and without prejudice hear what we say? It is not that the management committee consciously undermine the service users, in fact, they would see the opposite as true, that they put the service users' well-being first. But how can this be so when they do not acknowledge that service user participation in setting the agenda and in decision making is essential.

A recent decision shows how entrenched the management committee's 'do for' rather than 'do with' attitude is. After seven days' notice and no consultation, smoking was to be banned inside the house, and those still wishing to smoke could erect a portable marquee outside. This caused service users to feel that nowhere was safe, everywhere things are imposed on you when you have a mental health problem.

Yet this time it was different, this time service users felt strong enough in themselves to demand a postponement of that decision. They then called a members' meeting to discuss the matter, and set up a referendum to gauge the weight of feeling for and against a smoking ban. This clearly shows that there are many articulate and non-articulate service users with something to say, irrespective of the lack of structure within the system to empower us. *We can still find a way to be heard.*

My time on the management committee was good for me, although sometimes it was extremely hard work. Both disappointment and achievement inspired me to fight for what I know to be right. This in turn has given me the confidence to command respect. My experiences on the committee have given me the opportunity to view mental health care from many different angles, widening my perspective; It has taught me how easy it is to 'see the illness' and not the person, and how enabling, empowering and self-advocacy come a poor second when pitted against the *system*. It has taught me to question and to challenge those who place restrictions and limitations on the progress and development of people suffering from mental illness. All too often those the system fails get locked up or left in the gutter, when all they need is a little help aimed specifically at their needs, hopes and fears.

Listening in the Asylum

MARY NETTLE

Until entering the psychiatric system, in 1978, I was working in consumer market research. For many years I was a passive recipient of mental health services before realising, with the help and support of people who had also been through the system, that I could use my skills as a researcher to enable my fellow service users to comment, safe in the knowledge that they would not be misunderstood.

The confidence gained by being involved in the user/survivor movement meant that in 1992 I felt able to become self-employed as a mental health user consultant under the Enterprise Allowance scheme, with the help of my local TEC (Training and Enterprise Council).

My first piece of research was a project to find out the views of long-stay psychiatric patients about the quality of their lives in a hospital they had lived in for at !east one year and, in many cases, over thirty years.

I was commissioned to do this work, with a colleague, by two local health authorities and a regional health authority. As purchasers of a service, they had set quality standards that the provider, an NHS trust, was expected to meet. Our task was to ask a sample of long-stay patients about their lives in hospital – what it meant to them and how they felt the quality of their lives could be improved.

We had many meetings with the purchasers and providers before we set foot inside the wards to talk to patients. We were trying to agree ground rules for our work which were acceptable to ourselves, the staff and, primarily, the patients.

The representatives of the hospital psychiatric consultants expressed their concern that 'researchers talking to their patients could interfere with their treatment'. The purchasers supported us in our view that asking patients questions about how they liked living in the hospital was consumer, not medical, research and, therefore, we did not need the approval of the medical ethics committee. (This committee exists to safeguard the rights of patients involved in medical research and has to approve all medical research involving patients in the hospital.)

Having, in consultation with the ward managers, decided which wards would be included in our sample, we were made very welcome by the staff and given the use of an office. A link worker did her best to make sure we felt comfortable, and her support was essential to the success of the project.

We originally aimed to conduct small group discussions on the wards, but the patients were not used to talking in groups. Instead, we had to spend a lot of time building up their trust and confidence by talking to them individually. This meant that the research took longer and was more demanding than we had anticipated. Fortunately for us, the people who commissioned the research were flexible and willing to renegotiate our fee.

We stayed in nurses' accommodation in the main building of the hospital. This meant that we could easily observe all aspects of patients' lives, talking to them wherever they happened to be: the ward, the library, the canteen or the corridors. We could talk to them at any time, including evenings and weekends. By staying in the hospital, we saw how festive occasions such as Guy Fawkes night, Hallowe'en and New Year were celebrated.

We wrote our report and it was undoubtedly critical of the residents' quality of life. We found, for example, that privacy was severely lacking, opportunities for recreation were very limited and physical health care was poor.

It was at this point that we encountered problems with the project.

The purchasers were changing jobs as their health authorities were being merged, and none of the six people involved in commissioning the research were in the same jobs when we produced the final report. This lack of continuity has led to a very frustrating situation, as we do not know what impact the research project has had on the quality of life of the hospital residents. We were initially given permission to publish the research but, due to the changes in personnel, this permission was withdrawn. We wanted the patients and staff to attend a series of workshops where we would explain what we had written in our report and discuss what was going to be done about it. We did not want the report to be a secret document seen only by top management, but we are fairly sure it did not get wide circulation and we were not asked to do the follow-up workshops.

We were very aware that we could have raised the expectations of a vulnerable group of people. We tried hard to explain that we wanted to know what people felt about their lives in hospital and that we would put down what they said in our report 'to the bosses', but we could not guarantee that they would take any notice of what we said. We did guarantee individual's anonymity and were able to preserve patient confidentiality. We did not have ownership of the report and felt powerless to help the patients who felt confident enough to talk to us openly and who may have thought we were able to change things.

We did not have a contract – only a letter agreeing to our proposal for doing the work. Our proposal did not include any clauses about follow-up work and I think this is essential, particularly in a time of change. There is nothing worse than producing a report that lies on the shelf.

User researchers are able to use their personal experiences of the mental health system to produce high-quality work which people can relate to. This reality can sometimes be unpalatable and bring providers' attention to issues they have been resisting dealing with.

Negotiation by user researchers with the organisation commissioning the research should end with a contract which includes whether the recommendations resulting from the research will be acted on and monitored, and, if so, how. It needs to be established exactly what the aims of the organisation are in commissioning the work. There needs to be mutual respect, and delegation of power to the researchers. We were given keys that opened every door in the hospital, which was respectful and empowering.

User-led research is often commissioned by purchasers/providers of health and social care, in order to find out what users think about current or planned services. It is often qualitative work, dependent on asking individuals how they feel about the services and treatments they are or are not receiving.

Quantitative research involves counting, for example, the numbers of people using a service, their ethnic backgrounds, where they live, how far they have to travel, and so on. It often includes the use of rating scales in order to try and quantify attitudes and opinions. This data is collected by using questionnaires completed by the individuals themselves or by interviewers asking the questions and interpreting the answers to fit the questionnaire. This is a valid method of data collection, especially if the questions asked have been designed and piloted by user researchers. However, unlike qualitative research, the rigid format of quantitative research does not allow service users to fully express their opinions, and therefore gives an incomplete picture of their views.

When a service user is asked questions they will be inclined to say what they think the researcher wants to hear. This is because they have learned to do so as a way of placating authority figures such as doctors, nurses and social workers. A researcher who is also a mental health service user can establish a rapport by identifying themselves as someone who can understand an individual's experience of the mental health system because they have 'been there' themselves.

User researchers are more likely to be told what individuals really think about their situation than 'professional' researchers. User researchers are able to relate to similar situations within their own experience, and are likely to have the ability to reflect and interpret users' views to give a picture of the reality of their lives. An example of this would be the sexual harassment that can occur on mixed-sex wards, particularly where this is the result of the use of psychotropic medication which can lead to the relaxation of social inhibitions.

User researchers need to guard against subjectivity and be as objective as possible in their work. Their 'training' as users of psychiatric services influences their work no more or less than all professionals' training influences their work. In any situation where the service user is asked to express a view on the quality, nature or type of service they are receiving, be it housing, social care, health care or any other service, user-led research will be relevant. There should be no circumstances where research is commissioned but where to commission user-led research is deemed inappropriate.

Service users involved in research and training often work on their own. It is important to have a support network in place so that the issues raised by the work you are doing can be discussed and put into context. Many of the difficult issues raised revolve around the attitude of the medical staff to your interaction with their patients. This can bring up your own feelings of helplessness when reminded of how this power imbalance affected you. The issues bought up by the patients can be difficult to handle because you feel powerless to help. You may need to be reminded that your very presence, as a researcher who is open about having used mental health services, will have made an impact. Even if your report does not bring about immediate change, it may still have influenced the people who read it, with results that you may never know about.

It is all too easy to identify with the situation and feel you must get involved and sort it out. This is not what you are being paid to do, and you must provide a quality service to the organisation that has commissioned you to undertake the work. Sometimes compromises may have to be made. You must work within the agreed ground rules and if you are not happy with them you may have to decline the work.

Organisations are increasingly using service users to conduct quality audits of the services they provide, and this on-going monitoring and evaluating of services by experienced user researchers is a very welcome development. Unfortunately, in many areas the idea is accepted in principle but the resources are not available to pay for this (or any other kind of) research. Organisations do not have a budget heading where user-led research fits, and therefore it is often treated as a good idea that cannot be implemented.

Until funding for user-led research is made more readily available, the

views of service users, and especially those of long-stay patients, will not
be heard and acted upon as they should be.

Shaking Hands with the Devil

EDNA CONLAN

There are times when, as someone who has been and still is a recipient of mental health services trying to work with the mental health services to empower service users, I feel as though I am shaking hands with the devil. The feeling tends to be strongest when I find myself sitting on any high-powered committee which is intent on sending out signals that the mere presence of people using the services is evidence of its goodwill and obvious commitment to delivering user-centred services. Unfortunately, people who work at high levels in organisations are often more skilled at staging the appearance of change than they are at implementing real participative change, and the promise may be passed off as the deed.

We, who are committed to positive change, have to demonstrate continually that we can play a constructively critical part in the process of change itself without being pushed into roles defined by the people who want to hold on to power, and without becoming muted by the formality of procedures and professional mystique. This is very much easier to talk about than to do.

The line of least resistance is a tempting one to take. It can carry with it the hope of admission to a promised land of smiles and nods where one may be an 'insider', a co-optee of the system we set out to challenge. There are rewards for singing along with the devil's disciples, being seen as accommodatingly reasonable, saying what they want to hear, giving everybody around the table the opportunity to relax and feel good and get on with business as usual. Neither the agenda nor the language has to change to reflect wider interests. Of course the resolutions will lack integrity. Rubber-stamping the *status quo* bends the principles, but could do wonders for personal status.

For people who are asked to speak for fellow service users, the one true antidote to swallowing that line is to make sure they are accountable and accessible to them and grounded strongly in their local service contexts. Only then can they know what is happening, and understand that their first duty is to empower and not to control other people using those services. Otherwise, in the rarefied air breathed by the power-brokers, it becomes all too easy to forget that. Everyone knows that the devil has all the best tunes, and it can be difficult and uncomfortable not to sing along but to follow the sound of a different, user-centred drum.

Every day in working with the services in user forums, patients' councils and advocacy projects, people who have used services are taking part in meetings and discussions which often seek to re-define them as limited, or less than professional in their status. There is a vague recognition that they may have different priorities from professionals, but often not a clear understanding of why that should be or what to do about it, in any terms except their own. A recent example of research in hospitals listing the order of value of 'things that do recipients good' showed that nurses gave wholly different priorities to items preferred by patients. Users were more inclined to favour good human relationships, rather than ward rounds. The study recommended that the patients should be educated to know what was good for them.

Shaking hands with the devil, but not accepting his version of events without questioning his right to define situations and to judge, is sometimes the hardest thing to do. Even when the most we can do is to be there and to bear witness to what is going on, it seems to me to be well worth doing. Working with the system does not mean buying into it lock, stock and barrel. But at least when you shake hands with the devil, you can get close enough to look him straight in the eye.

What Has Disability Got to do with Psychiatric Survivors?

PETER BERESFORD, GLORIA GIFFORD and CHRIS HARRISON

The three of us are all survivors of the psychiatric system. One of us also has cerebral palsy, another is blind, so we have some first-hand knowledge of both disability and distress.

The two are both very different, yet also have similarities. So far, most emphasis has been placed on the differences. Many psychiatric survivors are unwilling to see themselves as disabled. They associate disability with the medicalisation of their distress and experience. They reject the biological and genetic explanations of their distress imposed by medical experts. They may not see themselves as emotionally or mentally distressed either, but instead celebrate their difference and their particular perceptions. Similarly, some disabled people do not feel that psychiatric survivors are disabled, because they do not have a physical impairment or their situation may not be permanent. There are also fears and anxieties on each side of being linked with the negatives that are often associated with the other.

In broader society, disability and distress still seem to be perceived differently. They figure differently on mainstream political agendas, with distress increasingly being associated with dangerousness. While there are now some attempts to educate children about disability, so far this has not extended in the same way to learning about mental distress .

When one of us goes to trade union meetings as a disabled member, there is a right to equal access. Facilitators and access are an accepted part of the philosophy because this trade union has come to realise that access is about *everyone's* needs. But so far there is not the same recognition of survivors' rights and needs around mental distress.

There are also important overlaps between disabled people and survivors. Some survivors also have physical or sensory impairments, often related to the chemical and other damaging 'treatments', like ECT, which they have received. Some people involved in the survivors' movement are also involved in the disability movement, as some are involved in the women's, Black people's, and lesbian and gay men's movements. Some people with impairments and people with learning difficulties also have experience as survivors which may be linked with the way they have been treated as disabled people.

In our experience there are many similarities in how you are treated as a survivor and as a disabled person. We have personal experience of both, as adults and as children. We have encountered the same harsh, uncomprehending treatment in both cases. We have discovered that having an adult's power of reasoning and an adult's knowledge of the world can count for nothing in these service systems. We have learnt that adult status is frequently a meaningless phrase in the world of psychiatry, where we can expect to be talked down to, ignored and patronised. This has routinely happened to all three of us.

While our experience tells us that distress and disability are very different in many ways, we also know that the struggle to live with each is very similar. Both are states which we are expected to keep under control – within acceptable social boundaries. We must look and act acceptably; not twitch, be awkward or ugly. This control is not of our own choosing, but is forced upon us by society as the price we must pay for qualifying as members of it. A series of assumptions are made about us and an invisible yet immensely powerful set of rules and values are brought into operation. They start with the assumption that we can't do things, are different, should be kept separate and need special treatment. We are judged according to these rules and values, and generally found to be lacking.

So far as civil rights are concerned, for us there is little difference between having a physical impairment and being a survivor of the psychiatric system. In both we have few rights as an individual and because the rights of disabled people and survivors are still not fully and effectively enshrined in law, the reality of the situation is a concept of 'normality' which we can expect always to fall short of, because we are stereotyped as defective, dependent, tragic and threatening.

In recent years strong and growing movements of disabled people and psychiatric system survivors have developed in Britain and other countries. These have challenged conventional understandings of disability and distress and forced both of them higher on mainstream public and political agendas. Two key common issues have emerged for these different movements and for us as individual survivors and disabled people. We both experience the medicalisation of our needs with destructive effects and we both have our civil rights restricted through discrimination – and in the case of survivors, through legal restrictions on our rights which may be applied arbitarily and without adequate safeguards.

There is still a lot of misunderstanding about the relationship between mental distress and disability. The social model of disability developed by the disabled people's movement can help us to make better sense of it. It no longer equates disability with personal deficiency. Instead it draws a distinction between *impairment* – the functional limitation within the individual caused by physical, mental or sensory impairment – and *disability* – the loss or limitation of opportunities owing to social, physical or attitudinal barriers. Thus people are disabled by society's reaction to impairment.

This highlights the common ground between survivors and disabled people – the oppression and discrimination we both experience. We are not trying to argue that as survivors we necessarily have some kind of impairment. But survivors do experience discrimination and oppression in response to their experiences and perceptions, and this is disabling. Both groups face discrimination in employment, housing, education, social situations and in personal relationships. We are disabled by the lack of appropriate social and personal support. We are disabled by society's barriers.

There are many things which we as survivors do not have in common with people form the disability movement, but there are also many ways in which we are different from each other as *survivors* too.

While it may not be helpful to try and extend the social model of disability to include survivors, it does offer us some helpful insights. The dominant interpretation placed upon survivors' experience is framed in terms of mental health and mental illness. This invariably stigmatises and pathologises us, and emphasises our abnormality and inadequacy. Perhaps what the social model of disability most helpfully emphasises is the value of survivors developing our own social model of madness and distress. This would highlight:

- the social causes of our madness and distress;
- the medicalisation of our experience and distress;
- the destructive and discriminatory response to it from both psychiatry and broader society;
- the need for a *social* response to the distress and disablement which survivors experience, addressing the social origins and relations of their distress, instead of being restricted to people's individual difficulties;
- the need for survivor-led alternatives to prevent distress and offer appropriate support for survivors

In the UK, the disabled people's movement is placing an increasing emphasis on building links between different movements. The Director of the British Council of Disabled People (BCODP) stresses the need for the disability movement to take on women's, Black and lesbian and gay men's issues, and develop links with survivors. As he says, the disabled people's movement is not a movement concerned with specific impairments, but a *civil rights* movement. Survivors face the same threats that he identifies facing disabled people; cuts in social provision, continuing economic recession and increasing support for eugenic policies. (The eugenics movement which has long been associated with the search for 'racial purity' and for physical and mental perfection, is most strongly linked with the Nazi Third Reich and other fascist regimes.)

As survivors, the three of us wanted to find out more about the disabled people's movement and explore links with it. The two movements have different traditions and experiences. Like other members of the survivors' movement, we value our own history and achievements. We recognise that we have a particular position within the struggle for civil rights, and do not want our identity as survivors to be weakened or lost.

We have sought to develop our links with the disabled people's movement through Survivors Speak Out (SSO), the national network of psychiatric system survivors of which we are members. SSO has committed itself to working more closely with disabled people. So far the response we have had from disabled people has been positive and supportive.

First, two of us spoke at a *Rights Now* rally in Trafalgar Square, campaigning for the Civil Rights Bill which the government eventually replaced with its own inadequate legislation. Thousands of disabled people who came seemed to value survivors' commitment to the broad disability movement. They recognised and acknowledged the central importance of the issues which currently affect and disempower survivors: being subjected to harmful and excessive doses of drugs and enforced 'treatment' with ECT, new legislation imposing increasing restrictions on us in our own homes, and generally only having unsafe and often unsympathetic services to turn to when what we need are support and asylum.

Then all three of us were invited to run a fringe meeting at the BCODP's annual general meeting. We went with some trepidation. Many members of BCODP were asking the same question that survivors were asking: what has disability got to do with survivors of the psychiatric system? We again encountered enthusiasm and interest. People talked about the tenuous links between the two movements, but the large areas of shared experience we have with each other. The meeting felt like another step towards recognising our differences, yet addressing our mutual goal – the achievement of civil rights for all of us.

Two other initiatives we have been involved in have both been international. First, one of us went as one of the two delegates from Survivors Speak Out to the World Assembly of Disabled People held in Australia and organised by Disabled People's International. This worldwide umbrella organisation, controlled by disabled people, sees survivors unequivocally as part of the broader disabled people's movement. We discovered that there seemed to be more readiness to accept this in other countries. We came away having made new contacts and strengthened our links with the disabled people's movement while still retaining our own unique identity as survivors.

Most recently, we took part in a European symposium on disability rights. If anything was needed to persuade us of the importance of building links this was it. Here we met survivors from Belgium as well as disabled people from all over Europe. We heard about the backlash disabled people are beginning to experience in the United States following their successes in achieving their civil rights and with the passing of the Americans With Disabilities Act. We learned about the obstacles placed in the way of disabled people and survivors struggling for their civil rights in some countries and the attacks made on the civil rights of those campaigning for reform in others. The message campaigner after campaigner repeated was the importance of working together at local level.

The dominant view of both disability and distress in societies like ours continues to be as individual problems which only affect a small proportion of the population. We know these are issues which affect *all* human beings. Traditional divisions between survivors and disabled people reflect the division made between mind and body which has been a feature of western society for centuries. So long as we, as survivors and disabled people, accept this view of each other, we are likely to remain divided and disempowered by our own ignorance and misunderstanding of one other.

Public policy is increasingly acting to divide people, as greater stress is laid on competing for resources, services and support The key lesson we have learned is the importance of being united if we are to achieve our civil rights. For example, SSO and BCODP are equally committed to ensuring that survivors have full access to the direct payments schemes introduced by government legislation, which enable people to run and control their own schemes for personal support. By joining forces in this way we can gain from each other's different experience and ways of working; and gain the greater strength that comes with campaigning together for our rights.

We are conscious too that the prejudice and discrimination which we must fight so hard to challenge and resist in society often also lies deep in our own hearts and minds. If we are to achieve full equality for ourselves and others, we must recognise and value both our differences and our similarities as survivors and disabled people.

Beyond Rage

TERRY SIMPSON

The first thing that really helped me start to get over my experiences as an in-patient on a psychiatric ward was to realise the depth of my anger about the experience. I think the whole subject of forced treatment is one that has been little researched, and one of the things that happened to me was a deep feeling of shame and humiliation. When I hear accounts of people who've experienced sexual abuse as children, some of the things they say – 'I felt I must have deserved it in some way/I felt it was my fault' – ring true for my experience of being treated against my will in the mental health system.

About six years after the first hospital admission, when I was having a hard time in a relationship, I sat down knowing I wanted to write something to express my feelings, but not knowing what it was I wanted to write. About thirty lines of white-hot anger about the mental health system came pouring out. I was amazed at myself to discover how enraged I still was after all that time, and at how I'd somehow lived with that level of anger completely suppressed.

I did have other admissions after this, but I was always clearer about who I was and what the system was, and I never got so completely lost as I did during that first admission.

I needed to talk about how it all was for me, but mostly I didn't. On the few occasions I did, I found I met with one of two responses. If people weren't themselves survivors, they were acutely embarrassed and shut me up. ('It was a long time ago. It's all behind you now. Try to think of something pleasant instead.') If they were survivors, they usually had so many of their own feelings about the experience that I would end up listening to *their* outrage or justifications. It was all pretty frustrating.

What turned it around for me was the discovery of a group of survivors meeting in my town to co-counsel. I joined the group, and once a month I'd go and spend the evening with these people. This was the only time I

215

ever saw them. We'd take it in turns to tell our stories, which process at first seemed very awkward and contrived. However, two things began to happen.

At last there was a place to bring the the thoughts and feelings I'd had for the last ten years without anyone telling me to shut up. Within a short space of time, I began to feel better about the whole thing and far less demoralised about it. Just having space to talk and think about it (or cry and rage, or just yawn away as I recalled the effects of drugs) meant I had new perspectives. I didn't feel so disempowered, and I began to see ways I could act and change the way the system operates (instead of just feeling bad about it).

The second thing was that I could hear how similar our stories were, and this helped me to see that I wasn't a freak.

When I started to get active in local user groups, it helped to have worked through some of the anger and negativity. It meant I didn't immediately have to jump and start attacking professionals, even when they were being provocative – especially when they were being provocative. I could *think* – 'What's the best way to handle this? What do I want to happen in this situation?'

It was specially useful if some big event was coming up, such as speaking at a meeting or conference, to have a time to be able to think about it and feel the feelings – all the terror and 'I'm not really any good' stuff. Acknowledging this and thinking about it in an environment that's safe means that those feelings have far less of a hold on you when you get out into the real situation.

As time goes on, I see that no one working in mental health gets enough support or is properly listened to. The impact of a well-organised system of peer support groups would be incalculable.

Recipe for a support group

1. Decide a few basic rules:
- What's said is confidential, is not to be referred to outside the group or outside a particular person's 'time'.
- People get the chance to talk without interruptions or having to hear someone else's views. The others can be supportive or encouraging if you get stuck.
2. Decide how much time you've got to spend on this and divide it between the number of you there are.
3. Listen to the others, enjoy their attention when it gets to your turn.

Good luck.